The Christian
in Complete Armour

THE CHRISTIAN IN COMPLETE ARMOUR

WILLIAM GURNALL

Abridged by Ruthanne Garlock, Kay King,
Karen Sloan and Candy Coan

Volume 3

THE BANNER OF TRUTH TRUST

THE BANNER OF TRUTH TRUST

3 Murrayfield Road, Edinburgh EH 12 6EL
P.O. Box 621, Carlisle, Pennsylvania 17013, U.S.A.

★

First published in three volumes in 1655, 1658 and 1662
Revised and reprinted in 1864 by Blackie & Son, Glasgow, Scotland
The 1864 edition (unabridged) republished by the Banner of Truth
    Trust, Edinburgh, Scotland in 1964, 1974 and 1979
The 1864 edition (Volume 1) revised and abridged, published by
    World Challenge, Inc., David Wilkerson Crusades, Lindale,
    Texas, U.S.A. in association with the Banner of Truth Trust, 1986
© World Challenge Inc., 1986

Volume 2 © World Challenge Inc., 1988

Volume 3 © World Challenge Inc., 1989
Reprinted 1992
ISBN 0 85151 560 6

★

Typeset in 10½ on 12 pt Linotron Plantin
at The Spartan Press Ltd, Lymington, Hants
Reproduced, printed and bound in Great Britain by
BPCC Hazells Ltd
Member of BPCC Ltd

Contents

The Several Pieces of the Whole Armour of God
(*continued*)

The Several Pieces of the Whole Armour of God

9: *Eighth Consideration: The Christian's Spiritual Shield*

Above all, taking the shield of faith, wherewith ye shall be able to quench all the fiery darts of the wicked (Eph. 6:16).

THE fourth piece in the Christian's armour presents itself in this verse – the shield of faith. It is a grace of graces, and is here fitly placed in the midst of its companions. It stands as the heart in the midst of the body; or as David when Samuel 'anointed him in the midst of his brethren' (*1 Sam. 16:13*). The apostle, when he speaks of this grace, anoints it above all its fellows – '*Above all*, take the shield of faith.'

THE KIND OF FAITH COMMENDED

We discover the kind of faith the apostle commended if we consider the use and end for which it is prescribed to the Christian – to enable him to 'quench all the fiery darts of the wicked' – that is, of the wicked one, the devil. Now, consider the several kinds of faith. Among them must be the faith which empowers the Christian to quench all of Satan's fiery darts.

Historical faith cannot do this. This kind is so far from quenching Satan's fiery darts that the devil himself, who shoots them, has this faith. 'The devils also believe' (*James 2:19*).

Temporary faith cannot do it. This is so far from quenching Satan's fiery darts that it is quenched by them. It displays a goodly blaze of profession and endures 'for a while' (*Matt. 13:21*) but soon disappears.

Miraculous faith falls as short as the others. Judas' miraculous faith, which he used alongside the other apostles, enabled him to cast out devils from others but left him possessed by the devils of covetousness, hypocrisy, and treason. A whole legion of lusts hurled him down the hill of despair into the bottomless pit of perdition.

There is only one kind of faith which remains, and that is *justifying faith*. This indeed is a grace which makes him who has it a match for the devil. Satan has not so much advantage of the Christian by the superiority of his natural abilities, as the Christian has of Satan by this faith, his weapon. The apostle is so confident that he gives the victory to the Christian before the fight is fully over: 'Ye have overcome the wicked one' (*1 John 2:13*). That is, you are as sure to do it as if you were now mounted on your triumphant chariot in heaven. The knight shall overcome the giant; the saint shall overcome Satan. And the same apostle tells us how this happens. 'This is the victory that overcometh the world, even our faith' (*1 John 5:4*).

THE NATURE OF JUSTIFYING FAITH

Justifying faith is not a simple assent to the truths of the gospel. Judas knew the Scriptures, and without doubt assented to the truth of them when he was a zealous preacher of the gospel; but he never had so much as one ounce of justifying faith in his soul. 'There are some of you that believe not. For Jesus knew from the beginning who they were that believed not, and who should betray him' (*John 6:64*).

Even Judas' master, the devil himself – one far enough, I suppose, from justifying faith – assents to the truth of the Word. He goes against his conscience when he denies it.

When he tempted Christ he did not dispute *against* Scripture, but *from* Scripture, drawing his arrows out of this very quiver (*Matt. 4:6*). And at another time, he makes as full a confession of Christ as Peter himself did (*Matt. 8:29*, compared with *Matt. 16:17*). Assent to the truth of the Word is but an act of the understanding, which reprobates and devils may exercise. But justifying faith has its substance both in the understanding and the will; therefore it is called a believing 'with the heart' (*Rom. 10:10*). 'Philip said, If thou believest with all thine heart, thou mayest' (*Acts 8:37*). It takes in all the powers of the soul.

There is a double object in the promise, which relates to both the understanding and the will. As the promise is true, so it calls for an act of assent from the understanding; and as it is good as well as true, so it calls for an act of the will to embrace it. Therefore, the person who knows the truth of the promise only intellectually, without clinging to it, does not believe savingly. That man no more receives benefit from the promise than a person who realizes food is nourishing but refuses to eat.

Justifying faith is not assurance. If it were, John might have spared himself the trouble of writing to 'you that believed on the name of the Son of God, that ye might know that ye have eternal life' (*1 John 5:13*). His readers might then have said, 'We already do this. Is it not faith to believe that we are among those pardoned through Christ, and that we shall be saved through Him?' But this cannot be so. If faith were assurance, then a man's sins would be pardoned before he believes, for surely he must be pardoned before he can know he is pardoned. The candle must be lighted before I can see it is lighted. The child must be born before I can be assured it is born. The object must be before the act.

Assurance is not faith itself, but rather the fruit of faith. Assurance is in faith as the flower is in the root. Faith, in time, after much communion with God, acquaintance with the Word, and experience of His fellowship with the soul, may flourish into assurance. But as the root truly lives before the flower appears, and continues after it and its beautiful petals are gone, so does true justifying faith live before assurance comes, and live on after it disappears. Assurance is like the sunflower, which opens with the day and shuts with the night. But faith is a plant that can grow in the shade, a grace that can find the way to heaven in a dark night. It 'walketh in darkness,' and yet will 'trust in the name of the Lord' (*Isa. 50:10*).

Now, to state it positively, justifying faith is that act of the soul by which it rests on Christ crucified for pardon and life, and trusts the guarantee of that promise. The whole truth of God is the object of justifying faith. It deals with the whole Word of God and firmly assents to it; but in its justifying act, it singles out Christ crucified for its object. Assurance says, 'I believe my sins are pardoned through Christ.' Faith's language is, 'I believe on Christ for the pardon of them.' The Word of God directs our faith to Christ and terminates it upon Him; it is called, therefore, a 'coming to Christ' (*Matt. 11:28*), a 'receiving of him' (*John 1:12*), a 'believing on him' (*John 17:20*).

The promise is only the dish in which Christ, the true food of the soul, is served up; and if faith's hand is on that promise, it is as one that draws the dish to him so he can be fed. The promise is the marriage ring on the hand of faith. Now we are not married to the ring but joined to Christ with it. 'For the promises of God,' Paul says, 'in him are yea, and in him Amen' (*2 Cor. 1:20*). They have their excellency from Him and their effectiveness in Him – I mean in a person's union with Him. To run away with a promise, and not unite with Christ and by faith become one in Him, is as if a man should tear a branch from a tree and expect it to bear fruit on the shelf. Promises are dead branches severed from Christ. But when a soul by faith becomes one with Him, then it partakes of all His life; every promise yields sweetness.

When we say Christ is the primary object of faith, we mean Christ crucified. Not Christ in all His personal excellence – for as such He is the end of our love rather than of our faith – but as bleeding to death, under the hand of divine justice to make atonement by God's own appointment for the sins of the world. As the handmaid's eye watches her mistress's hand for direction, faith's eye is on God revealing Himself in His Word; and wherever God's Word points the soul, that is where it goes. In the Word, faith finds God ready to save sinners and clings to Christ for the transacting and accomplishing of that salvation. Faith, then, chooses to lay her burden of confidence upon that divine Man whom God has entrusted with His work.

Again, faith sees how Christ performed this great redeeming work and how the promise holds Him forth to be applied for pardon and salvation. Faith finds that Christ made the full payment to God's justice for sin when He poured out His blood. All the preceding acts of His humiliation were preparation for this. He was born to die; He was sent into the world as a sacrificial lamb bound with the cords of an irreversible decree. When Christ Himself came into the world, He understood that this was His errand: 'When he cometh into the world, he saith, Sacrifice and offering thou wouldest not, but a body hast thou prepared me' (*Heb. 10:5*); Christ was the atoning sacrifice. Without this, all He had done would have been unfruitful. There is no redemption but by the blood of

Jesus: 'In whom we have redemption through his blood, the forgiveness of sins' (*Eph. 1:7*).

Just as redemption is impossible without Christ's blood neither can the church exist without it: 'The church of God, which he hath purchased with his own blood' (*Acts 20:28*). The church is taken out of the dying Jesus' side, as Eve was brought from Adam's body. Christ did not redeem and save man by sitting in majesty on His heavenly throne but by hanging on the shameful cross, under the tormenting hand of man's fury and God's wrath. Therefore the person who wants his sins pardoned is directed to place his faith not only on Christ, but on the bleeding Christ: 'Whom God hath set forth to be a propitiation through faith in his blood' (*Rom. 3:25*).

Faith, then, becomes active when it rests on Christ crucified for pardon and life. There are many acts of the soul which must precede this, for a person can never truly exercise this faith unless he first has knowledge of Christ and relies on His authority. Only then can he say, 'I know whom I have believed' (*2 Tim. 1:12*). Most people are reluctant to trust a complete stranger. Abraham did not know where he was going, but he knew with whom he was going! God worked with Abraham to teach him the knowledge of His own glorious self – who He was – so that His child could rely on His word, assenting to the truth of it no matter how harsh and improbable and impossible it seemed. 'I am the Almighty God; walk before me, and be thou perfect' (*Gen. 17:1*).

God also wanted Abraham to recognize his own emptiness and inadequacy. He means us to see what we deserve – hell and damnation. But He also intends us to recognize our own impotence and how little – indeed, nothing – we can contribute to our own reconciliation. I join them together, because one arises out of the other. Our sense of emptiness comes from the deep apprehension we feel as we see God's fullness and our own insufficiency. One never encounters a man full of self-confidence and self-abasement together. The conscience cannot abound with the sense of sin and the heart abound with self-conceit at the same time. Both are necessary to faith – a sense of sin, like the pain of a wound, to make the creature think of medicine to cure it; and a sense of emptiness and insufficiency in himself to make him turn to Christ for cure. We would not go abroad to beg what we already have in the house.

However it is not these preliminaries but the receiving of Christ, and resting on Him, which comprise the act of faith to which justification is promised. 'He that believeth on him is not condemned: but he that believeth not is condemned already, because he hath not believed in the name of the only begotten Son of God' (*John 3:18*). Not everyone who assents to the truth of what the Scripture says of Christ believes on Him. This believing on Christ implies a union of the soul to Christ and a security in leaning on Him. Therefore we are told to take hold of Christ: 'Let him take hold of my strength, that he may make peace with me; and he shall make peace with me' (*Isa. 27:5*). Christ is also referred to as God's 'arm.' It is not seeing an arm stretched out over the water that will save a man from drowning, but the taking hold of it.

Still another lesson Abraham had to learn was the absolute security and reliability of God's covenant with him. There is no way God can be understood as contracting a debt to one of His creatures but by His promise. There are ways for men to become debtors to one another without ever actually making promises. A father is a debtor to his child and owes him love, provision, and nurture. The child is a debtor to his parent and owes him honor and obedience, though neither of them promised this to the other. Much more does the creature stand deep in God's debt-book and owe himself, with all he has, to God his Maker, although he does not have the grace voluntarily to make these promises and covenants to God. But the great God is so absolute a Sovereign that none can make a law to bind Him but Himself. Until He is pleased to pass an act of grace of His own good will, to give this or do that good thing to and for His poor creatures, no claim can be laid to the least mercy at His hands. There are two things therefore which the person must obey if he wants to believe: First, he must seek out a promise for his faith and the authority to expect such a mercy at God's hand. Secondly, when he has found this promise and observed the terms on which it stands, the Christian is not to wait for any further encouragement but, upon the basis of the naked promise, to put his faith to work.

He is to seek out the promise and observe its terms. To believe without a promise, or to believe on a promise but not observe the terms of it – both are presumptuous. A prince has as much reason to be angry with a man who does not obey his command as with another who acts without any command at all. Many who boldly lean on God's arm for pardon and salvation never realize that the promise which presents Christ to be leaned on as Savior presents Him at the same time to be exalted as Lord! The rebellious Israelites dared make God and His promise a leaning-stock for their foul elbows to rest on. 'They call themselves of the holy city, and stay themselves upon the God of Israel' (*Isa. 48:2*); but they were more bold than welcome. God rejected their confidence and loathed their sauciness. Although a prince would not hesitate to let a poor wounded man, weak and faint with bleeding, lean on his arm rather than die in the street; yet he would indignantly reject the same request from a filthy, staggering drunkard. The humble soul who lies bleeding for his sins at the mouth of hell would be welcomed by God when he comes on the encouragement of the promise to lean on Christ. But the profane wretch who rushes to Christ by his own merits shall be rejected by a holy God for abusing His promise.

When a poor sinner finds a promise and observes the terms with a heart willing to embrace them, he is to put forth an act of faith upon the credit of the naked promise, without looking for any other encouragement. Old Jacob gave no credit to his children when they told him Joseph was still alive and governor over all the land of Egypt. This news was too good and too great to enter into his belief, because he had thought for so long that Joseph was dead. It is said, 'And Jacob's heart fainted, for he believed them not' (*Gen. 45:26*). But when he saw the wagons that Joseph had sent to carry him on, then it is said, 'The spirit of Jacob their father revived' (*verse 27*). In similar fashion, the promise tells the poor humbled sinner that Christ is alive and is Governor of heaven itself, with all power there and on earth to give eternal life to all who believe on Him. The sinner is therefore urged to rest upon Christ in the promise; yet his heart faints and believes not. It is the wagons he insists upon seeing – some tangible expression of God's love that he listens for. If only he knew that he is one whom God does love, then he would believe. But God has little reason to be pleased with him in the mean time for suspending his faith until the wagons come.

WHY FAITH IS COMPARED TO A SHIELD
The apostle compares faith to a shield because of a double resemblance between this grace and that particular piece of armour.

The first likeness is that the shield is not for the defense of any one part of the body, as most other pieces are. The helmet is fitted for the head and the plate designed for the breast, but the shield is intended for the defense of the whole body. Therefore it was to be made very large and was called a 'gate' or 'door' because it was so long and large that it covered the whole body. The psalmist alludes to this meaning when he says, 'Thou, Lord, wilt bless the righteous; with favour wilt thou compass him as with a shield' (*Ps. 5:12*). And if the shield was not large enough to cover every part at once, the skillful soldier could turn it this way or that way, to stop the swords or the arrows, no matter where they were directed. This resemblance reminds us of the importance of faith in the life of a Christian. It defends the whole man – every part of the Christian is preserved by it.

Sometimes the temptation is leveled at the head – at the saint's *reasoning*. Satan will dispute truth and, if he can, will make a Christian question the validity of faith merely because his understanding cannot comprehend it. And sometimes he prevails, blotting out a person's beliefs in the deity of Christ and in other great and profound truths of the gospel. But faith intervenes between the believer and this arrow, coming to the relief of the Christian's weak understanding.

Abraham, 'being not weak in faith . . . considered not his own body now dead' (*Rom. 4:19*). If reason had had the upper hand in that business, if that holy man had put the promise to a test of sense and reason, he would have been in danger of questioning the truth of it, although God Himself was the messenger. But faith brought him through the test. 'I will trust the Word of God,' says the believer, 'not my own blind reason.'

Again, is it *conscience* that the tempter assaults? Satan

often shoots his fiery darts of horror and terror at this mark. But faith can endure the shock: 'I had fainted, unless I had believed,' said David (*Ps. 27:13*). When false witnesses rose up against him and breathed out cruelty, faith was his best defense against man's accusations. And so it is against Satan's charge, and conscience's also.

Never was a man in a sadder condition than the Philippian jailer. The only thing that kept him from suicide was the strong determination of his prisoners. Who, having seen him fall at the feet of Paul and Silas with the question, 'Sirs, what must I do to be saved?' (*Acts 16:30*), would have thought this deep wound to his conscience could so soon be closed and healed? The earthquake of horror which had so dreadfully shaken his conscience was quiet, and his trembling turned into rejoicing. Notice what it was that caused such a blessed calm: 'Believe on the Lord Jesus Christ, and thou shalt be saved' (*verse 31*). And he 'rejoiced, believing in God with all his house' (*verse 34*). Faith stilled the storm which sin had raised. It was faith that changed his grief into joy and gladness.

Again, is it the *will* that temptation tries to snare? Some of God's commands cannot be obeyed without self-denial, because they cross us in circumstances where our wills adamantly desire to rule. Thus we must deny our own wills before we can do God's will. Now a temptation becomes very forceful when it runs with the tide of our human wills. 'What!' says Satan, 'Will you serve a God who thwarts you in everything?' It seems that God always asks you to give up what you love the most. No lamb in all the flock would serve for a sacrifice but Isaac, Abraham's only child.

God was not content until Abraham served Him in a place of banishment from his closest family and friends.

'Will you yield to such hard terms as these?' Satan taunted. Now faith is the grace which serves the soul admirably during such a crisis as this. It is able to still the tumult which temptation stirs in the soul and finally, to dismiss all thoughts of mutiny. And further, faith can keep the King of heaven's peace so sweetly in the Christian's heart that such a temptation, when it comes, finds nothing to welcome it. 'By faith,' it is written, 'Abraham . . . obeyed; and . . . went out, not knowing whither he went' (*Heb. 11:8*). And we do not read of a single wistful look he cast back toward his native country, because faith had made him satisfied with his path.

It was hard work for Moses to strip himself of the magistrate's robes and allow someone else to take over his work and reap the honor of planting the Israelites' colors in Canaan, after it had cost him so much to bring them within sight of it. Yet faith made him willing; he saw better robes in heaven that he would put on than those he was called to put off on earth. The lowest place in glory is, beyond all compare, greater than the highest place of honor here on earth. For Moses to stand before the throne and minister to God in heaven was more to be desired than to sit on an earthly throne and have all the world bowing at his feet.

The second resemblance between faith and a shield is this: not only does the shield defend the whole body, but it defends the soldier's other armour also. It keeps the arrow from the helmet as well as from the head, from both breast and breastplate alike. Thus faith is armour upon armour, a grace that preserves all the other graces.

THE MEANING OF THE EXPRESSION 'ABOVE ALL'

There are various views among interpreters as to the

meaning of this phrase. Jerome has it mean: 'In all duties, enterprises, temptations, or afflictions – in whatever you are called to do or suffer – take faith.' Indeed, faith to the Christian is like fire to the chemist; nothing can be done in the name of Christ without it. 'Without faith it is impossible to please him' (*Heb. 11:6*). And how can the Christian please himself if he does not please God? Others interpret the passage like this: 'Over all, take the shield of faith as that which will cover all your graces.' Every grace derives its safety from faith; each one lies secure under the shadow of faith, as an army is protected under the command of a strong castle fitted with cannon. But let me follow the translation I feel is most comprehensive: 'Above all, take' – that is, among all the pieces of armour which you are to wear for your defense, let this one be the one you purpose most earnestly to acquire; and having acquired it, most carefully to keep. We see, then, that the apostle compared faith to the shield because he meant to give it pre-eminence.

In old times the shield was prized by a soldier above all other pieces of armour. He counted it a greater shame to lose his shield than to lose the battle; and therefore he would not part with it even when he was under the very foot of the enemy, but esteemed it an honor to die with his shield in his hand. It was the charge which one mother laid upon her son going into war: 'Either bring your shield home with you or be brought home upon your shield.' She would rather have seen her son dead with his shield than alive without it.

The apostle further attached another noble effect to faith. We are commanded to take the girdle of truth, the breastplate of righteousness, and so on, but it is not specified what each one of them could do. Yet when the apostle spoke of faith he ascribed the whole victory to it.

This quenches 'all the fiery darts of the wicked.' And why is this true? Are the other graces useless, and does faith do everything? If so, why must the Christian arm himself with more than this one piece?

I answer that every piece has its vital use in the Christian's warfare. No one part can be spared in the day of battle. But the reason that no single effect is attributed to each of these, but that all is ascribed to faith, is to let us know that these graces – their power and our benefit from them – must operate in conjunction with faith.

Plainly it is the design of God's Spirit to give faith the precedence among all those graces entrusted to our keeping. But be careful not to become indifferent or careless in your dealings with the other graces just because you are more excited about getting and keeping this one. Could we warn a soldier to beware of a wound at his heart but forget to guard his head? Truly, we would deserve cracked crowns to cure us of such foolishness.

I. The Pre-eminence of Faith Above Other Graces

Of all graces faith is the most important. The Christian must fight to keep it because there is a pre-eminence peculiar to faith. It is among graces as the sun is among the planets, or as Solomon's virtuous woman among the daughters.

In one Scripture the apostle gives precedence to love and sets faith on a lower level: 'And now abideth faith, hope, charity, these three; but the greatest of these is charity' (*1 Cor. 13:3*). Here his placing of love before faith points to the saints' blissful home in heaven, where love remains and faith disappears. In that regard love is clearly the greater, because it is the end of our faith. We see by faith so that we may enjoy by love.

Before the Christian can enjoy heaven's rewards,

however, he must live in a spiritually militant state here on earth. From this practical perspective love must give way to faith. It is true – love is the grace which will triumph in heaven. But it is faith, not love, which is the conquering grace on earth. 'This is the victory that overcometh the world, even our faith' (*1 John 5:4*).

Certainly love has its place in battle and contends valiantly, but it moves under faith, its leader: 'faith which worketh by love' (*Gal. 5:6*). Even as the captain fights by his soldiers whom he leads, so faith works by the love which it arouses. Love is the grace which ultimately possesses the inheritance, but it is faith that gives the Christian the right to it. Without faith he could never enjoy it.

Love is the grace which unites God and the glorified saints in heaven; but it is faith which first unites them to Christ while they are in the world – 'that Christ may dwell in your hearts by faith' (*Eph. 3:17*). And if Christ never dwells in them by faith on earth, they can never dwell with God in heaven.

WHY FAITH IS PRE-EMINENT

Why does faith have such pre-eminence over the other graces?

I. THE GREAT INQUIRY GOD MAKES OF FAITH

Nothing else shows how important persons or things are to us more than how frequently we ask after them. We inquire most often about those whom we love the most. 'Is your father well,' asked Joseph, 'the old man of whom ye spake? Is he yet alive?' (*Gen. 43:27*). Surely Joseph was interested in other people too, but because of his deep affection for his father, he wanted to find out about him first.

Now we come to the great inquiry which God makes for

faith: 'When the Son of man cometh, shall he find faith on the earth?' (*Luke 18:8*). He implies here that faith is the grace which He especially wants to find in His people.

Christ further illustrates the pre-eminence of faith in the account of His restoring sight to the blind man by the pool of Siloam. This healing so enraged the malicious Pharisees that they excommunicated the man for no fault other than giving glory to his merciful Physician. And the presence and tenderness of Jesus more than compensated for this man's sudden new role as an outcast. But to our present purpose, let us note Christ's words to this person at their first meeting: 'Dost thou believe on the Son of God?' (*John 9:35*). The man had already expressed some enthusiasm in vindicating Christ and in speaking favorably of Him to the bitterest enemies He had on earth. But the one thing which Christ prized even more highly than the man's loyalty was his faith, a fact which we find in His inquiry: 'Dost thou believe?' It is as if He had said, 'All this zeal in speaking for Me, and your patience in suffering, are worth absolutely nothing if you do not have faith.'

As we see in Jesus' encounter with the blind man, most of God's dealings with His people are questions concerning their faith, either the presence or the strength of it. And even when He afflicts, it is for 'the trial of your faith' (*1 Pet. 1:7*).

Afflictions are a spade which God uses to dig into His people's hearts to find the gold of faith. Not that He does not seek out the other graces also, but faith is the most precious of them all. Even when God delays and seems to withdraw His hand before coming with the mercy He promises, it is so that He can explore our faith.

Jesus carefully but thoroughly examined the Canaanite woman's faith while she struggled to believe: 'O woman, great is thy faith: be it unto thee even as thou wilt' (*Matt.*

15:28). In answering this woman's plea for Him to heal her daughter, Jesus gave her the evidence of her faith and more mercy by far than she had expected.

II. THE FAVOR GIVEN TO FAITH

Even when other graces are working along with faith in the Christian's life, it is faith that receives the crown of supremacy. We hear almost nothing, for example, about any grace except faith in the eleventh chapter of Hebrews. 'By faith Abraham,' 'by faith Jacob,' and 'by faith' the rest of those saints did their great exploits. In each of their accomplishments the other graces were present with faith. But here all come under the name of faith. Each soldier in an army fights the battle, but the honor of that victory goes to the general or captain.

Faith is the captain grace. All the notable acts of saints are recorded as achievements under its command. Thus Christ says of the centurion, 'Verily I say unto you, I have not found so great faith, no, not in Israel' (*Matt. 8:10*). Other graces besides faith were eminent in the centurion, such as his devotion for his servant, whom he cared for as conscientiously as if he had been his own son.

The centurion's humility first became obvious in the self-abasing attitude he expressed: 'Lord, I am not worthy that thou shouldest come under my roof' (*verse 8*). When we consider this man's military prominence as a swordsman and commander, his humility becomes even more conspicuous. Power is seldom such a companion to humility. Surely the centurion was a man of unusual character to humble himself in approaching Christ; yet faith outshines humility as his greatest virtue.

Christ did not say, 'I have not found such *humility*,' but 'such *faith*.' It is as if He had said, 'I know the exact measure of faith in every believer in all Israel; but I have

[35]

not found so much of this heavenly treasure in any one hand as in this centurion's.'

Indeed the Christian's most priceless riches are held in faith's hand. 'Hath not God chosen the poor of this world rich in faith?' (*James 2:5*). Why does God say 'rich in faith' rather than rich in patience, rich in love, or any other grace? When a sinner claims pardon of sin, favor of God, and heaven itself, it is not love or patience but faith alone which lays down the price of all these benefits. Not, 'Lord, pardon and save me – here are my love and patience for it'; but, 'Here is Christ and the price of His blood, which faith presents for the full payment of them all.' This understanding, then, leads to a third reason for the pre-eminence of faith.

III. THE IMPORTANCE OF OUR JUSTIFICATION

'Therefore being justified by faith, we have peace with God through our Lord Jesus Christ' (*Rom. 5:1*). We are not justified by love, repentance, patience, or any other grace besides faith. 'Justifying patience,' 'justifying repentance' – how jarring these words sound to a Christian. Rather, we find that justification is appropriated by faith and the rest of the graces hedged out from this act, although they are included and assumed in the person who is justified.

Paul's job was to prove that faith justifies without works. But the faith which justifies is not idle or dead but a lively working faith, which seems to be James's design in the second chapter of his epistle. As God singled out Christ from all others to be the only mediator between Himself and man, and His righteousness to be the worthy cause of our justification; so He has singled out faith from all the other graces to be the instrument for appropriating this righteousness of Christ to us. This righteousness is called 'the righteousness of God' as opposed to our 'own righteousness,' although it is worked by God in us (*Rom. 10:3*). It is wrought for us by Christ.

It is also called 'the righteousness of faith' (*Rom. 4:11, 13*). Why does God call it 'the righteousness of faith' and not of love or repentance? Surely faith itself is not our righteousness. If this were true, we would be justified by works *and* by faith. We would be justified by a righteousness of our own; for faith is a grace inherent in us, and as much our own work as any other grace. But this is contrary to the apostle's doctrine, wherein he clearly contrasts faith and works. Scripture sets forth 'the righteousness of faith' for this reason and no other – faith is the only grace whose role it is to lay hold on Christ, and so to secure His righteousness for our justification (*Rom. 4:11*).

Christ and faith are relatives which must not be severed. Christ is the treasure, and faith the hand which receives it. Christ's righteousness is the robe, and faith the hand which puts it on. It is by His blood, not by our faith, that He discharges our debt. Our part is only to receive Christ by faith, so that He becomes ours. It is Christ's righteousness that is the robe which covers our nakedness and makes us beautiful in God's sight; faith has the honor of putting the robe on.

God blessed Moses exceedingly above the rest of the Israelites when He called him up the mountain to receive the law from His own mouth, while the rest of the Israelites had to wait until he brought it down to them. Accordingly, God highly honors faith as the grace by which He conveys the glorious privilege of justification. But why does God choose to use faith rather than any other grace to complete this act of justification? We see at least two reasons.

First, no other grace besides faith is so appropriately designed for this purpose. Why has God appointed the eye instead of the ear to see? Why the hand rather than the foot to take our food? This is easily answered – because these members have a particular fitness for these functions. Thus faith has a fitness for this work peculiar to itself. We are justified not by giving anything to God but by receiving from Him what Christ has already done for us. Faith is the only receiving grace and therefore the only one appropriate for justification.

Secondly, there is no grace God could trust His honor so safely with in the business of justification as with faith. The great design of God in justifying a helpless sinner is to magnify His free mercy in the eyes of that creature.

Because God is determined that His mercy should keep all the honor, He protects the person from any pretension to partnership with Him regarding justification. There is no way like being justified by faith for securing and safe-guarding the glory of God's free grace. When the apostle discusses the free justification of a sinner before God, he shows how this cuts through the very fiber of all self-exalting thoughts: 'Where is boasting then? It is excluded. By what law? of works? Nay: but by the law of faith' (*Rom. 3:27*).

Throughout history, kings have closely guarded their own and their queens' reputation for sexual purity. They have been so protective in this respect that they avoided accusations by hiring eunuchs to attend themselves and their queens. By the very nature of the eunuchs' disability, all suspicion is displaced. God is even more jealous of having the glory of His grace ravished by pride and self-glorying, and to defend it from such abuse, He has chosen faith, this 'eunuch grace' with a self-emptying nature, to stand near Him and labor to safeguard the glory of His grace.

Faith has two hands. With one it pulls off its own righteousness and throws it away, as David discarded

Saul's armour; with the other it puts on Christ's righteousness to cover the soul's shame. 'This makes it impossible,' said one Bible scholar, 'to conceive that faith and works should be joined in justification. Faith attributes all to the free grace of God, but works draw attention to themselves. Faith aspires no higher than to be the instrumental cause of free remission; works can sit no lower, but insist on being seen as the source of justification.'

IV. THE INFLUENCE FAITH HAS ON THE OTHER GRACES
The sun is glorious because it serves all the lower world with light and influence. Faith is a grace which God uses as much for the good of the spiritual world – in the 'new creature' – as He uses the sun for the physical world (*Gal. 6:15*). Just as nothing is hidden from the heat of the sun, there is no grace which faith's influence cannot touch.

HOW FAITH'S INFLUENCE REACHES THE OTHER GRACES

I. FAITH SUPPLIES ALL THE GRACES WITH WORK
Faith is like a wealthy owner of wool who supplies material to men who weave cloth. When the tradesman does not furnish supplies, the spinners must stop their production. They have nothing to work with except what the tradesman gives them. Thus faith gives out to each grace what it must have to act upon.

Let us review one or two graces as an example of all the rest. *Repentance* is a sweet grace but faith has to make it work. For instance, Nineveh's repentance can be traced to faith: 'The people of Nineveh believed God, and proclaimed a fast, and put on sackcloth' (*Jonah 3:5*). Their repentance may have been nothing more than legalism, but it was as good as their faith. If their faith had been better, their repentance would have been of a deeper quality too.

In the same way as light causes the eye to focus on an object, faith uncovers sin in the conscience. Thoughts soon arise like clouds and thicken into a storm until they fill the soul with heavy black horror and trembling for sin. But at this point the person is at a loss and cannot go any further into repentance until faith sends in more support from the promise of pardon. When the sinner hears and believes the promise, repentance can continue. And finally, the cloud of terror which the fear of wrath had gathered in the conscience dissolves into a soft rain of evangelical sorrow.

Love is another heavenly grace, but faith finds the fuel that makes it blaze. Was your soul always flaming with love for God the way it is now? Undoubtedly there was a time when your hearth was cold – not a spark of this fire could be found. How is it that you love God so much now? Surely you have heard some good news from heaven!

Faith is the only messenger which can bring good news from heaven to the heart. It is faith that proclaims the promise, opens Christ's riches, and pours out His name to increase love in believers. Whenever faith wins the character of Christ out of the Word and presents Him to us in all His loveliness, we are sweetly drawn to Him. 'Unto you therefore which believe he is precious' (*1 Pet. 2:7*).

We cannot really give our love to the Savior until we see Him for who He is. If we should sit by our dearest friend in a darkened room, we would pay no more attention to him than we would to a stranger. But if someone whispered that this is the one who laid down his life to save ours and then made us heir to all his personal estate, would we not show our respect for him? Our hearts would throb immediately with the longing to show strong affection to that person!

As long as faith's eye is closed or asleep, the Christian may sit very close to Christ in the shelter of His divine care and be completely unaffected by Him. But when faith sees

Him and reveals the sweetness in His bleeding love, the Christian has no choice but to respond with personal love.

II. FAITH HELPS ALL THE GRACES TO RECEIVE STRENGTH FROM CHRIST

Not only is faith the instrument to receive the righteousness of Christ for our *justification*, but it is also the great instrument to receive grace from Him for our *sanctification*. 'Of his fullness have all we received, and grace for grace' (*John 1:16*). But we must receive this fullness by faith. The faith that unites a soul with Christ is like a pipe by the mouth of a fountain which carries water into several houses for the supply of the whole neighborhood. Jesus said of the believer, 'Out of his belly shall flow rivers of living water' (*John 7:38*).

The Savior presented His disciples with a very hard lesson when He taught them to stir up enough love to forgive their offending brother 'seven times in a day' (*Luke 17:4*). Since his followers realized at once that it would be almost impossible for them to obey this teaching, they asked the Lord to increase their faith. But why did they not say, 'Increase our love'? If they had more faith in Christ they could love their brother more also. The more strongly they could believe on Christ for the pardon of their own sins – seventy times a day – the more easily they could forgive their brother who sinned against them seven times a day.

Notice how Christ responded to His disciples' prayer for more faith: 'If ye have faith as a grain of mustard seed, ye shall say unto this mountain, Remove hence to yonder place, and it shall remove' (*Matt. 17:20*). It is as if He had said, 'You have hit on the right way to get a forgiving spirit; it is faith that will enable you to conquer the unmercifulness of your hearts. Even if it is as deeply rooted as this mountain is in the earth, your faith can remove it.'

III. FAITH DEFENDS THE CHRISTIAN IN THE EXERCISE OF ALL HIS GRACES

'Thou standest by faith' (*Rom. 11:20*). A soldier stands his ground under the protection of his shield and does his duty even when the enemy opens fire to drive him back. If faith should fail, then every grace will be put to flight. Job's patience was wounded when his hand got too tired to hold up his shield of faith as a covering.

Similarly, no grace is safe if it is out from under the wing of faith. At a time when Peter's zeal surpassed his faith, Christ kept him from falling from all grace by saying, 'I have prayed for thee, that thy faith fail not' (*Luke 22:32*). Peter's faith was the reserve that the Savior took care should be kept in order to recover his other graces when the enemy foiled him, and to deliver him, bruised and broken, from that encounter.

Christ could not do many miracles for His own countrymen 'because of their unbelief' (*Matt. 13:58*). And neither can Satan harm the Christian seriously when faith is in its place. It is true that the devil skillfully aims to fight faith above all, because it is the grace which keeps him from conquering the rest of the graces. Although a saint may be humble, patient, and devout, Satan can easily tear a hole in these graces and break in if faith does not completely cover each piece of armour. But God's design is still our best defense; He causes faith to be the grace which makes Satan turn and run.

IV. FAITH ALONE GAINS ACCEPTANCE WITH GOD FOR ALL THE OTHER GRACES AND THEIR WORKS

Even the obedient Christian who works hard all day does not expect to take his accomplishment home at night and find God's acceptance for the sake of his human effort. It is only by faith that he can present it through Christ to God. We 'offer up spiritual sacrifices, acceptable to God by Jesus Christ' (*1 Pet. 2:5*) – that is, by faith in Christ. Faith can so prevail with God that He will take even the smallest broken pieces of human effort from its hand. But He takes nothing unless the hand of faith brings it to Him.

V. FAITH BRINGS HELP WHEN OTHER GRACES FAIL

There are two ways the Christian's graces may fail – in their activity and in their evidence.

Sometimes the various graces perform with such overcoming strength that the Christian breaks the bonds of temptation as easily as Samson snapped his cords of flax; but at other times, he is held prisoner because he cannot even begin to shake them off. Faith strengthens the Christian especially in his season of weakness. Just as Joseph drew his brothers to him and nourished each one out of his storehouses during famine, so faith sustains the Christian when his supply of grace seems to fail.

In time of need the Christian can claim the fullness of Christ's grace as his own. 'Why are you dejected because of your weak grace?' asks the Christian's faith. 'All fullness dwells in Christ and there is enough in Him to be the supply in your emptiness.' As the clouds do not carry rain for their own sake but for the good of the earth, so Christ offers His fullness of grace for us. 'But of him are ye in Christ Jesus, who of God is made unto us wisdom, and righteousness, and sanctification, and redemption' (*1 Cor. 1:30*).

Faith also supports the Christian by applying promises for perseverance in grace. Although a sick man may be faltering and helpless, he receives great comfort when his doctor tells him he will not die. The weakness of grace is sad, but the fear of falling away is even sadder. Now faith, and only faith, is the messenger to bring this good news to the soul, that it can persevere.

[43]

In this matter of perseverance, sense and reason are outsmarted. It seems impossible to them that such a bruised reed could hold up against all the counterblasts of hell. Since it is so overmatched by Satan's power and policy, they think it only rational to give the victory to the stronger side. But when faith sees symptoms of death in the saint's grace, it finds life in the promise and comforts the soul. Our God is faithful and will not let His grace see corruption; He has undertaken the *eternal* life of His saints.

When the Christian consults his faith and asks whether his weak grace will fail or hold out, faith's answer is, 'Your feeble grace may possibly die and fall away, but the Lord has showed me it will live and persevere.' Because of its own frailty and the changeableness of man's nature, the Christian's grace might certainly die; but God has shown faith in the promise that it will recover even from the most serious infirmity.

When we must admit our grace is far from being sufficient, God sends His Word to give us new courage. Listen to David's last words regarding his household: 'Although my house be not so with God; yet he hath made with me an everlasting covenant, ordered in all things, and sure: for this is all my salvation, and all my desire' (*2 Sam. 23:5*). He saw God's eternal covenant with him as being the same as all his salvation, even though he could not see the solution to his problem at that moment.

The salt of this 'everlasting covenant' is that it preserves our weak grace from corruption. 'Why art thou cast down, O my soul?' asked the psalmist, 'Hope in God: for I shall yet praise him, who is the health of my countenance, and my God' (*Ps. 43:5*). The health of David's countenance was not in his own human outlook nor in what he had to face in life, but in his God – security that causes faith to silence fears.

A second way the Christian's graces can fail is in the evidence of them. Sometimes these graces fade as stars do in a cloudy night. When the Christian is tempted he says, 'I do not know whether I love God sincerely or not; I cannot say I have any true godly sorrow for sin. I am at a loss what to think, but sometimes I am ready to think the worst.' Even in this kind of darkness, faith undergirds the soul's ship and throws out two unyielding anchors to rescue the Christian from the devouring quicksands of despair.

(a) *Faith finds rich mercy in Christ and invites the sinner to look up to it when he loses sight of his own grace*

God is full of grace and mercy; if you have lost the evidence of your grace He is ready to restore it. But David did more than ask God for restoration – he prayed for Him to *create*: 'Create in me a clean heart, O God; and renew a right spirit within me' (*Ps. 51:10*). 'Yes,' says faith, 'if it were true what you fear – that your grace was never real in the first place – there is enough mercy in God's heart to pardon even your hypocrisy, as long as you come to Him in repentance.'

Faith, then, persuades the soul by an act of adventure to cast itself upon God in Christ. It is not beyond God's mercy to forgive many unkindnesses, much falseness, and great unfaithfulness when a sinner humbly confesses his wrong. The world is full of parents who do as much for their children. Is it hard for God to do what is easy for humans? Faith vindicates God's name. And as long as we do not lose sight of God's merciful heart, our heads will be kept above water, even though we cannot see any evidence of our own grace.

(b) *Further, when the Christian cannot see any evidence of grace in himself, faith discovers it in the promise of Scripture*

A man who has no bread left in his kitchen is relieved to

[45]

hear there is bread available in the market. A Christian may regret that he has a hard heart with no genuine sorrow for his sin. If he could experience brokenness, he reasons with himself, then he might run to Christ and take comfort from His promise: 'Blessed are they that mourn: for they shall be comforted' (*Matt. 5:4*).

Faith intervenes to insist, 'There are not only promises to the mourning and broken-hearted, but promises for those who need brokenness and a spirit of mourning.' God reveals how He gathers the erring person to Himself: 'A new heart also will I give you, and a new spirit will I put within you: and I will take away the stony heart out of your flesh . . . and cause you to walk in my statutes' (*Ezek. 36:26–27*).

Thus faith arouses the Christian out of troubled thoughts, where he cowers without hope, and turns his complaints into fervent prayer for the grace he wants so much. 'There is bread in the promise,' says faith. 'Do not keep sitting here in despondency but get down on your knees and boldly, yet humbly, ask for grace in your time of need.' The Christian will get new evidence for his grace sooner by remembering and believing God's promise than he will by giving in to unbelieving thoughts. Satan delights in watching the Christian's strength and time melt away into bitterness without realizing that what he wants is ready to hand. But God purposes that the Christian should find help and freely put that help into action.

VI. FAITH COMFORTS THE CHRISTIAN WHEN OTHER GRACES ABOUND

Of all the graces, faith is the Christian's cup-bearer. The Christian takes the wine of joy out of faith's hand, rather than from any other grace. 'Now the God of hope fill you with all joy and peace in believing, that ye may abound in hope, through the power of the Holy Ghost' (*Rom. 15:13*).

The apostle Paul gives pre-eminence to faith, attributing the Christian's joy to his faith rather than to his love. 'Whom having not seen, ye love; in whom, though now ye see him not, yet believing, ye rejoice with joy unspeakable and full of glory' (*1 Pet. 1:8*). Mark the key word in that passage: '*believing*, ye rejoice.' Here is the door where the Christian's joy comes in. God allows us to rejoice only in Christ. 'For we are the circumcision, which worship God in the spirit, and rejoice in Christ Jesus, and have no confidence in the flesh' (*Phil. 3:3*).

Christ's blood is the only wine which gladdens God's heart and satisfies his justice at the same time. Therefore it is all that can bring true gladness into the heart of man. When Christ promises the Comforter, He tells His disciples about the vessel He will use to draw the wine of joy. 'He shall take of mine, and shall shew it unto you' (*John 16:15*). No grape of our own harvest is pressed into this sweet cup. It is as if Christ says, 'When He comes to comfort you with the forgiveness of your sins, He will take of mine, not anything of yours. I purchased your peace with God with My blood, not by your tears of repentance or mourning for your sins.'

The Christian's joy flows from Christ alone, not from any human source. But faith discovers unsearchable riches in Christ and reveals to the Christian all that it sees and knows of Him. And it is faith that makes an opening in our hearts for the promises and then pours in the sweet realities of God's Word (see *Rom. 10:17*).

Not only does faith show the soul how wonderful Christ Jesus is, and the pleasures in God's promises; but it also makes Christ real to the soul in practical ways. Faith carves out sweet servings of life-giving meat from God's

Word, puts them into the mouth of the soul, and grinds these promises into fine particles so that the saint receives strength and stability (see *John 6:63*). Because of faith, the Christian enjoys satisfying nourishment by tasting every dish at the table which his Father spreads before him.

THE PRE-EMINENCE OF UNBELIEF AMONG SINS

Unbelief deserves as high a place among sins as faith has among graces. Unbelief is the Beelzebub, or prince of sins, which makes others sin. God branded Jeroboam as one 'who did sin, and who made Israel to sin' (*1 Kings 14:16*). Unbelief is a sin-making sin.

The first poisonous breath which Eve took in from the tempter was sent in these words: 'Yea, hath God said, Ye shall not eat of every tree of the garden?' (*Gen. 3:1*). It is as if he had said, 'Think about this now. Do you really believe God would keep back the best fruit in the whole garden from you?' This was the traitor's gate whereby all other sins rushed into Eve's heart; and even now Satan continues to hold this same gate wide open.

The devil sets up a blind of unbelief between the sinner and God so that he will not fear the Father's warning and chastening aimed at his heart. Then once there is a barricade between him and these merciful bullets, the sinner can be bold with his lust. Unbelief not only diverts the bullets of wrath which are sent out of the law's fiery mouth, but it also retards the actions of grace coming from the gospel. All the offers of love which God makes to an unbelieving heart fall like sparks into a river; they are put out as soon as they fall into it.

'The word preached did not profit them, not being mixed with faith in them that heard it' (*Heb. 4:2*). The secret of sin's strong hold upon a person is unbelief. There is no mastering a sinner while unbelief overpowers him. This sin will break down all reasoning as easily as Samson did the doors and posts, bar and all, from the city of Gaza (*Judg. 16:3*). It is a sin which holds out last on the battlefield, the one which the sinner is least aware of, and which the saint ordinarily conquers last. It is one of the chief fortresses to which the devil retreats when other sins are routed.

How often a poor sinner will confess other sins he has lived in, but will not accept Christ's mercy! We beg him to believe on Christ and be saved – which was the doctrine Paul and Silas preached to the trembling jailer (*Acts 16:31*). But it is hard to persuade him to do this when the devil has already taken himself into this city of gates and bars and stands guard. To keep sinners with him there, Satan uses the most superficially plausible of all sins – the fear of sinning with presumptuous faith. Satan intends to use this sin to put the greatest scorn upon God and unfold all his diseased malice against Him at once.

It is by faith that the saints have all 'obtained a good report' (*Heb. 11:39*). And by the saints' faith God has a good report in the world. Yet by unbelief the devil does his worst to raise an evil report of God. In a word, hell gapes wide to swallow the sin of unbelief.

There are two sins which claim pre-eminence in hell – hypocrisy and unbelief. Therefore sinners are warned not to have their 'portion with the hypocrites' (*Matt. 24:51*) or with 'unbelievers' (*Luke 12:46*). It seems that infernal mansions are reserved principally for the sins of hypocrisy and unbelief and that all others are inferior prisoners. But of the two unbelief is the greater, for it is called 'the damning sin.' 'He that believeth not is condemned already' (*John 3:18*). The unbelieving person carries his own warrant to jail; in a sense he is already imprisoned, for he wears the brand of a damned person. The apostle said the Jews are to be shut up 'in unbelief' (*Rom. 11:32*), and surely there is no more confining prison the devil can keep sinners in.

Faith, on the other hand, shuts the soul up in the promise of life and happiness even as God shut Noah into the ark: 'The Lord shut him in' (*Gen. 7:16*). Thus faith shuts up the soul in Christ and the ark of His covenant, from all fear of danger from heaven or hell. On the contrary, unbelief shuts up a soul in guilt and wrath. And once he is held slave to unbelief, there is no more possibility for an unbeliever to escape damnation than for one shut up in a fiery oven to escape burning. No help can come to the sinner as long as unbelief bolts the door of his heart.

As our salvation is attributed to faith rather than to other graces – though none is absent in a saved person – so a sinner's damnation is attributed to his unbelief, although other sins also are found within the condemned person. The Spirit of God passes over the Jews' hypocrisy, murmuring, and rebellion and lays their destruction at the door of this one sin – unbelief.

Suppose a judge offers life to a condemned man on the condition that the prisoner read a psalm of mercy. If the person refuses to do this, his refusal is what hangs him. The promise of the gospel is this psalm of mercy, which God offers in His Son to sinners condemned by the law. Believing is reading the psalm of mercy. If you refuse to believe and are damned, you go to hell for unbelief, not for any other sin. Freedom is offered if you receive Christ and believe on Him. Let this cause us all to rise up against this sin as the Philistines did against Samson, whom they called the 'destroyer of our country' (*Judg. 16:24*). Unbelief is the destroyer of your souls, and that is worse; it destroys them with a bloodier hand than other sins do.

We find two principal indictments by which sinners will be condemned at the great day of judgment. Those who fall under Christ's condemning sentence are those who 'know not God' and those who 'obey not the gospel of our Lord Jesus Christ' (*2 Thess. 1:8*). The heathens' ignorant unbelief of the gospel will not be held against them, because they never had it preached to them. They will be sent to hell for not knowing God and thus escape with a lighter punishment than Jews or Christian Gentiles who have heard the gospel.

The somber charge brought against these men will be that they have not obeyed the gospel of Jesus. And certainly there must be a more severe torment in hell for those who refuse the gospel than for those who never received the offer of grace. These unbelievers reject God's greatest measure of mercy and therefore must expect the greatest proportion of His wrath. Because their unbelief shames Christ and the grace of God in Him, it is only right that God should put them and their unbelief to the utmost shame before men and angels.

WHY WE SHOULD BE SERIOUS IN THE TRIAL OF OUR FAITH

Some things are of such meager value that they are not worth the trouble we take to get them. But other things are worth so much that no one but the fool would risk not getting them. Suppose, for instance, that a terminally ill patient could save his life only by taking some scarce drug. How hard would he try to get exactly the right one? Will the devil's drugs, which are sure to kill, meet your need when God Himself offers a rich drug that will completely cure you? The apostle has labeled this life-giving gift the 'faith of God's elect' (*Tit. 1:1*).

When you shop for a garment you ask for the best

quality. In the market you look for the best meat; when with the lawyer, the best counsel; and with the physician, the best care for your health. Do you seek the very best in everything except for your soul? If a man receives false money, who does he cheat but himself? If you are deceived with false faith, the loss is yours.

When you come to the bar of judgment, God will demand that you pay the debt you owe Him or writhe painfully in hell's prison. If you hold false faith in your heart, He will not accept your payment, even though it is Christ Himself you believe in. He will give you over to the tormentor's hand not only for not believing but for counterfeiting the King of heaven's coin and placing His name on your false money. The judgment scene itself should be enough to stir our earnest determination to have true faith. But there are three additional important reasons why the Christian must be serious in his trial of faith.

1. AS YOUR FAITH IS, SO ARE ALL YOUR OTHER GRACES
As a man's marriage is, so are all his children – legitimate or illegitimate. Thus, as our marriage is to Christ, so all our graces are. Now it is faith by which we are married to Christ. 'I have espoused you to one husband,' said Paul to the Corinthians (*2 Cor. 11:2*). It is by faith that the soul gives consent to take Christ for her husband. If our faith is false, then our marriage to Christ is also false; and if the marriage is illicit, then all our assumed graces are illegitimate also.

No matter how handsome a bastard's face may be, he is still illegitimate. Our humility, patience, temperance – they are all illegitimate. Just as 'a bastard shall not enter into the congregation of the Lord' (*Deut. 23:2*), no bastard grace can enter the congregation of the redeemed in heaven. A man who has children of his own will not make another's bastard his heir. God has children of His own to inherit heaven's glory. And by His Spirit He has begotten heavenly graces in their hearts which resemble His own holy nature. Surely, then, He will never give His glory to mere strangers, counterfeit believers who are the devil's brats.

II. THE EXCELLENCY OF TRUE FAITH MAKES FALSE FAITH THE MORE REPULSIVE

Because a king's son holds such an exceptional position, it is a serious crime for a commoner to impersonate him. It is by faith that we 'become the sons of God' (*John 1:12*). A man blasphemes, therefore, when he pretends to be God's child but has no heaven-blood in his veins. Such a person traces his pedigree to Satan and must expect to meet his kinsfolk in hell. Because a false friend is worse than an open enemy, God abhors a hypocritical Judas more than a bloody Pilate.

Since an ape has the face but not the soul of a man, he is the most ridiculous of all creatures. And of all sinners, none will be subjected to more shame at the last day than those who have imitated the believers in profession but who have not performed a single act of faith. As for the prideful pretenders to godliness, the psalmist tells us God will 'despise their image' (*Ps. 73:20*).

But there is another sort of person whose image God hates even more than these, and that is the image of temporary believers who have an imaginary faith, which they set up like an image in their own imaginations. But in due time this self-pleasing idol will be shattered and its worshipers plummeted into hell.

III. FLATTERING FALSE FAITH SCREENS OUT THE OPERATION OF TRUE FAITH

'Seest thou a man wise in his own conceit? there is more hope of a fool than of him' (*Prov. 26:12*). Of all fools the conceited fool is the worst, in that pride makes a man incapable of receiving counsel. For example, Nebuchadnezzar's mind was 'hardened in pride' (*Dan. 5:20*). A proud man castles himself in his own opinion of himself and there settles in to defend himself against all reason. He thanks God that he does not have to seek faith and revels in the false hope that he is in good spiritual condition. But God knows that this man 'feedeth on ashes: a deceived heart hath turned him aside, that he cannot deliver his soul' (*Isa. 44:20*).

It is not hard for the ignorant sinner to admit he deserves nothing but hell, but the man who pretends to have faith lives a lie. Satan delights in stalling this man's search for fulfillment by cheating him along the way with a counterfeit faith. The Israelites longed for the true worship of God in Jerusalem, but Jeroboam kept them from going there by setting up something *like* religious worship at home. He substituted golden calves and satisfied many Israelites to such a degree that they never took the first step to Jerusalem.

Be careful not to let Satan cheat you with false faith. Everyone, I know, would have the living child, and not the dead one, to be hers. All of us want true faith. But do not be your own judges; appeal to the Spirit of God and let Him decide the controversy by using the sword of His Word. You say you have faith, but which kind is it – false or true?

HOW TO JUDGE THE TRUTH OF FAITH

By this time you may want to know what your faith is and how you can judge the truth of it. In your search there are two directions you can take – one, how the Spirit works faith in the soul; and the other, the characteristics of this faith.

1. HOW THE SPIRIT WORKS FAITH IN THE SOUL

Faith is the greatest work which the Spirit of Christ accomplishes in the human spirit. The apostle calls it 'the exceeding greatness of his power to us-ward who believe' (*Eph. 1:19*). Notice the expressions of the Spirit of God describing this work of the Spirit: 'power,' 'greatness of power,' 'exceeding greatness,' and 'exceeding greatness of his power.' What angel in heaven can understand the command of faith's power in the human spirit?

God assigns His whole being to this work. It is compared to 'the working of his mighty power, which he wrought in Christ, when he raised him from the dead, and set him at his own right hand in the heavenly places, far above all principality, and power' (*Eph. 1:19–21*). To raise anyone from the dead is a mighty, an almighty work; but to raise Christ from the dead implies more authority than to raise any other. He had a heavier gravestone to keep Him down – the weight of a world's sin upon Him. But regardless of this, He is raised with power by the Spirit, not just out of the grave but into glory. The power God expends in working faith in the soul is like raising Christ, for the sinner's soul is as dead in sin as Christ's body was in the grave for sin.

Many people who look for true faith find they do not have it. They have assumed that receiving Christ into their souls is as simple as putting a crumb of bread into their mouths. But since they have never experienced God's power humbling them because of personal sin, they have not laid down empty lives before Him. They have not been effectually drawn to Christ by the Holy Spirit. Should they be questioned about the experience of repentance and saving faith, they must give the same answer which Paul heard when he asked the Ephesians if they had received the Holy Spirit: 'We have not so much as heard whether there be any Holy Ghost' (*Acts 19:2*). So these persons might say, 'We did not know there was any such power required for faith to work.'

To see how God produces faith in the soul, we must consider two particular works of the Holy Spirit: the condition of the soul when the Spirit of Christ begins His work of grace, and the approach He uses to complete His work.

(a) *The condition of the soul when the Spirit begins His work of grace*

The Spirit finds the sinner in such a state of spiritual helplessness that he will not and cannot contribute anything to the work. As the 'prince of this world' found nothing in Christ to further his tempting design, so the Spirit of Christ finds as little co-operation from the sinner. On the contrary, the frequent response to God's gentle summons is: 'He came unto his own, and his own received him not' (*John 1:11*). No military bulwark ever fought against enemy batteries more sharply than the carnal heart resists God's efforts to reduce it to obedience. Because even the noblest operations of the soul are 'earthly, sensual, devilish' (*James 3:15*), unless heaven and earth can meet – God and the devil agree – there is no hope that a sinner could be won over to Christ through his own efforts.

(b) *How the Spirit approaches the soul and completes His work*

The Spirit addresses several faculties of the soul, the principal ones being understanding, conscience, and will. These attributes are like three forts, one within the other, which must all be captured before the town is taken – the sinner subdued to the obedience of faith. The Spirit must demonstrate at least three acts of almighty power upon every one of them.

(i) *The Spirit illuminates the understanding.* He will not work in a dark shop; the first thing He does to produce faith is to open a window in the soul and let in some light from heaven. Thus Scripture speaks of being 'renewed in the spirit of your mind' (*Eph. 4:23*). By our human nature we know little of God and nothing of Christ or the way of salvation by Him. The eye of the creature therefore must be opened to see the way of life before he can enter into it by faith. God does not transport souls to heaven like a ship's passengers who are shut under the hatches and see nothing all the way they are sailing to their port.

As faith is not just blind assent without leaning on Christ, neither is it assent without some knowledge. If you prefer your own ignorance and do not know who Christ is and what He has done for your salvation, you are far from believing. If this light of day has not broken into your soul, neither has the Sun of righteousness risen by faith to bring healing salvation into your spirit.

(ii) *The Spirit of God convicts the conscience.* When the Comforter comes, 'he will reprove the world of sin' (*John 16:8*). Now this conviction of the conscience is nothing but reflection of the light which is in the understanding. Because of it the sinner feels the weight and force of those things he knows are wrong in his life. Most people who hear the gospel realize that unbelief is a damning sin and that there is no name by which to be saved but the name of Christ; yet how many are convinced enough to apply repentance to their consciences?

By law a man is a convicted drunkard who is judged to be one by clear testimony and by a lawful authority. Likewise, a person is a convicted sinner who, upon the clear evidence of the Word brought against him by the Spirit, is found by his own conscience – God's officer in his heart – to be so. Has the Spirit of God come to try you in this way? There are at least four ways to determine whether or not you are a convicted sinner.

First, a convicted sinner is convicted not of one particular sin only, but of the evil of *all* sin. It is a bad sign when a person passionately condemns one sin but ignores another. A part-boiled conscience is not right, soft in one part and hard in another. The Spirit of God is uniform in His work.

Secondly, the convicted sinner is convicted of the state of sin as well as of acts of sin. He is affected not only by what he has done – this law broken and that mercy abused – but also by his present condition. Peter leads Simon Magus from that one foul act he committed to the recognition of something far worse – the dangerous position he was in: 'I perceive that thou art in the gall of bitterness, and in the bond of iniquity' (*Acts 8:23*). While many people are willing to confess they have sinned, they would not think of admitting they live in a state of sin and death. The convicted soul, however, freely accepts this sentence of death and owns up to his condition: 'I am a limb of Satan, full of sin. My whole nature lies in wickedness even as a rotten carcass lies in slime and decay. Because I am a child of wrath, the only inheritance I deserve is a flaming hell; and if God puts me there, I do not have one righteous syllable to argue against His decision. Even when it is doomed, my conscience clears Him from having done me any wrong.'

Thirdly, the convicted sinner not only condemns himself for what he has done and for what he is, but he realizes he cannot do anything to save himself. Although many condemned people will go so far as to confess their sin and wickedness, they hope to cut the rope from their neck at the last minute by repentance and good works.

Faith is not lazy; it does not lull the soul to sleep but stirs it up to work; it does not send the creature to bed but out into the field. The night of ignorance and unbelief was once the sleeping time; but when the Sun of righteousness arises, and it is day in the soul, then the creature rises to work. The first words that open faith's lips are those of Saul at his conversion: 'Lord, what wilt thou have me to do?' (*Acts 9:6*). Do not pretend to have faith if you do not freely bow to put on this yoke of obedience. The devil himself can pass for a believer as well as a disobedient soul.

(b) *True faith is prayerful*

Prayer is the child of faith. As the child bears his father's name, prayer wears the name of faith. If prayer is the very natural breath of faith, the two parts of prayer are supplication and thanksgiving. By supplication the Christian takes in God's mercy and then breathes out that mercy in praise. But without faith he can do neither. He cannot draw mercy from God by supplication, 'for he that cometh to God must believe that he is, and that he is a rewarder of them that diligently seek him' (*Heb. 11:6*). Neither can he return praises to God without faith. Thanksgiving is an act of self-denial, and it is faith alone that shows us the way out of our own self-centeredness. Therefore as the Christian cannot pray – acceptably, I mean – without faith, so with faith he cannot help but pray.

The new creature, like infants at natural birth, comes crying into the world; and therefore Christ tells this news to Ananias about Saul, a new-born believer: 'Behold, he prayeth' (*Acts 9:11*). Is it so strange, though, that one brought up at the feet of Gamaliel, and such a strict Pharisee, should kneel in prayer? No, his sect gloried in fasting and praying and works – but he never had the spirit of prayer until the Spirit of grace caused him to believe on Jesus Christ.

Therefore if you want to test your faith, you need to do more than pray. You must also understand how faith infuses its power into prayer. To gain this understanding, let us analyse three relationships of faith and prayer.

(i) *Faith kindles the Christian's desire to pray.* To provoke the soul to pray, faith reveals the destitute condition of the soul and the fullness of God's supply in Christ. The lepers asked each other why they should sit still and die. It was faith that roused up their souls to prayer. If you stay at the door of your own soul you will surely starve. What do you see in yourself but hunger and famine? You have neither bread nor money for bread. Get up, then, and hurry to God. Your soul will live.

Do you feel dejected because of your own weakness? Press to the throne of grace as the only way left for your supply of spiritual strength. Faith is the principle of our new life: 'I live,' says Paul, 'by the faith of the Son of God' (*Gal. 2:20*).

Faith also arouses a person to pray from an inward delight which it has in communion with God. 'It is good for me,' the psalmist says, 'to draw near to God.' And notice his next words: 'I have put my trust in the Lord God' (*Ps. 73:28*). It is a pleasure to look often at the place where we have laid up our treasure. By faith David invested his soul and all he had in God, to be kept safely for him; and now he delights to be with the Father. By faith the soul is joined to Christ. Being married to Him, there is no wonder that it should desire this communion. And since prayer is the place of meeting where Christ and the soul come together this side of heaven, the believer often walks that way. Can anything less, or anything more, satisfy you? Certainly God treasures your faith, or else you could not so freely give your love to Him and take delight in Him.

(ii) *Faith puts forth an assisting act in prayer*. And it does this in two ways. First, it assists the soul with persistence. Faith is the wrestling grace. It comes up close to God, reaches out to Him, and will not easily take a denial. Faith is the soul's eye by which it sees the filth and hell in every sin. It is this insight which makes the heart sorrowful when the soul spreads its abominations before the Lord. Tears come as freely as water from a flowing spring when faith finds Jesus in His love and graces reflected in the mirror of promise.

Never before could the Christian know what to do with a promise in prayer until faith teaches him to press in to God with it, humbly yet boldly. 'What wilt thou do unto thy great name?' asks believing Joshua (*Josh. 7:9*). It is as if he had said, 'You are so inseparably bound to Your people by promise that You cannot leave them to die unless Your name suffers with them.'

The second way faith assists in prayer is that it empowers the soul to persevere. As the wheel wears out with turning until it breaks, the hypocrite prays until he gets tired. Sooner or later something will make him abandon the duty which he never really liked anyway. But it is impossible for the sincere believer to stop praying unless he also stops believing. Prayer is the very breath of faith. Stop a man's breath and where is he then?

Are you compelled to pray? As a baby cannot help but cry when it is hurt or wants something – because there is no other way to get help – so the Christian's wants, sins, and temptations return to him and he cannot do anything but pray about them. 'From the end of the earth will I cry unto thee,' says David (*Ps. 61:2*). He was saying, 'Wherever I am I will find You. Imprison me, banish me, or do with me what You will – You will never be rid of me.' 'I will abide in thy tabernacle for ever' (*Ps. 61:4*). How

THE CHRISTIAN IN COMPLETE ARMOUR

could David do that when he was banished from it? Surely he means by prayer, for the praying Christian carries a 'tabernacle' with him. As long as David can come to the tabernacle he will not neglect it; but when he cannot get there then he will look towards it and as devoutly worship God in the open fields as if he were in the temple. 'Let my prayer be set forth before thee as incense, and the lifting up of my hands as the evening sacrifice' (*Ps. 141:2*).

(iii) *Faith prompts the soul to expect a gracious answer*. 'In the morning will I direct my prayer unto thee, and will look up' (*Ps. 5:3*). Faith fills the soul with expectation. A merchant, when he appraises his estate, counts what he has sent overseas as well as what he has at home; likewise, the believer claims what he has sent to heaven in prayer and has not received as well as those mercies in his hand. Further, faith heightens expectation through power to quieten the soul until the ship of prayer returns full of the rich cargo it traveled to bring home.

Rest depends on faith's strength. Sometimes faith triumphantly bursts from prayer and shouts 'victory!' It gives such substance to the answer before it appears to the sense and reason that the Christian silences all his troubled thoughts with the expectation of it. Hannah prayed like this and 'her countenance was no more sad' (*1 Sam. 1:18*). Faith makes the Christian pay his debt of praise long before he receives the mercy he prayed for. It was this high faith effectually working in David's heart which confessed, 'What time I am afraid, I will trust in thee.' And his next vow to the Father was to 'praise his word' (*Ps. 56:3–4*). David praised God for His promise when it had no existence except in God's faithfulness and his faith.

While we may not attain to David's heroic level of faith we can be Christ's faithful soldiers and exercise the measure of faith which we do have. There is a lesser act of

[64]

faith which does not immediately relieve the soul of all disturbing thoughts, as David's faith did; but it keeps the soul's head above the waves of anxiety until the tide of trouble subsides. When God took the flood from the earth, He did not do it in a moment of time. 'And the waters returned from off the earth continually' (*Gen. 8:3*) – that is, the water settled from day to day until it was all gone. Do you not find peace when you send out disturbing thoughts through the channel of prayer and empty your sorrowful heart into the heart of God? While praying does not always make all your fears evaporate, it protects you from being drowned.

A soul wholly void of faith prays and leaves none of its burden with God but rather takes every problem back upon itself. Calling on God furnishes no more relief to such a person than an anchor without hooks does for a sinking ship. If you throw out your anchor of faith in prayer and it takes such hold on Christ in the promise as to keep you from being driven by the fury of Satan's temptations, or your own despairing thoughts, then bless God for it. Although the ship that rides at anchor may be tossed about at times, it remains safe nevertheless. Do not be disappointed if your faith is not strong enough to free you from all fears. Remember that it will save you from hell.

(c) *In addition to its obedient and prayerful nature, true faith respects all God's precepts alike*

As sincere obedience does not take one commandment and leave another alone, but respects every precept of God, so faith respects all God's truths. It believes one promise as much as it believes another. God has invested His honor as deeply to perform one promise as He has for another promise. And just as breaking one commandment would make us guilty of the whole law, so God's failure to keep one promise – which is blasphemous to consider – would be the breaking of His whole covenant. Promises, like commands, are merged with God's being; He cannot keep one unless He performs them all. And neither can we believe one without believing all. God has spoken these New Testament promises as He did the Old Testament precepts; His seal is upon all of them, and He expects us to embrace each one with our faith.

Notice how David bears witness to the whole truth of God: 'Thy word is true from the beginning: and every one of thy righteous judgments endureth for ever' (*Ps. 119:160*). Try your faith in the light of this passage. You may believe God's promise for pardon, and enjoy meditating on it; but how much faith do you put in His promise to work sanctification in your everyday life?

But David did more than agree with the whole truth of God; he heartily prayed and expected God to perform His promise: 'Order my steps in thy word: and let not any iniquity have dominion over me' (*Ps. 119:133*). David was determined not to lose any privilege that God has promised for His children. 'Look thou upon me,' he says, 'as thou usest to do' (*Ps. 119:132*). This is no more than family conversation – 'Do what You promised to do for all who love You; and do not let me be more poorly clothed than the rest of my brothers.'

You may have faith for eternal salvation, but do you have enough faith to rely on God for the daily circumstances of this life? It is a strange believer who lives by faith for heaven but by his own ingenuity schemes for success in the world. Christ rebuked the unbelieving Jews because they refused to trust Him with their earthly concerns (*John 5:44*). If we cannot trust Him in small matters, how can we trust Him in great things?

Even the Christian with faith strong enough for heaven

may sometimes stumble and find his faith frustrated about a temporal promise. But we should not judge this trial to be an accurate indicator of the spiritual health of the believer, for God leaves even His most stable children in places of trouble for a season to humble and strengthen them. Although Abraham once acted in pretense to save his life, yet at other times his actions proved that he trusted God in temporal situations as well as for eternal salvation. You should not, therefore, question the truth of your faith every time weakness comes. In wartime a man may forfeit some of his property to the enemy's power for a time, and during that period he shows no profit from it; but still he knows it is his. And although he is troubled for his present loss, he tries as soon as he can to rescue it from his enemy's hand. So when Satan brings temptation and God withdraws His assistance, the believer may feel little support from some particular promise; but he counts that promise as his portion still and seeks to reinforce it with new strength from heaven so that he may live upon it and turn it more to his comfort.

It is even more tragic, on the other hand, to pretend to trust God for the things of this life and yet fail to receive Christ as Lord and Savior. What gives the woman legal right to her husband's estate but her marriage covenant? And what gives the creature true claim to these promises, or any other promise in the covenant of grace, except union with Christ? The first act of God's love to the sinner is that He chooses him to be His and sets him apart, in His unchangeable purpose, to be an object of His special love in Christ. God's choice, therefore, is called 'the foundation' on which He structures all other mercies: 'The foundation of God standeth sure, having this seal, The Lord knoweth them that are his' (*2 Tim. 2:19*).

EXHORTATION TO UNBELIEVERS TO OBTAIN THE SHIELD OF FAITH

Faith is a precious grace. Can you hear about this pearl and not want it for yourself? Why has the Spirit spoken such glorious things in the Word about faith except to make it more desirable in your eyes?

Is there any way to have Christ except by faith? There is a generation of men in the world who would almost make one think so. Their corrupt, profane life-styles have been decorated with flowers of morality, leaving a sweet reputation among their neighbors. Yet why do they continually ignore the gospel of Christ? Surely it is not because they are more willing to go to hell than other people, but because they think their 'morality' will get them into heaven. They are deceived.

Did Christ come to help only the sensual, defiled sinners such as drunkards, liars, and prostitutes find heaven? And are civil, moral men left to walk there the best way they can? God's Word opens only one way to heaven. There is but 'one God, and one mediator between God and men, the man Christ Jesus' (1 Tim. 2:5). And since Christ is the only bridge over the gulf between earth and heaven, judge what will happen to the self-righteous man and his sweet-scented life if he misses this one bridge.

The man who thinks he does not need faith to accept Christ's offer of salvation as much as the bloodiest murderer or filthiest Sodomite in the world is treading in hopeless deception. If a group of men and children were to wade through a brook no deeper than a man's head, the men would have a definite advantage over the children. But if they tried to cross the ocean, the men as well as the children would need a ship to carry them. And only the insane would try to wade through without the help of a ship just because they are a little taller than the rest.

[68]

Nothing deserves precedency before faith in your thoughts. David resolved, 'I will not give sleep to mine eyes, or slumber to mine eyelids, until I find out a place for the Lord, an habitation for the mighty God of Jacob' (*Ps. 132:4–5*). The habitation which pleases God most is your heart; but it must be a believing heart, 'that Christ may dwell in your hearts by faith' (*Eph. 3:17*).

How can you sleep at night in that house where God does not dwell? And He does not live in you if you have an unbelieving heart. Every time you hear a gospel sermon He stands at your door to be let in. Because unbelief keeps closing the door when Christ knocks, how can you be sure God will not suddenly seal you up under final unbelief?

DIRECTIONS TO UNBELIEVERS FOR ATTAINING FAITH

You may be wondering how to get this precious gift of faith for yourself. The answer lies in five directions.

I. LET YOUR HEART BE CONVICTED OF UNBELIEF
Until this is done your efforts to have faith will be sluggish and impotent. When a drunkard is convicted of his drunkenness and turns away from it he feels relieved. He enjoys this improvement because that one sin was all that bothered his conscience. But when the Spirit of God convicts the sinner of his unbelief, He gets between him and all man-made hiding places of vindication. In his spirit he has no peace from the efforts at reformation which formerly pacified him and thus kept him from coming to Christ.

Many people try to change their habits in order to patch up peace in their consciences, even as some remodel an old rotten house by stopping up gaps, a tile here and a stone there, until a loud wind comes and blows the whole house down. But once the creature has the load of unbelief heaped upon his spirit, then it does not help at all for him to recall that he is no longer a drunkard. 'Your present state,' says God's Spirit, 'is just as damning as if you were still a drunkard, because you are an unbeliever.' What you were, you still are; and you will be found at the judgment day to be the drunkard and atheist, regardless of your reformation, unless intervening faith has caused you to take a new name. What if you do not get drunk anymore? Guilt still stains you until faith washes it away with the blood of Jesus. Make no mistake; God will be paid – by you, or by Christ for you. But Christ makes no payment for unbelievers.

Again, guilt remains as long as the power of lusts remains – although they may disappear outwardly – if you are still an unbeliever. Your heart is not emptied of one sin, but the vent stopped by restraining grace. A tightly closed bottle full of wine shows no more of its contents than does an empty bottle. And that is your case. How is it possible for you mortally to wound one particular lust and let that be the only valid victory in the world, when you still have no faith? In a word, if you are convicted of unbelief you will find there is more evil in this sin than in all your other sins.

Have you been a liar? That is a serious sin. Hell gapes for every one who loves and tells a lie (*Rev. 22:15*). But the loudest lie which you have ever told is what your unbelief says. Here you bear false witness against God Himself and tell a lie not *to* the Holy Ghost, as Ananias did, but a lie *of* the Holy Ghost. Unbelief acts as if not a word were true which He promises in the gospel.

Have you been a murderer? Of course this too is a dreadful sin. But unbelief pronounces you an even bloodier murderer because God's blood is more precious than the blood of mere men. By your unbelief you kill Christ over again and then tread His blood under your feet; worst of all, you throw it under Satan's feet to be trampled on by him.

II. DO NOT RESIST THE HOLY SPIRIT WHEN HE OFFERS HIS HELP

You cannot ever believe unless the Holy Spirit empowers you to do so. Because such a Master Workman does not want to be controlled or manipulated, it is important that we see two of the ways in which the Spirit of God may be opposed.

(a) *Do not oppose the Spirit by refusing to attend to the way He works faith*

Ordinarily, Christ's sheep conceive while they are drinking the water of life – the ministry of the Word. The hearing of the gospel is called 'the hearing of faith' (*Gal. 3:2*) because by hearing the doctrine of faith, the Spirit works the grace of faith. In a still voice He speaks to the souls of sinners. 'Thine eyes shall see thy teachers: and thine ears shall hear a word behind thee, saying, This is the way, walk ye in it' (*Isa. 30:20–21*). Here God and man are teaching together, and if you neglect man's teaching, then you resist the Spirit's instruction also. Concerning this indifference the apostle warns: 'Quench not the spirit'; and in the following verse: 'Despise not prophesyings' (*1 Thess. 5:19–20*).

The most serious way of despising prophesyings or preaching is turning away from them. When God sets up the ministry of the Word in a place, His Spirit opens His school and expects those who want to learn to come together. Is it more appropriate that the student should wait on his teacher at school or that the master should run after his truant pupil on the playground? You be the judge.

(b) *Be careful not to interfere with the Holy Spirit as He produces faith in your soul*

There is nothing we can do to gain grace, but the Holy Spirit has His own steps in preparing our souls to receive this gift. It is extremely important to submit to the Spirit's gradual approach to your soul from the Word, because resistance to His work may result in His withdrawing temporarily or permanently.

We read how 'it came into [the heart of Moses] to visit his brethren the children of Israel' (*Acts 7:23*). There he begins to show his zeal for them by slaying an Egyptian who had wronged an Israelite. By this hint, Moses supposed his brothers would understand how 'God by his hand would deliver them' (*verse 25*). But instead of co-operating they opposed him; therefore he withdrew and they heard no more of Moses or of their deliverance for forty years. Thus the Spirit of God may direct a word to speak to your specific situation, to make you understand that He is ready to help you come out of your bondage. Your part in His work is to hear His counsel and obey whatever He says. But if you rebel you may never hear Him knock at your door again.

God makes short work of some of His judiciary proceedings. 'I say unto you, That none of those men which were bidden shall taste of my supper' (*Luke 14:24*). These guests were invited only once, but for their first denial God punished them with a dreadful curse. He did not say they would never *come* to the supper; He said they would not *taste*. Many people hear precious truths from the gospel but because their hearts are sealed up in unbelief they never taste of Christ set forth before them in all their life.

There is a kind of mental illness in which a man speaks rationally until you mention the one subject that caused his disorder in the first place; here he loses his reason and cannot continue a coherent conversation. How many men and women who regularly attend church services can knowledgeably discuss anything in the world; but when you say something about God, Christ, and heaven, they suddenly appear deaf and dumb. Some who have heard the gospel and have been drawn by the Spirit suffer this burden as a consequence of a curse put upon them for rejecting the ways of the Holy Spirit.

I warn you again – beware of opposing the Spirit. Does He beam light from His Word into your understanding? Be careful what you do with this candle of the Lord that lights your mind; do not pride yourself in this new insight, or it may be snuffed out in an instant. If the Holy Spirit confirms the light in your understanding so that it sets your conscience on fire with the awareness of sin, do not resist Him. He is mercifully kindling fire in your soul to keep you out of a hotter fire in hell. But you must expect Satan – whose house is on fire over his head – to do everything he can to quench it; your greatest danger is listening to him. Instead, draw water freely from God's Word to control this blaze.

Satan longs for you to quench the Spirit by trying to calm your own conscience. There is more hope for a sick man when his disease is discovered than when it is hidden in the heart and cannot be seen outwardly. Satan is so afraid of losing his throne inside you that he tries to smother your conscience with carnal lukewarmness and extinguish the Holy Spirit's convicting work. But it is God's goodness which sends these convictions to effect your spiritual delivery, and you should welcome them as much as a woman in labor welcomes pain. Without the travail she could not be delivered of her child, and neither can God bring forth the new creature in your soul without repentance.

Sometimes the Spirit of God not only furnishes light for your mind and hell-fire in your conscience, but heaven-fire in your affections. From the Word He makes Christ so visible in His excellencies and sufficiency for all your needs that your affections begin to desire Him. These glimpses of Jesus and of God's mercy through Him are so luscious that you begin to taste sweetness in hearing of them, which stirs up further desire in you so that finally you must have the desire of your heart: 'I must have Christ!' Possibly in the earnestness of your affections you renounce both your lusts and Satan, the obstacles which for so long kept you from Christ.

Now the kingdom of God is near indeed. You are only a breath away from new life in Christ, but be careful not to miscarry. If your sudden desires did ripen into a deliberate choice of Christ, and these purposes settle into a permanent decision to renounce sin and self, as you cast yourself on Christ, then I salute with joy the birth of this babe of grace – faith – in your soul.

III. CRY ALOUD IN PRAYER TO GOD FOR FAITH

May an unbeliever pray? Some think he should not. But 'prayer is the soul's motion God-ward,' says Richard Baxter; and to forbid an unbeliever to pray is to say he should not obey God's direction to the man lost in wickedness: 'Seek ye the Lord while he may be found, call ye upon him while he is near' (*Isa. 55:6*). 'Desire is the soul of prayer,' continues Mr Baxter, 'and who dares say to the wicked, Desire not faith, desire not Christ or God'?

It is true that an unbeliever sins each time he prays. Praying is not his sin, but praying unbelievingly. Therefore he sins less in praying than in failing to pray. When he prays his sin lies in the manner of it; but when he does not pray, he defies the duty God has commanded him to perform and rejects the way God provides for finding grace. I must urge you, poor sinner, to go on praying; but go on in the awareness of your vileness. Only the wickedest of sinners approaches the throne of grace with the resolve to go on sinning.

But perhaps you cannot see how such a sinful person as yourself could ever believe on Christ. It is not the love of any present sin in your heart but the fear of your past sins in your conscience which keeps you from believing. Let me gather the best encouragements I can find out of God's Word and so make a path for you to find the throne of grace.

Poor sinner, do not be afraid to pray for faith. God will not reprimand me for sending such customers to His door. You have a Friend in God's own breast who will ensure your welcome. He who could give Christ before anyone ever prayed is more than willing to give faith to you when you ask. Remember that what you ask God to *give*, He commands you to *do*: 'This is his commandment, That we should believe on the name of his Son Jesus Christ' (*1 John 3:23*). How glad God must be to answer prayer which fulfills His highest purpose for you.

By this time you can promise yourself a joyful return on your prayer sent to heaven. But so that you can be even more hopeful, remember that this grace which you want so much and ask God for is the main part of Christ's purchase. His blood, which is the price of pardon, is the full price of faith also. Not only has He canceled man's debt of sin but He has also made a way for us to approach Christ's bank of grace for sinners who see they have nothing of their own. 'Thou hast ascended on high, thou hast led captivity captive: thou hast received gifts for men; yea, for the rebellious also, that the Lord God might dwell among them' (*Ps. 68:18*).

Scripture tells us the reason these gifts are given: 'that God may dwell among them.' Nothing but faith can make a soul who has been rebellious an acceptable place for the holy God to dwell. This is the gift He received all other gifts for. Now let this understanding give you boldness to humble yourself and press God for that which Christ has already bought: 'Lord, I have been a rebellious person; but did not Christ receive anything for such? I have an unbelieving heart; but I hear there is faith paid for in Your covenant. Christ shed His blood so You could pour out Your Spirit on a sinner like me.'

While you are pleading like this with God and using His Son's name in prayer, Christ Himself can hear, agree, and give favor to your prayer. And when you beg for faith because of Christ's death, He will intercede for you. He went to heaven so that you would have a Friend there waiting to receive and understand your prayer (see *Heb. 7:25*).

IV. MEDITATE OFTEN ON THE PROMISE

It is the Spirit's work, and only His, to ground your soul in the promise and give substance to His Word by faith in your heart. You cannot do this. Yet, as fire came down from heaven upon Elijah's sacrifice after he had gone as far as he could, God's Spirit will come to quicken the promise in your heart after you have diligently meditated on it. For when Elijah had laid everything in order he lifted up his heart and prayed, expecting God to act in his behalf (*1 Kings 18:36*). I know of no more trustworthy way to invite God's Spirit to help.

As the man who surrenders to lust invites Satan's temptation, the person who makes his thoughts stay on heavenly themes invites the Holy Spirit's perfect peace. The Spirit of God is as willing to cherish any good motive as the wicked spirit is to nourish evil intentions.

We find the spouse sitting under the shadow of her beloved, as one under an apple tree; and soon she says that 'his fruit was sweet to my taste' (*Song of Sol. 2:3*). Her sitting under his shadow signifies a soul resting under the thoughts of Christ and the precious promises growing out of Him as branches out of a tree. O Christian, stay here awhile and see if the Spirit will not shake some fruit from one branch or another into your lap. As Isaac met his bride when he went into the fields to meditate, so you may find your Beloved walking through this garden of promises.

V. URGE YOUR SOUL WITH STRONG OBLIGATION TO BELIEVE

Many humbled sinners tremble with tender conscience toward other sins but express little or no sorrow for their unbelief. They think they offend God in these sins and wrong only themselves by unbelief. If this is true in your life, your thoughts greatly abuse you; for you have dishonored God more by unbelief than by all your other sins put together!

Possibly you might like it better if you could keep your sins and have Christ too. Do you think it is too hard to give up these lusts and gain Him? God Himself could not have set aside this requirement and truly loved you. The man values gold little who complains that the labor it costs him to get it is too much. So too does the man who is unwilling to surrender his lusts that he may make Christ his treasure. Surely you can trust Christ to more than compensate for anything you must give up for Him.

Would you rather give up the presence of God and Christ in hell, where your lusts will surely lead you, or the company of your lusts in heaven, where faith in Christ will just as certainly transport you? Take your choice then, and leave it for your work in hell to repent if you make the wrong decision.

But maybe the choice between Christ and sin is not what keeps you from believing. Although you agree to the terms of Christ's covenant, it does not seem possible for God to perform His promise for such an unworthy person

[77]

as you. And of the two, it is better that the obstacle to Christ should be the difficulty which your understanding conceives rather than the refusal of your will to receive what God offers in Him. A careful consideration of two special works in your soul will now satisfy your doubts and scatter your fears about this particular stumbling-block to Christ.

(a) *Work to get a right understanding of God*

When this happens it will not appear strange at all that a great God should do such great things for sinners. If a beggar promises you a million dollars, you might discount his offer and ask where he would get that much money. But if a prince guarantees an even larger sum you would not hesitate to believe him, because he has wealth proportionate to his promise. God never promises more than His infinite mercy, power, and faithfulness can perform. 'Be still, and know that I am God' (*Ps. 46:10*). In times of great confusion in the church Martin Luther would say of this psalm: 'Let us sing the six and fortieth psalm, in spite of the devil and all his instruments.' And, humbled Christian, you too may sing with comfort, in spite of Satan and sin: 'Be still, my soul, and know that He who offers you mercy is God.'

(b) *Study the securities God gives the believer for the performance of His promise*

They are many, although his bare Word deserves to be taken for more than our souls are worth. If we had the most fraudulent cheat in the world under bonds for paying a sum of money, we would assume our business agreement was secure enough. Can you not be satisfied when the true and faithful God puts Himself under the bonds of His Word for your security? His truth is so immutable that it is more possible for light to send forth darkness than it is for a lie to come out of His blessed lips.

EXHORTATION TO BELIEVERS TO PRESERVE THE SHIELD OF FAITH

I now speak a double exhortation to you who are believers. First, seeing that faith is such a choice grace, be stirred up to preserve it; and secondly, if you have this faith, do not deny what God has done for you.

FAITH MUST BE PRESERVED WITH GREAT CARE BECAUSE OF ITS PRE-EMINENCE AMONG GRACES

Keep your faith and it will keep you and all your other graces. You stand by faith; if that fails, you fall. Where will you be then but under your enemies' feet? Be aware of any potential danger to your faith; be like that Grecian captain who, when he was knocked down in battle, asked as soon as he regained consciousness where his shield was.

Faith is the chief grace which God would have us value ourselves by, because there is the least danger of pride in this self-emptying grace. 'For I say, through the grace [of God] given unto me, to every man that is among you, not to think of himself more highly than he ought to think; but to think soberly, according as God hath dealt to every man the measure of faith' (*Rom. 12:3*). The Corinthians received various gifts from God, but He wanted them to judge themselves rather by their faith so they could 'think soberly.'

Indeed all other graces are to be measured by our faith; and if these are not fruits of faith they have no true worth. This is the difference between a Christian and an honest heathen. The heathen values himself by his patience, temperance, liberality, and other moral virtues. While he lives he brags about his morality; and he expects God to commend him and to guarantee him happiness after he dies. But the Christian has found Christ, whose righteousness and holiness by faith become his; and he values himself by these more than by inherent traits.

Let me illustrate this by two men – the one a courtier, the other a countryman and stranger to court – both having sizeable estates, but the courtier the greater by far. Ask the country gentleman, who has no relation to the court or place in the prince's favor, what he is worth, and he will tell you the sum of his lands and monies. He values himself by these. But ask the courtier what he is worth, and although he has more property and money than the other, he will tell you he values himself by the favor of his prince more than by all his other assets. He says, 'What my prince has is mine, except his crown and royalty, his treasure mine to take care of me, his love to embrace me, his power to defend me.'

The poor heathen – strangers to God and His favor in Christ – bless themselves only by their natural resources and the stockpile of moral values which they gather with great effort. But the believer, having access by faith into this grace because he stands high in God's favor by Jesus Christ, values himself by his faith rather than by any other grace. And he cherishes this grace of God in himself above all the world's treasure or pleasure – he had rather be the ragged saint than the robed sinner. He prefers security in his spiritual life to stability in his natural life, which he is willing to lose and count himself no loser.

But not only is the believer a partaker of the divine nature by the holiness which is infused into him; he is also heir to all the glorious perfections that are in God Himself. He can call all that God is, has, and does his very own. And God is pleased to be called His people's God – 'The God of Israel' (*2 Sam. 23:3*). As a man's house and land bear the owner's name, so God is pleased to carry His people's name so that all the world may know. God has kept nothing back from His people except His crown and glory. That He 'will not give to another' (*Isa. 42:8*).

If the Christian needs strength, God wants him to use His; and he may do so boldly and confidently, for the Lord calls Himself His people's strength: 'The Strength of Israel will not lie' (*1 Sam. 15:29*). If the believer lacks righteousness and holiness, these are brought to him—Christ 'is made unto us righteousness' (*1 Cor. 1:30*). Is it love and mercy? All the mercy in God is at their service. 'Oh how great is thy goodness which thou hast laid up for them that fear thee' (*Ps. 31:19*). Mark the phrase, 'laid up for them.' God's mercy and goodness are intended for His chosen ones in the same way that a parent saves a sum of money and writes on the envelope, 'This is for a certain child of mine.'

That which makes the believer a child also makes him an heir. And faith is what makes him a child of God. 'As many as received him, to them gave he power to become the sons of God, even to them that believe on his name' (*John 1:12*). But Christian, let us now study five directions for preserving your faith.

DIRECTIONS TO BELIEVERS FOR THE PRESERVING OF FAITH

I. GOD'S WORD IS INSTRUMENTAL IN PRODUCING AND PRESERVING FAITH

As it was seed for your conversion, so now the Word of God is milk for the preserving of your faith. Make use often of this breast. Babies cannot suck long nor digest much at a time; they need to return for frequent feedings. 'Precept must be upon precept; line upon line; here a little, and there a little' (*Isa. 28:10*).

He who taught Christians to pray for their daily bread knew they needed it; and surely He did not mean natural bread only. For in the same chapter He says, 'Seek ye first the kingdom of God' (*Matt. 6:33*). Prize the Word, Christian; feed on it, whether it be in a sermon, in a conference with some friend in private, or in a special time of reading and meditating by yourself.

If only Christians who complain about their weak faith would turn their murmuring into an investigation of why it is so weak! It is because faith has missed its meals from the Word. In earlier days you went through many pressures to keep yourself in the fellowship of God's Word; and you were always rewarded for the time taken from other schedules. But now that you have gradually stopped coming to God in His Word, there is a sad change. It is not easy for you to trust Him; and you have little authority over your unbelief.

The best counsel I have is what doctors recommend for healthy bodies. They find out where a patient was born and send him back there. Let me ask you – if you ever had faith, where was it born and brought up? Was it not in the sweet air of hearing, meditating, and praying over the Word? Go as fast as you can into your native air, where you drew your first Christian breath, where your faith thrived and grew from the beginning.

II. LOOK TO YOUR CONSCIENCE

A good conscience is the vessel faith sails in. If the conscience is wrecked, how can faith be safe? Now you know what sins destroy the conscience – sins deliberately committed or impenitently repeated. Guard against these deliberate sins! Like a stone thrown into a clear stream, they will so muddy the conscience that you cannot see the reflection of the promise.

But even if you have fallen into the pit of sin, do not stay there. The sheep may fall into a ditch, but it is the swine that wallow in it. Therefore, how hard will it be to stir up faith in the promise when your garment is filthy and your countenance smeared with sin? It is dangerous to drink poison, but far more lethal to let it stay in the body for a long time. Although you are a believer you cannot act on faith until you have cleansed your heart by repentance.

III. EXERCISE YOUR FAITH

We live by faith, and faith lives by exercise. As we say of some strong men, they are not satisfied unless they are working hard. Confine them to their chair and you kill them. So then if you hinder your faith from working, you threaten its very life.

We fail to experience glorious victories in prayer because we do not allow faith to pray very often. Let a child seldom see his parents, and when he comes into their presence he will not be very excited to see them. Why are we unable to live on a promise during a crisis? Surely it is because we do not live with the promise every day. The more we consult the promise the more confidence we put in it. We do not trust strangers as we do our next-door neighbor.

But how many ventures are undertaken where faith is not even called in, nor the promise considered from one end of the business to the other? Therefore when we need faith in some particular emergency, our faith itself is at a loss. It is like a servant who wanders away because his master seldom employs him. And so when his master does call for him during some extreme situation he cannot find him. Christian, do not let your faith be so long out of work. If you do not use it when you should, it may fail you when you need to act upon it.

IV. DEAL WITH ANY RESIDUAL UNBELIEF

Repentance recovers what faith loses by unbelief. David fervently shamed himself for his unbelief and confessed how 'foolish and ignorant' he was: 'I was as a beast before thee' (*Ps. 73:22*). And by this humble confession, David's sin breathes out its venom so his faith can regain its control. 'Thou hast holden me by my right hand. Thou shalt guide me with thy counsel, and afterward receive me to glory' (*verses 23–24*).

You have a judge in your heart whom God Himself commissions to reprove and shame you when you sin. There is no sin which dishonors God more than unbelief; and this sword cuts His name deepest when it is in a saint's hand. The wound in the house of His friends painfully touches the tender heart of God. There is a reason why the sin of unbelief causes God to suffer, if we consider the close kinship a believer has with God.

Think of this, Christian, again and again – by unbelief you bear false witness against God. And when the world hears you speak unkindly of your Father it may harden its opinion of God, even to final unbelief and unrepentance. The way to degrade a man's reputation to the lowest possible point is to say, 'Even his own children dare not trust him or give him a good word.' Ask yourself whether you are willing to be an instrument for taking away God's good name in the world. Certainly your heart must shudder at the thought of it; and surely your unbelief which caused you to do this so often will wound you to the very heart. And bleeding for what you have done, you will not take up that sword against God again.

V. LABOR TO INCREASE FAITH

None are in more danger of losing their faith than those men who are content with what they have. A spark is sooner smothered than a flame, a drop more easily dried up than a river. The stronger your faith, the safer your faith is from enemies' attacks. When reconnaissance reveals a poorly protected fort, this is usually all the enemy needs to come against it. The devil is a coward and loves to fight at the point of his greatest advantage;

and he can have no greater advantage than weak Christian faith.

If only you knew the many advantages of strong faith over weak faith you would not rest a minute until it was yours. Strong faith conquers those temptations which take weak faith a prisoner. When David's faith prevailed, he looked death in the face fearlessly. 'For the people spake of stoning him, but David encouraged himself in the Lord his God' (*1 Sam. 30:6*). Yet when his faith was weak, he was ready to run and hide in the nearest hole to save himself (*1 Sam. 21:13*).

Strong faith frees the Christian from those thoughts which oppress weak faith. 'Thou wilt keep him in perfect peace, whose mind is stayed on thee' (*Isa. 26:3*). The more faith, the more inward peace and quietness; if little faith, then little peace and serenity through the storms that unbelieving fears will surely gather.

Weak faith will as surely take the Christian to heaven as strong faith; for it is impossible that the least ounce of true grace should perish, since it is all incorruptible seed. But the doubting Christian will not have as pleasant a voyage there as will the believer with strong faith. Although everyone aboard the ship will arrive safely at the shore, yet the seasick traveler will not have so comfortable a trip as the man who is healthy. The sick person misses pleasant surprises during the delightful parts of the journey. But the strong man views it all with abundance of expectation; and while he wishes with all his heart he were already home, yet the joy he has shortens and sweetens his way to him.

Thus, Christian, there are many delights which saints traveling to heaven meet on their way there, besides what God has for them at the journey's end. It is the Christian whose faith is strong enough to act upon the promise who finds and possesses these pleasures. He who sees spiritual glories in the promise sings all the way; but the doubting Christian's eye of faith is so gummed up with unbelieving fear that he sees nothing to make him joyful and sighs from heavy, unsettled thoughts. If you do not want a ponderous, melancholy walk to heaven, labor to strengthen your faith.

But you may want to know for sure whether your faith is strong or weak. The following characteristics will show you the difference.

HOW WE KNOW IF FAITH IS WEAK OR STRONG

I. THE MORE ENTIRELY THE CHRISTIAN CAN RELY ON GOD'S PROMISES, THE STRONGER IS HIS FAITH

When we trust God for His bare promise we trust Him on His own credit; and this is faith indeed. He who walks without a crutch is stronger than the man who needs one to lean on. The promise is the ground which faith walks on, but sense and reason are the crutches which weak faith depends on too much.

(a) *Can you believe without the crutch of sense and feeling?* Maybe in days past you have basked in God's love and the rays of His favor; and as long as the sun shone in at your window, your heart was light. You thought you could never distrust God again or listen to unbelieving ideas. But how is your heart now that these demonstrations of His favor have stopped? Because you can no longer *see* His love, does your eye of faith lose sight of His mercy and truth in the promise?

The little child thinks his mother is lost if she goes out of the room where he is; but as the child grows older and wiser, he realizes this is not true. And so it is with the believer. Christian, bless God for the experiences when you tasted His love; but know that we cannot judge our faith, whether weak or strong, by these. Experiences, says Parisiensis, are like crutches which help a lame man walk; but they do not make him sound or strong. Food and exercise must do that. So labor to lean more on the promise and less on tangible expressions of God's love.

Although a strong man does not rely on his cane all the way – as the lame person leans on his crutch – yet he may use it now and then to defend himself from a thief or dog in his path. Thus the maturing Christian may make good use of his experiences in some temptations, although he does not lay the weight of his faith upon them, but upon the promise.

(b) *Can you believe when reason breaks down?*
Or does your faith fall to the ground with the broken crutch of reason? It is a strong faith indeed which can trample on the improbabilities and impossibilities which reason puts forward against the performance of the promise. Thus Noah worked hard on the ark because he believed God meant what He said and never bothered to clear the matter with his reasoning to see *how* these strange things might come to pass.

Skillful swimmers are not afraid to get into water over their heads, whereas young learners feel for the ground and stay close to the bank. Strong faith does not fear when God carries the creature beyond the depth of reason: 'Neither know we what to do,' said Jehoshaphat, 'but our eyes are upon thee' (*2 Chron. 20:12*). It is as if he had said, 'We are swallowed up in a sea that is bigger than we are. We have no idea how to get out of this trouble, but our eyes are upon You. We will not give up as long as there is strength in Your arm, tenderness in Your heart, and truth in Your promise.'

Weak faith that gropes for some footing for reason to stand on tries desperately to reconcile God's promise and human reasoning. And weak faith asks many questions. When Christ says, 'Give ye them to eat,' His disciples ask in return, 'Shall we go and buy two hundred pennyworth of bread?' (*Mark 6:37*). As if Christ's bare word could not spare them that cost and trouble! 'Whereby shall I know this?' says Zacharias to the angel, 'for I am an old man' (*Luke 1:18*). His faith was too feeble to stand up to such wonderful news.

II. THE MORE CONTENTED THE CHRISTIAN'S HEART UNDER THE CHANGES WHICH PROVIDENCE BRINGS ON HIS STATE AND CONDITION IN THE WORLD, THE STRONGER IS HIS FAITH

Weak bodies cannot tolerate change of weather as well as healthy ones. Heat and cold, fair and foul weather cause no great change in the strong man's constitution. But the weak person complains of them. Thus strong faith can live in any climate, travel in all weather, and handle any unpredictable condition. 'I have learned, in whatsoever state I am, therewith to be content,' says Paul (*Phil. 4:11*). Unfortunately, however, not all Christ's followers are like Paul in this; and weak faith has not yet mastered this hard lesson.

When God turns your health into sickness, your abundance into poverty, and your honor into contempt, how do you talk to Him about it? Is your spirit bitter and discontented? Do you vent your feelings in whining or grumbling? Or are you satisfied to agree with God's sovereignty in your present situation, not from ignorance of the affliction but in assurance that He is working these things together for good because He has called you and you love Him?

(a) *Contentment shows that God reigns in your heart*

You reverence His authority and trust His sovereignty, or else you would not obey His orders. 'I was dumb, I opened not my mouth; because thou didst it' (*Ps. 39:9*). If the blow had come from any other hand, David could not have taken it so silently. When a servant slaps a child he runs immediately to tell his father; but although the father himself punishes his child more severely than the servant did, the child does not complain because he respects his father's authority. Thus your comfort comes from God alone: 'Be still, and know that I am God' (*Ps. 46:10*). We must know God *believingly* before our hearts will 'be still.'

(b) *A surrendered heart trusts God's mercy and goodness during trouble*

You believe He can work through your trouble for good or else you could not sacrifice your immediate pleasures so easily. The child goes to bed willingly while others are going to a family dinner if the mother promises to save something for him in the morning. The child believes the promise and is content to obey his parent.

Surely the eye of your faith sees something which will recompense your present loss; and this makes you willing to fast while others feast, or be sick when others are well. Paul tells why he and his brothers in affliction did not faint – they saw heaven coming to them while earth was going from them. 'For which cause we faint not . . . For our light affliction, which is but for a moment, worketh for us a far more exceeding and eternal weight of glory' (*2 Cor. 4:16–17*).

III. THE LONGER A CHRISTIAN CAN WAIT FOR ANSWERS, THE STRONGER IS HIS FAITH

Only the poorest tradesman must demand cash for what he sells. Weak faith is all for the present; if it cannot have its desires met instantly it grows jealous and comes to sad conclusions – the prayer was not heard, or he must be one whom God does not love. But faith strong enough to do business with God can wait. 'He that believeth shall not make haste' (*Isa. 28:16*). His investment is in good hands, and he is not anxious to call it home, knowing well that the longest voyages have the richest returns.

IV. THE MORE A CHRISTIAN SUFFERS WILLINGLY BECAUSE OF A PROMISE, THE STRONGER IS HIS FAITH

If a man gives up an ample inheritance, leaves his family, and follows a friend into foreign, dangerous ventures, we assume this man has great love for his friend. But if he should throw away all his present possessions for a friend whom he has never seen, based only upon a written invitation promising great things to come, we would be even more amazed at the confidence he has in his friend.

It is not as far-fetched as it may seem. In Scripture we read of such a Friend, 'Whom having not seen, ye love; in whom, though now ye see him not, yet believing, ye rejoice' (*1 Pet. 1:8*). The setting of this passage is 'in heaviness through manifold temptations' (*verse 6*); yet because the believers' path goes through rugged wilderness to come to the enjoyment of Christ, they will go joyfully through the deepest of temptations. Here is glorious faith indeed. It is not praising heaven and wishing we were there, but surrendering prized pleasures and embracing great sufferings when God calls us to them, which supplies proof that our faith is both true and strong.

V. THE MORE EASILY A CHRISTIAN RESISTS TEMPTATIONS TO SIN, THE STRONGER IS HIS FAITH

A big fish easily breaks through the same net which holds a little fish captive. The Christian's faith is strong or weak as he finds it easy or hard to break from temptations to sin. When an ordinary temptation entangles you like a fly in a spider's web your faith is very frail. Peter's faith was weak when nothing more than a maid's voice drove him to deny Christ; but it became strong when he withstood and refuted the threats of a whole council (*Acts 4:20*). Even when faith does not have a hand to throw down an enemy, it still has a hand to lift up against it and a voice to cry out to heaven for help. True faith finds a way to combat sin.

Christian, compare yourself with yourself. Do lusts snare your heart and lure it away from God as forcefully as they did several months ago? Or can you honestly say your heart is overcoming them? Since you now know more about Christ and have glimpsed His spiritual glories, can you now pass by their door and not look in? And when temptation knocks, can you shut the door in its face? If the power of sin dies, you can be sure your faith is lively and vigorous. The harder the blow, the stronger the arm that gives it. A child cannot deliver such a wound as a man. And while weak faith cannot deliver a fatal blow to sin, strong faith is both willing and able to do this.

VI. THE MORE OBEDIENCE AND LOVE IN THE CHRIST-
IAN'S WALK, THE STRONGER IS HIS FAITH

Faith works by love, and therefore its strength or weakness can be gauged by the strength or weakness of the love which it activates in a Christian's behavior. The strength of a man's arm that draws a bow is proved by the force in the arrow's flight. And certainly the strength of our faith may be known by the force with which our love mounts to God. It is impossible that weak faith – which is unable to draw the promise as strong faith can – should as powerfully impress the heart to love God as stronger faith can.

Therefore, if your love for God causes you to abandon sin, perform duty, and obey His command, you are a graduate in the art of believing. The Christian's love advances by equal degrees with his faith, as the heat of day increases with the blinding sun; the higher the sun mounts toward its meridian, the hotter the day grows. So the higher faith lifts Christ up in the Christian, the more intense his love to Christ becomes.

Formerly when the Christian deplored his sins he was moved by fear and made an ugly face at the remorse, as does one taking a dose of bitter medicine. But now his acts of repentance are not so distasteful since faith has found the personal reality of God's mercy. He no longer hates the word 'repentance' as Luther once did. Instead, he goes about the work of repentance with sweet attitudes toward a good God who stands ready with a sponge dipped into Christ's mercy to blot out his sins as fast as he confesses them.

And the same might be said concerning another aspect of faith and love. Strong faith sets the soul free. It does not perform duties as an oppressed subject pays heavy taxes – regretfully, to think how much he is giving up. Instead he gives as freely as a child presents his father with an apple from the family orchard. As a younger child he obeyed and served his father more because he was afraid of punishment than because he loved him. But as his relationship to his father develops, with full awareness of expected parental obedience, his selfishness wears off and his natural affection prevails to please his father. So it is with the Christian whose faith is growing and ripening.

VII. THE SWEETER THE CHRISTIAN'S ATTITUDE TOWARD DEATH, THE STRONGER IS HIS FAITH

Things that are very sharp or sour require much sugar to make them sweet. Death is one of those things which often leaves a bad taste in the person's soul. Only strong faith can make serious thoughts of it sweet and desirable! When some people get tired of their present situation they say they want to die. But a man who knows the unchangeableness of death, whether of bliss or misery, never calls for death until he understands what he may expect from God when he comes into that other world. Weak faith cannot do this without a deluge of doubts and fears.

Sometimes, however, a Christian with very weak faith meets death with as little fear, indeed with more joy, than one of far stronger faith, when he is sustained by some remarkable measure of comfort from God. Should God withdraw this, however, the dying man's fears would return and he would again feel languid, like a sick man strangely but temporarily braced with a strong drink.

But the ordinary way Christians' hearts are lifted above fear into an ardent desire of death is by attaining to strong faith. God can still make a feast of a few loaves and instantly multiply the dying Christian's meager faith into a table spread with a variety of consolations. But I fear God will not do this miracle for that person who satisfies himself with the little faith he has and does not try to increase his supply against that spending time.

THE BELIEVER MUST ACKNOWLEDGE FAITH

Which is worse, the sinner who hides his sin and denies it or the Christian who hides and denies his faith? The first is worse, if we consider the person's intention, for the sinner hides his sin because of a wicked purpose. The doubting soul means well: he is afraid to play the hypocrite and liar in saying he has something which he fears he does not really have. But if we consider the consequence of a Christian's disowning God's grace, and how Satan uses it to lead him into other sins, it is not so easy to resolve whose sin is the greater.

Joseph's intention was pure when he decided to put away his espoused Mary, assuming she had fallen into sexual sin. Yet it would have been tragic if he had persisted in that thought, especially after the angel had told him that that which was conceived in her was of the Holy Ghost.

Thus you may be thinking about putting away your faith as some base-born counterfeit grace begotten in your hypocritical heart by the father of lies. Have you not had a vision – not necessarily of an angel or immediate revelation, but by God's Spirit – encouraging you to take and own your faith as that which is conceived in you by the Holy Ghost? Truly your faith is not a bastard formed by the delusion of Satan in the womb of your imagination. Do not rob yourself by drawing back from this grace when in reality you can freely draw an inexhaustible supply from your rich storehouse in Christ.

SUSPICIONS WHICH LEAD TO A PERSON'S DENYING HIS FAITH

Our blessed Savior tells His disciples what wonders they will do if they believe and 'doubt not' (*Matt. 21:21*); and that which is 'faith without doubting' in Matthew is faith as a 'grain of mustard seed' in Luke (*Luke 17:6*). The doubt against which Christ warned His followers is the kind which tries to steal the assurance of their faith's genuineness.

For example, you may have inward peace but no joy; and this apparent paradox may cause you to doubt your faith. The day may be still and calm though not all glorious and bright with sunshine. And although the Comforter may not come with emotional consolations, He has already hushed the storm of your troubled spirit. And true peace, as well as joy, is evidence of 'unfeigned faith' (*2 Tim. 1:5*).

Another way doubt tries to cheat the Christian and prod him to deny his faith is through the absence of peace itself. We have peace with God as soon as we believe on Christ but we do not always have peace with ourselves. The pardon may be past the prince's hand and seal, yet not placed in the prisoner's hand. Do you not think the islanders were rash who accused Paul of being a murderer because the snake fastened itself on him? Then why do you condemn yourself as an unbeliever when afflictions and inward agonies fasten themselves on the spirit of the most gracious child God has on earth?

Yet Scripture relates doubt to the *strength* of faith, not to the *existence* of it. 'O thou of little faith, wherefore didst thou doubt?' (*Matt. 14:31*). These are Christ's words to the sinking Peter, in which He chides doubt and at the same time acknowledges the reality of faith, even though it is very weak. All doubting is evil by its nature; but some doubting, though evil in itself, evidences grace in the person who doubts.

Irritability in a sick person who previously lay unconscious is a sure sign of healing. And it is good for the doubting soul to know that his doubts can tell him whether his faith is true, although weak, or whether faith is absent. Because this is so, I shall lay down four characteristics of the doubtings which accompany true faith.

CHARACTERISTICS OF THE DOUBT WHICH MAY ACCOMPANY TRUE FAITH

I. A TRUE BELIEVER FEELS SHAME AND SORROW BECAUSE OF DOUBT

When you think about how much you actually doubt God instead of believe Him, do you not feel like crying? Where does this sorrow come from? Will unbelief mourn for itself? No, it shows there is faith in your soul which grieves because unbelief has wronged God's name.

As the law cleared the young woman in distress who cried out in the field (*Deut. 22:27*), so the gospel will clear you when you repent of unbelief. The psalmist was almost consumed by the disease of doubt: 'Can God furnish a table in the wilderness?' (Ps. 78:19). How often do we find this unbelief questioning God's faithfulness. He may as well have asked whether there was a God! But at last he admits his foolishness: 'And I said, This is my infirmity' (Ps. 77:10). He might have said, 'Thank you, unbelief! You are my enemy and God's enemy; and your goal was to make me fear. But what you actually did was prove there is faith at the bottom of my unbelief.'

II. A SINCERE BELIEVER EARNESTLY DESIRES GOD'S GOODNESS IN SPITE OF HIS DOUBTS

The weak believer may question whether or not God loves him, but he desires it more than life itself. This is the language of a seeking soul: 'Thy lovingkindness is better than life' (Ps. 63:3). He doubts if Christ is his; yet if you ask him what Christ is worth, and what he would give for Him, he tells you that no price would be too much. 'Unto you therefore which believe he is precious' (1 Pet. 2:7). In a word, he doubts whether he is holy or counterfeit; but his soul pants and thirsts after those graces which he can barely see.

This desire gives a good testimony of grace in the heart. David's words evidence this grace when he says: 'My soul breaketh for the longing that it hath unto thy judgments at all times'; 'Thy word is very pure: therefore thy servant loveth it' (Ps. 119:20, 140). Can you really let your heart run after Christ and His grace and fail to see that you have an interest in both? Be encouraged, for your doubts are not coming from an absolute void of faith but from your dissatisfaction with the weak quality of the faith you have.

It is common for excessive love to produce excessive fear. The wife who loves her husband earnestly fears when he is away that she may never see him again. One doubt tells her he is sick and another says he is dead; thus her love torments her without just cause, for her husband is well and on his way home. If we have mislaid an expensive ring we fear it might be lost. It is the nature of strong passions to disturb our reason and hide things from our eye which ordinarily we would see clearly. Thus many doubting souls hunt for that faith which they already have in their hearts. It has been hidden from their view because of their strong desire for it.

Rhoda 'opened not the gate for gladness' to Peter because her joy made her forget what she had been praying for (*Acts 12:14*). So then the high value which the doubting Christian sets on faith, together with an excess of longing for it, make him unaware that he already has that jewel which he has set his heart on.

III. DOUBTS MOTIVATE THE BELIEVER TO SEEK GOD
FOR WHAT HE FEARS HE MAY LACK

The doubting Christian has so much turmoil in his spirit that he cannot rest until he lets God's Word settle the questions for him. As Ahasuerus could not sleep and called for the chronicles of his kingdom, so the doubting soul goes to the records of heaven. And he looks now into the Word and now into his own heart to see if he can find there anything which answers to the description of Scripture faith, as the countenance in the mirror reflects the face of the man.

When David's doubts clogged up his faith he did not give up and let the ship run, as we say, before the storm. Instead of doubting if God loved him he communed with his own heart and his spirit searched diligently: 'In the day of my trouble I sought the Lord' (*Ps. 77:2*). A person should no more sit down and be content in his unresolved doubt than one who thinks he smells fire in his house would go to bed and sleep. He will look in every room and corner until he is satisfied that everything is safe.

The doubting soul is much more afraid of waking with hell-fire about it; but a soul under the power of unbelief is falsely secure and careless. Because the old world did not believe in an impending flood, the men settled down into a lethargic refusal to consider God's warning. And water reached their windows before they had the means to escape.

IV. IN SPITE OF HIS DOUBTS THE TRUE BELIEVER
LEANS ON AND DESIRES STILL TO CLING TO CHRIST

While Peter's feet were faltering beneath the water he was lifting up prayer to Christ; and this proved the truth of his faith. Although Jonah had many fears, yet even in these his faith had some little secret hold on God: 'Then I said, I am cast out of thy sight; yet I will look again toward thy holy temple' (*Jonah 2:4*). 'When my soul fainted within me I remembered the Lord' (*verse 7*). And David also, though he could not get rid of all the fears which came in through his weak faith, as water into a leaking ship, raised a firm hand and cut them off: 'What time I am afraid, I will trust in thee' (*Ps. 56:3*).

The weak Christian's doubting is like the wavering of a ship at anchor – he is moved, yet not removed from his hold on Christ; but the unbeliever's doubting is like the wavering of a wave which has nothing to anchor it and is wholly at the mercy of the wind. 'But let him ask in faith, nothing wavering. For he that wavereth is like a wave of the sea driven with the wind and tossed' (*James 1:6*).

CHARACTERISTICS OF PRESUMPTUOUS FAITH

Sometimes, however, the fear of doubting Christians is that their faith may be presumptuous. For those who struggle with this problem, let me set forth three characteristics of presumptuous faith.

I. PRESUMPTUOUS FAITH IS AN EASY FAITH

Because Satan does not bother to oppose presumptuous

faith, it shoots up like a wild weed in fertile ground. The devil is never more pleased than when the sinner walks around in his sleep, in a fool's paradise of vain hopes about Christ and about salvation. Satan would not think of waking him but instead smugly draws the curtain so that no light or noise can disturb his dozing conscience. Does a thief ever call in the night to warn his victim he is about to rob and kill him? No, sleep is his advantage.

The devil is a sworn enemy against true faith. He persecutes it in the cradle, as Herod did Christ in the manger; he pours a flood of wrath on it as soon as it announces its own birth by crying after the Lord. If your faith is legitimate, 'Naphtali' may be its name, and you may say, 'I have wrestled with Satan and with my own heart, and at last I have prevailed.' You know the answer Rebecca received when she asked God about the scuffle and striving of the children in her womb. 'Two nations,' God told her, 'are in thy womb' (*Gen. 25:23*). If you find strife in your soul, comfort yourself because of it, Christian. This dispute is from two contrary principles, faith and unbelief, which lust against each other; and your unbelief, which is the elder – no matter how hard it fights for mastery – shall serve faith, the younger.

II. PRESUMPTUOUS FAITH LACKS BALANCE

It has one lame hand. It has a hand to receive pardon from God but no hand to give itself up to Him. But true faith has the use of both hands. 'My beloved is mine' – there the soul takes Christ – 'and I am his' – there she surrenders herself to His purposes (*Song of Sol. 2:16*). Have you ever freely given yourself to Him? Everybody professes this, but the presumptuous soul, like Ananias, lies to the Holy Ghost by keeping back the most important part of what he promised to lay at Christ's feet. The enjoyment of lust is entwined about his heart and he cannot persuade himself to deliver it up to God's justice. His life is bound up in it, and if God will have it from him He must take it by force; there is no hope of gaining his consent. Is this the picture of your faith? If it is, you have blessed yourself in an idol; you have mistaken a bold face for a believing heart.

On the other hand, if you count it a privilege that Christ should have a throne in your heart, as you have a room in His mercy, you prove yourself a sound believer. And Satan may as well call himself a Christian as accuse you of having presumptuous faith. Let the devil nickname you and your faith whenever he wants to; perfume from rose petals is no less sweet because someone scribbles 'vinegar' on the label. The Lord knows who are His and claims them for His true children and their graces for the sweet fruits of His Spirit, though Satan or the world may give them a false title. No father rejects his child who in the delirium of a fever denies that he is his father.

III. PRESUMPTUOUS FAITH FAILS TO ENJOY THE SAVIOR'S FELLOWSHIP

When an unsound heart pretends to have faith in Christ it tastes very little sweetness in Him. If he were honest, he would admit he prefers the servants' table, with scraps of carnal treasure, to the pleasures of holy communion with Christ and His children.

The man with presumptuous faith brags about his interest in God but does not want to be in God's presence; he does not sip the wine of joy from the heavenly cup. It is not thoughts of heaven which comfort him, but what he has in and of the world – these dregs furnish his joy.

True faith, however, changes a person's appetite. No feast is so sweet as Christ to the believer. If God takes all other dishes off the table and leaves only Christ, the man still has all he wants. But if worldly priorities – health, friends, money – remain and Christ withdraws, the man cries out, 'Who has taken away my Lord?' Only Christ seasons all the believer's enjoyments and makes them sweet to the taste.

II. A Powerful Argument to Quench the Fiery Darts of the Wicked

We are fully persuaded of the pre-eminence of faith; now let us see why we must take up the shield of faith. The most powerful argument is contained in these words – 'Wherewith ye shall be able to quench all the fiery darts of the wicked' (*Eph. 6:16*). 'Ye shall be able' – not an uncertain 'maybe you shall'; it is absolute. But able to do what? 'Able to quench' – not only to resist and repel, but to extinguish. What then shall we quench? Not ordinary temptations only, but the most lethal arrows the devil has in his quiver – 'fiery darts'; and not just a few of them but *all* the fiery darts of the wicked. Part 2 explores two particular aspects of spiritual warfare: a description of the enemy – 'the wicked'; and the power of faith to overcome him – 'Ye shall be able to quench all the fiery darts of the wicked.'

DESCRIPTION OF THE ENEMY

Scripture describes the saint's enemy in three ways – his nature, his unity, and his fiery darts.

I. THE NATURE OF THE ENEMY

Satan is called 'spiritual wickednesses' in Ephesians 6:12. Certainly God must have a special lesson for His people to learn from this attribute of the devil in representing him by this name. We see at least two reasons for His using the word 'wicked' to describe the enemy of every Christian.

First, God chooses the word 'wicked' to remind His children to hate sin and resist Satan. The name which exalts God the highest is 'the holy One.' Accordingly, Scripture gives the devil the blackest brand of infamy – he is 'the wicked one.' If holiness could be separated from God's other characteristics – which would be the height of blasphemy – their glory would be gone. And if the devil's wickedness could be removed from his torments and misery, this case too would be exceedingly altered. We must hate him with a perfect hatred.

If you are not ashamed to live in sin you look like the devil himself. Do not attempt to mock or fear Satan's name, for inside you carry the truest possible picture of him – imprinted in your choice of sin. It is said that Cain was 'of that wicked one' (*1 John 3:12*). If you are wicked you are of the devil. Every sin you commit is a new line which the devil sketches on your soul. And if God's image in a saint – which the Spirit of God draws for many years in him – will be such an amazing portrait of Christlikeness when the last line has been drawn in heaven, think how fearful and horrible you will look after all the devil's efforts here on earth to impose his image upon you when you find yourself in hell, where you will have time to see the fullness of death and wickedness reflected unmistakably in yourself.

How pitiful are the souls here on earth who are controlled by the power of this wicked devil. David classifies it among other great curses: 'Set thou a wicked man over him: and let Satan stand at his right hand' (*Ps. 109:6*). He would rather be the worst prisoner in the nation than to be the best servant of sin or Satan. Solomon tells us, 'When the righteous are in authority, the people rejoice: but when the wicked beareth rule, the people mourn' (*Prov. 29:2*). Deceived sinners laugh when the devil rules. But you can mourn for them who laugh at sin and go to hell because of it.

Remember that Satan is wicked and can come for no good. And because you know the happiness of serving a holy God, surely you have an answer ready when this evil one comes to entice you to sin. Can you think of staining your hands to do his nasty drudgery after they have been used for the pure and fine service of God? Do not even listen to Satan's excuses unless you want your name to be 'wicked'.

The second reason God calls Satan wicked is to encourage believers in their combat with him. It is as if God says, 'Do not be afraid of him; it is a wicked company you go against. And they who defend it are wicked too.' If the saints must have enemies, the worse they are, the better! It would put courage into a coward to fight with such a crew.

Wickedness must be weak. The devils' guilt tells them their cause is lost before the battle is ever fought. They fear you, Christian, because you are holy; so you do not need to fear them at all. When you see them as subtle, mighty, and many, your heart beats fast. But look on all these spirits as ungodly wretches who hate God more than they hate you. And the only reason they detest you at all is your kinship to Him. Whose side is God on? In the past He rebuked kings for touching His anointed ones. Will He stand still now and let those wicked spirits threaten His life in you without coming to your rescue? It is impossible.

II. THE UNITY OF THE ENEMY

All the legions of devils and multitudes of wicked men and women form a single mystical body of wickedness, as Christ and His saints are one mystical holy body. One Spirit unites Christ and His saints and one spirit unites the devils and ungodly men. Their darts are all shot from the same bow and by the same hand. The Christian's fight, then, is a single duel with one great enemy. But this enemy unites all forces to arm themselves with darts of the worst kind.

III. THE WARLIKE PROVISION OF THE ENEMY

The devil's darts are temptations which he aims with remarkable accuracy at the souls of men and women. These temptations are called 'darts' for three reasons.

(a) *Darts are swift*

The psalmist names lightning God's arrow because it flies so swiftly. 'He sent out his arrows, and scattered them; and he shot out lightnings, and discomfited them' (*Ps. 18:14*). Satan's temptations travel like a flash of irrevocable lightning. He needs no more time than the blink of an eye for the delivery of a temptation. David looks upon Bathsheba and the devil's arrow is in his heart before he can close his window.

Sometimes a word or two accelerates Satan's arrow of temptation. When David's servants report that Nabal has wronged him, David's anger is the agent that causes an arrow of revenge to pierce his own heart. What is quicker than a thought? One foolish idea rises and our hearts are suddenly carried away like a spaniel after a bird that springs up before him as he goes after his master. If one temptation does not wound, Satan sends another straight after it; no sooner is one arrow delivered than the skillful archer draws another on the string.

(b) *Darts fly secretly*

So do temptations. The arrow comes from so far away that often a man may be wounded but never see who has shot him. The wicked shoot their arrows 'in secret' (*Ps. 64:4*). Thus Satan lets a temptation fly – sometimes he uses a wife's tongue to do his errand; another time he gets behind the back of a husband or friend and is not seen while he works. For instance, who would have suspected that Abraham would be Satan's instrument to betray his wife into the hands of a sin?

Sometimes the devil is so secretive that he borrows

God's bow to shoot his arrows, and the Christian thinks it is God who chides him. Job cries out because of 'the arrows of the Almighty' and their 'poison' (*Job 6:4*), when all the time Satan is practicing his malice upon him. God is a good Friend to this man but He gives Satan permission to test him. And poor Job protests as if God has thrown away their friendship and become his enemy.

Satan's darts not only fly swiftly and secretly but they make little noise as they go – they cut their passage through the air without warning us they are coming. Thus temptation makes its approach insensibly – the thief is in the house before we think to shut the doors. The wind is secret in its motion, as our Savior says, we know not 'whence it cometh, and whither it goeth,' yet we hear 'the sound thereof' (*John 3:8*). And just as silently Satan schemes to aim temptations at the unsuspecting Christian.

(c) *Darts have a wounding, killing nature*
This is especially true when they are shot out of a strong bow by one who is forceful enough to draw it. Satan's temptations are like that – headed with deadly malice and drawn by a strength little short of angelical. If God had not provided good armour, it would be impossible for us to outlast Satan's power and arrive safely in heaven.

Jesus wants us to be aware of the might of Satan's alluring attacks, for He teaches us to ask the Father: 'Lead us not into temptation' (*Matt. 6:13*). When Christ prays these words He has just tasted Satan's tempting skill and strength – which by His wisdom and power He is well able to defeat – yet how well He knows they are able to conquer even the strongest of His saints!

Apart from Christ, however, Satan has successfully deceived every man who ever lived. It was Christ's prerogative to be tempted but not to be led into temptation. And Job, a chief in God's army of saints, whom the

Father calls 'perfect and upright' (*Job 1:1*), is himself seriously injured by Satan's arrow. Yet in His time God is faithful to pluck him out of the devil's grip and bring healing and restoration to His servant.

Satan's warlike provision includes not just arrows but 'fiery darts.' Some scholars believe the term 'fiery' denotes a particular kind of temptation, such as blasphemy or despair; but since faith is a shield for *all* temptations, we see that every one of Satan's arrows is fiery. But why does Scripture call these darts 'fiery'?

First, Satan shoots them in fiery wrath. This dragon spits fire full of indignation against God and every one of His saints. Saul breathes out 'threatenings and slaughter against the disciples of the Lord' (*Acts 9:1*). As one who is inwardly inflamed, his breath is hot – a fiery stream of persecuting rage comes out of him like a burning furnace. Such temptation is the breath of the devil's fury.

Further, these darts are called fiery because they lead to hell-fire if they are not quenched. There is a spark of hell in every temptation; and all sparks fly to their own element. So then all temptations are bound for hell and damnation, according to Satan's intent and purpose.

Finally and most important, the devil's darts are said to be fiery because of the malignant effect they have on men's spirits, kindling a fire in their hearts and consciences. The apostle alludes to the custom of cruel enemies who used to dip the heads of their arrows in poison, making them even more deadly. They not only wounded the part where they penetrated the victim, but infected the whole body, a condition which made healing almost impossible.

FAITH'S POWER OVER THE ENEMY

Satan's fiery darts – which by faith the Christian can quench – may be described according to two of their characteristics: those which entice with false promises of satisfaction; and those which carry fear and terror in them.

FIERY DARTS OF PLEASING TEMPTATIONS

Satan's fiery darts of enticing temptations have a blistering quality. In every heart there is a secret tendency to sin. Temptations do not fall on us as a ball of fire on ice or snow, but as a spark or lightning on a thatched roof, which later bursts into flames. It is Satan who tempts, yet the sin is charged to us. 'Every man is tempted, when he is drawn away of his own lust, and enticed' (*James 1:14*). Satan tempts but our lust draws us. The hunter lays the net but the bird's own desire is what betrays it into the trap.

Man's heart is vulnerable to receive fire from Satan's darts. 'Where no wood is, there the fire goeth out' (*Prov. 26:20*). Because Christ extinguished the fiery darts they could not hurt Him. Satan found no combustible fuel of corruption in Him. But our hearts were once heated in Adam and have not cooled since. The Old Testament compares a sinner's heart to an oven: 'They are all adulterers, as an oven heated by the baker' (*Hos. 7:4*). The heart of man is the oven, the devil the baker, and temptation the fire with which he heats it.

David says, 'I lie even among them that are set on fire' (*Ps. 57:4*). And who sets them on fire? The apostle James resolves this question: '. . . set on fire of hell' (*James 3:6*). When the heart is inflamed by temptation, it is hard to quench such a fire, even in a gracious person. David himself, under the power of temptation so apparent that a carnal eye could see it, was responsible for the death of seventy thousand men; one sin cost that much. And if hell roars like that in a David, what damage will it cause where there is no grace in the heart to quench it? A soul possessed by flames of temptation runs into the mouth of death and hell and will not easily be stopped.

We should be afraid of embracing temptation when there are such bewitching qualities in it. Some people are too confident, as if they could not be overtaken by such a disease and therefore will inhale any air. And sometimes God lets such an atmosphere be invaded by one of Satan's darts, to make them know their own hearts. Who pities the man whose house is blown up, when he keeps his powder in the chimney corner?

Stand away from the devil's bull's-eye unless you want one of his arrows in your side! Keep as far from temptation's targets as you can. For if Satan gets you within his circle, your head will soon be dizzy. One sin ignites another, as brush kindles logs.

Because one sin kindles another, we must not let Satan use us as fuel to set fire to another person. Idolaters, for instance, decorate their temples and altars with gold and silver pictures to draw the spectator to them. They are infatuated with their idols as much as any lover with his mistress. And the drunkard stirs his neighbor's lust by giving his 'bottle to him' (*Hab. 2:15*). It is against the law to set fire to a neighbor's house. But what about a person who sets fire to the soul of a man, and hell-fire at that?

Some people start fires on purpose, but it is possible for it to be done unintentionally. A silly child playing with a lighted straw may set a house on fire which many wise men cannot put out. And truly Satan may use your carelessness to kindle lust in another's heart. It might be an idle word which you consider harmless; but a gust of temptation may carry this spark into your friend's heart and start a fatal fire there. Or perhaps it is inappropriate attire. Even if you wear it with a pure heart, and only because it is the style, this may ensnare another person.

Surely your brother's soul is more important to you than high fashion.

Scripture warns us not to be prideful in our decisions to overcome temptation: 'Wherefore let him that thinketh he standeth take heed lest he fall' (*1 Cor. 10:12*). Any temptation which we resist is common to all men. But 'God is faithful, who will not suffer you to be tempted above that ye are able; but will with the temptation also make a way to escape' (*verse 13*). And God makes this way for us through the power of faith.

FAITH'S POWER TO QUENCH PLEASING TEMPTATIONS

Faith empowers a soul to quench the pleasing temptations of the wicked one. This is called our 'victory that overcometh the world, even our faith' (*1 John 5:4*). Faith plants its triumphant banner on the world's head. And John tells us what God means by 'the world': 'Love not the world . . . For all that is in the world, the lust of the flesh, and the lust of the eyes, and the pride of life, is not of the Father, but is of the world' (*1 John 2:15–16*). All that is in the world is food and fuel for lust. Now faith enables the soul to quench those darts which Satan dips into the poison of worldly lusts – called by some the world's 'trinity.'

1. 'THE LUST OF THE FLESH'

This is temptation which promises pleasure to the flesh. It carries such fire in it that when it finds a carnal heart, it quickly inflames with unruly passions and coarse affections. The adulterer burns in his lust and the drunkard is inflamed with his wine.

No temptations work more eagerly than those which promise delight to the flesh. Sinners are said to 'work all uncleanness with greediness' – with a kind of covetousness; for the Word suggests they can never have enough

(*Eph. 4:19*). No drink will quench a poisoned man's thirst. Nothing but faith can help a soul in these flames. In hell Dives burns without a drop of water to cool the tip of his tongue. The unbelieving sinner is in a hell above ground; he burns in his lust without a drop of water, for lack of faith, to quench the fire.

By faith the martyrs 'quenched the violence of fire' (*Heb. 11:34*). 'We ourselves also were sometimes foolish, disobedient, deceived, serving divers lusts and pleasures. . . . But after that the kindness and love of God our Saviour toward man appeared . . . he saved us' (*Tit. 3:3-5*). No one can ever shake off the old companions of lust until by faith he becomes intimate with the grace of God revealed in the gospel.

II. HOW FAITH QUENCHES 'THE LUST OF THE FLESH'

Faith strips away the veil from the Christian's eyes so he can see sin in its nakedness before Satan disguises it with flattering costumes. Faith's piercing eye sees 'the evidence of things not seen' (*Heb. 11:1*). It looks behind the curtain of sense and sees sin, before it is dressed for the stage, to be a brat from hell that brings hell hidden with it. Let Satan come and present a lust ever so enticing – the Christian's answer is: 'I won't be cheated by a lying spirit. It shows you a fair Rachel but intends to give you a weak-eyed Leah; it promises joy but pays sorrow.'

The costumes which make lust so attractive are not its own. 'Why hast thou deceived me?' says the woman of Endor, 'for thou art Saul' (*1 Sam. 28:12*). Thus faith can call sin and Satan by their own names even when they are disguised. 'You are Satan,' says faith, 'Why do you try to deceive me? God has said sin is bitter as gall and wormwood. And you cannot make me believe I can gather sweet fruits of true delight from your root of bitterness or grapes from your thorns!'

Faith enables the soul to recognize not only the nature of sin void of all true pleasure, but also the temporal quality of its frivolous elation. Faith persuades us not to give up God's sure mercies for Satan's transient thrills. This persuasion makes Moses run from the enchantments of the Egyptian court into the fire of 'affliction' because he knows them for what they are – 'pleasures . . . for a season' (*Heb. 11:25*). If you saw a man jump from a ship into the sea, at first you might think him insane; but later if you saw him standing on the shore, and the ship swallowed up by the waves, you would know he took the wise course.

Faith sees the world and all the stimulus of sin sinking; there is a leak in them which the wisdom of man cannot repair. Now is it not better to swim by faith through an ocean of trouble and get safely to heaven than to sit in the lap of sinful pleasures until we drown in hell's gulf?

Sin's enjoyment cannot last long because it is not natural. Whatever is not natural soon decays. The nature of sugar, for example, is to be sweet and therefore it holds its sweetness; but artificially sweetened wine loses its good taste in just a few days. The pleasure of sin is foreign to its nature and will corrupt the life it touches. None of the sweetness which now satisfies sinners will be tasted in hell; only bitterness will spice the sinner's cup there.

Another reason sin's exhilaration must be short-lived is that life itself does not last long, and they both end together. Many times the pleasure of sin dies before the man dies. Sinners live to bury their worldly joy. The worm breeds in their conscience before it breeds in their flesh by death. But be sure the advantages of sin never survive this world. The word has gone out of God's mouth: He 'distributeth sorrows in his anger' (*Job 21:17*). Hell's climate is too hot for evil delights to survive.

Faith is the wise grace which makes the soul consider how it will live in eternity. The carnal heart is all for the present; his snout is in the trough and as he wallows he thinks it will never end. But faith has a large stride; at one pace it can reach over a whole lifetime of years and see the end while they are only beginning. 'I have seen an end of all perfection,' says David (*Ps. 119:96*). He envisions the wicked, while thriving on their beds of sensuality, cut down and burning in God's oven as if it were done already (*Ps. 37:2*). And according to its strength faith will sharpen the vision of every Christian. For who envies the condemned man his feast on his way to execution?

Finally, faith outwits Satan's 'bargains' by showing the soul where quality enjoyments are available at a more reasonable price. Customers shop where they find the very best of what they want. This principle holds true among sinners as well. The drunkard goes where he can have the best beer, the glutton where he finds the biggest platter. Yet faith presents rewards to the soul which are beyond all compare. It leads to the promise and entertains the believer there at Christ's expense, with every rich course the gospel affords.

Faith sets before the Christian a taste of that full supper he will enjoy in heaven. And even this small sample melts into 'joy unspeakable and full of glory' (*1 Pet. 1:8*). Surely this truth must quench temptation's appetite. When Satan invites the Christian to his glittering orgy, the soul can say, 'Should I give up those pleasures which fill all my desire and corrupt myself with sin's moldy bread? Then I would be like Judas, who rose from his Master's table to sit at the devil's.'

III. 'THE LUST OF THE EYES'

The apostle refers here to those temptations drawn from the world's treasury. And it is the eye which first commits adultery with them. As the unclean eye looks upon another man's wife, so the covetous eye looks on another's wealth to lust after it. Consider what tragic effects this temptation has on Ahab when he covets Naboth's vineyard. To gain only a few acres which do not add much to a king's revenues, he swims to it in the owner's blood. Only faith can permanently blind lusting eyes and give clear insight into the sufficiency of God's grace.

IV. HOW FAITH QUENCHES 'THE LUST OF THE EYES'

Satan lures the soul to venture out into lying and taking the wedge of gold like a carrot dangled before a donkey; but faith simply convinces the soul of God's fatherly care. Thus faith teaches the soul to counter, 'I am well provided for already, Satan; I do not need your donation; why should I play the thief for something which God has promised to give me?' 'Let your conversation be without covetousness; and be content with such things as ye have: for he hath said, I will never leave thee, nor forsake thee' (*Heb. 13:5*). How can you possibly lack anything when God's promise commands His riches? Let him who is without God in the world struggle to survive in Satan's worthless will; but Christian, you are free to live on the inheritance of your faith.

Another way in which faith quenches the lust of the eyes is by teaching us that our comfort comes from God's blessing, not from material abundance. 'A faithful man shall abound with blessings: but he that maketh haste to be rich shall not be innocent' (*Prov. 28:20*). Faith warns, 'If you heap up the world's goods in the wrong way you will never be content in the way you expected.' It is impossible to steal something and then ask God to bless it. Satan cannot give you quiet possession of what you get by sin, and neither can he acquit you from the proceedings which God will surely bring against you.

Finally, faith lifts the Christian to seek higher goals than anything the world has to offer. It discovers that faith's merchandise lies beyond the heavens and leaves the clay of this earth in order to trade for grace and glory. Faith can bring its riches from far away.

David brands the worldly man as foolish who troubles himself so much for nothing. He says, 'Surely they are disquieted in vain: he heapeth up riches, and knoweth not who shall gather them' (*Ps. 39:6*). And then he turns his back on the world as not being worth his effort: 'And now, Lord, what wait I for?' (*verse 7*). He asks, 'Is this my prize? To sit upon a bigger collection of wealth than my neighbor has?' 'My hope is in thee. Deliver me from all my transgressions' (*verses 7–8*). His attitude is, 'Let those who love the world take the world; Lord, do not pay my wages in gold or silver, but in pardon of sin.'

V. 'THE PRIDE OF LIFE'

There is a place in man's heart which itches with pride because of the world's honors; and the devil works hard to scratch and irritate man's proud flesh by fascinating offers. Thus when temptation and lust finally meet, Satan accomplishes his purpose.

Even after the Jews are convinced that Christ's doctrine is true, they part with Christ and remain slaves to their pride, 'for they loved the praise of men more than the praise of God' (*John 12:43*). Faith quenches this temptation of pride and with holy scorn turns from all that the world uses as a bribe to sin.

But pride has not taken everyone captive through the years. 'By faith Moses, when he was come to years, refused to be called the son of Pharaoh's daughter' (*Heb. 11:24*). Although this adoption might have made him heir to the crown, he threw it down. Honors swept toward him as the waters of a flowing tide; and for him to stand against this flood of preferment was admirable indeed. But he did not give up one court position for a better one. He did it to join a remnant of poor, reproached people. By rejecting royal favors he incurred the king's anger; but faith carried him through the heights and depths of disgrace and favor, honor and dishonor. And wherever this grace is today, in its strength or weakness, it does the same thing.

Believers of later days have been tempted too. When they were about to suffer, these men and women were offered attractive alternatives to cause them to bend to the times by retreating from the bold profession of their faith; but they chose the flames of martyrdom rather than the favor of princes on Satan's terms. How is faith able to quench such a strong temptation as this?

VI. HOW FAITH QUENCHES 'THE PRIDE OF LIFE'

There are several distinctive ways in which faith quenches the pride of life: it takes away the fuel that feeds the temptation; it causes the Christian to expect all honor from Christ; it shows the dangers of bargaining with Satan for worldly glory; and it reveals precedents to believers.

(a) *Faith takes away the fuel that feeds this temptation*
Pride is the fuel for temptation. Take away the oil and the lamp goes out. Where this lust is present in any strength, the creature's eyes are dazzled with the sight of something which suits the desires of the heart. By temptation the devil gives vent to what the heart itself is full of. Simon Magus had a haughty spirit; and when he first saw the chance to upstage the apostle, his desire was on fire to have a gift to work miracles himself. On the other hand, a man of humble spirit loves a low seat; he is not ambitious to tower above the thoughts of others; and while he stoops in his own opinion of himself, the same bullet flies over his head which hits the proud man in the chest. Faith settles the heart down. Pride and faith are opposites; like a pair of

balance scales, if one goes up, the other must go down. 'Behold, his soul which is lifted up is not upright in him: but the just shall live by his faith' (*Hab. 2:4*).

(b) *Faith is Christ's favorite and makes the Christian expect all his honor from Him*

When temptation comes, faith casts the soul on Christ as being all-sufficient to make it happy. And when temptation promises to bring you to honor if you will allow a sin, faith chokes the bullet. Remember whose you are. Princes will not let their subjects become indebted to a foreign prince – least of all to one who is hostile to them. Faith declares that the honor or applause you get by sin makes you subject to the devil himself, who is God's greatest enemy.

(c) *Faith shows the danger of bargaining with Satan to gain the glory of the world for one sin*

Faith urges you to realize that the world's glory can never satisfy you. It may kindle thirst but it quenches none; it will beget a thousand fears but quiet none of them. But the sin which buys these glories has the power to torture your soul for ever.

(d) *Faith reminds the Christian of the exploits of former saints, who have renounced the world's honor*

These saints refused to prostitute their souls by selling themselves into sin. Faith clearly calls the roll of Scripture saints and the exploits of their faith so that the Christian may be stirred by the same gallant spirit. This was plainly the apostle's design in recording these saints' choices along with the trophies of their faith (*Heb. 11*). 'Seeing we also are compassed about with so great a cloud of witnesses, let us lay aside every weight, and the sin that doth so easily beset us' (*Heb. 12:1*).

What courage it puts into the soldier to see the man beside him run into the face of death! Elisha, having seen the miracles God worked by Elijah, smites the waters of Jordan with his mantle, saying, 'Where is the Lord God of Elijah? and . . . they parted' (*2 Kings 2:14*). Faith uses the exploits of former saints to encourage us to pray.

'O God, You are the God of the valleys – the smallest of saints, as well as of the mountains – the more famous heroes. Does not the same blood run in the veins of all believers? Were they victorious, and shall I be the only slave, to cower under my burden of corruption without shaking it off? Help me, my God!' Faith says, 'Awake, Christian! Prove that you are kin to these holy men, that you are born of God as they were, by your victory over the world.'

FAITH'S VICTORY DISTINGUISHED FROM HEATHENS' VICTORY

Some say that faith's victory over the world is really no more than that of some well-behaved heathens. They have trampled on worldly pleasures and resisted temptations to cheat their fellow men. Yet their achievement is as much excelled by faith's victory as the sad example of looser Christians is outdone by them, and in the following ways:

I. THE UNIFORMITY OF FAITH'S VICTORY

Scripture calls sin a 'body' (*Rom. 6:6*) because it is made up of several members, consisting of as many troops and regiments as military forces. It is one thing to defeat one division but quite another to break up the entire army. The moral principles of a heathen may gain some minor victories and overcome a few surface sins; but then they are fearfully beaten by another wing of sin's soldiers. When they seem to triumph over 'the lust of the flesh' and 'of the eyes' – the world's profits and pleasures – they are at the same time becoming slaves to 'the pride of life,' kept in chains by the credit and applause of the world.

As the sea which, it is said, loses as much land on one shore as it gains on another, so the heathen's moral principles gain in a seeming victory over one sin but lose again by falling into bondage to another. But faith is uniform and routs the whole body of sin so that not one single lust stands in its unbroken strength.

'Sin shall not have dominion over you: for ye are not under the law, but under grace' (*Rom. 6:14*). 'Sin shall not' – that is, no sin shall be your commander. Sin may stir like a wounded soldier on his knees, and many of them may rally like scattered troops; but they will never take the battlefield where true faith is moving.

II. THE SECURITY OF FAITH'S VICTORY

Many men say they believe; they thank God they are not infidels. But what can your faith *do*? Can it defend you in battle and cover your soul when Satan's darts fly all around you? Or is it such a sorry shield that it lets every arrow of temptation through to wound your heart?

If Satan tells you to lie or cheat in your business and your passive faith makes no resistance, you are sinning not only against your fellow men but against faith itself. God forbid that you should think your faith is saving faith. Will faith which cannot bring you out of hell ever take you to heaven? Do not venture out in life with such a paper shield. To get faith that keeps you secure and strong, come to Him who is the Faith Maker – God, I mean.

It is not the possession of a shield itself that defends the Christian; we must hold it up and use it in battle against Satan's fiery darts. Do not let him take you when your faith is not ready to hand, as David found Saul unarmed in the cave, with his spear on the ground when it should have been in his hand.

HOW TO USE THE SHIELD OF FAITH TO QUENCH ENTICING TEMPTATIONS

Let your faith ask God to come and defend you against Satan's fiery darts. There are three particular acts of faith which will require God to help – and we say this with reverence – because He binds Himself to do so.

I. FAITH'S PRAYERFUL ACT

Open your case to God in prayer and call in help from heaven, as the commander of a station under fire sends a secret messenger to let his general know the seriousness of his need. The apostle James says, 'Ye fight and war, yet ye have not, because ye ask not' (*James 4:2*). If we have any victory it must drop from heaven – but it will stay there until believing prayer comes for it.

Although God purposed to deliver Israel out of Egypt, there was no sign of His coming until the groans of His people rang in His ears. This gave heaven the alarm: 'Their cry came up unto God . . . And God heard their groaning, and God remembered his covenant' (*Exod. 2:23–24*). To prevail in this act of faith, apply the following scriptural principles to your prayer.

(a) *Show God His promise*

Prayer is nothing but the promise reversed, or God's Word formed into a request and returned by faith to Him again. Show God His own hand in such promises as these: 'Sin shall not have dominion over you' (*Rom. 6:14*); and 'He will subdue our iniquities' (*Mic. 7:19*). A good man is as good as his word, and is not this true of God also?

(b) *Plead with God as His child when you pray against any sin*

Has God accepted you into His family? Have you chosen Him for your God? Who will take care of the child if the father will not? God does not receive glory when one of His children is a slave to sin. 'Order my steps in thy word:

[119]

and let not any iniquity have dominion over me' (*Ps. 119:133*).

(c) *Engage God from His Son's bloody death to free you from lusts*

Christ died to 'redeem us from all iniquity, and purify unto himself a peculiar people' (*Tit. 2:14*). Shall He not have full benefit of the price of His blood and the purchase of His death? In a word, what is Christ praying for in heaven? The same thing His mouth prayed for on earth – that His Father would sanctify and keep us from the evil of the world. You come in a good time when you ask God for something which Christ has already asked Him to give you.

II. FAITH'S EXPECTING ACT

When you have been with God, expect good from Him. 'I will direct my prayer unto thee, and will look up' (*Ps. 5:3*). If you do not believe, why do you pray? And if you believe, why do you not expect? By praying, you seem to depend on God; by not expecting, you again renounce your confidence and undo your prayer. What is this but to take His name in vain and to play games with God? It is as if someone should knock at your door but turn away before you can open it and speak with him.

For a man to break into your house after you have closed the door would be presumptuous; but for him to come out of a storm into your house when you invite him is no presumption. This is graciousness. And if God will not open the door of His promise to be a sanctuary to humbled sinners escaping from the rage of their sins, I know of no one this side of heaven who can expect welcome. God has promised to be a king to His people. And it is no presumption for subjects to come under their prince's shadow and expect protection from him. God says He 'will be unto us a place of broad rivers and streams; wherein shall go no galley with oars, neither shall gallant ship pass thereby' (*Isa. 33:21*).

You have the saints for precedents. When they are in combat with corruption they act upon their faith and expect God to ruin those enemies which overrun them. At the very time their enemies seem to prevail, their faith sees God destroying them.

David spoke not only for his own faith but also for that of all believers – and you are, I suppose, one of these. 'As for our transgressions, thou shalt purge them away' (*Ps. 65:3*). And mark the ground of his confidence: 'Blessed is the man whom thou choosest, and causest to approach unto thee, that he may dwell in thy courts' (*verse 4*). It is as if he had said, 'Surely the Father will not let those so close to Him waste away under the power of sin without His gracious help.' This is Christ's own argument against Satan on behalf of His people. 'The Lord rebuke thee, O Satan; even the Lord that hath chosen Jerusalem rebuke thee' (*Zech. 3:2*).

Surely this expecting act of faith must encourage you to see what God has already empowered you to do. If you are a believer sin does not have the same strength in your soul that it did before you knew Christ, His Word, and His ways. Although you are not what you want to be, yet you are not what you have been.

There was a time when sin played king in your heart. You went to sin as a ship to sea before the wind and tide; you spread your affections to receive the gale of temptation. But now the tide has turned and you find a secret strength to wrestle with temptation. And because it is God who helps, Satan cannot loose all his will on you. Here is a sweet beginning, and this promises a readiness in God to perfect the victory. But He wants your faith to improve into a confidence for total deliverance.

'God broke my heart,' says the Christian, 'when it was like flint, and brought me home when I was walking in the pride of my heart against Him; but can He give bread to nourish my weak grace? I have come out of Egypt; but can He master those giants in iron chariots which stand between me and Canaan? He helped me in one temptation; but what will I do the next time?' Do not grieve a good God with such heart-breaking questions. You have 'the former rain.' Why should you question 'the latter'? The grace which God has given you is a sure pledge that more is on the way.

III. FAITH'S CONFIDENCE IN GOD

After Jehoshaphat had prayed and anchored his faith on the word of promise, he marched out under this victorious banner against his enemies (*2 Chron. 20*). Christian, do what he did; hasten as he did. And I give you the same counsel which David gave his son Solomon: 'Arise therefore, and be doing, and the Lord be with thee' (*1 Chron. 22:16*). The same faith which caused you to work against your sins as God's enemies will undoubtedly move Him to work for you against them.

The lepers in the Gospel were cured not as they sat but as they walked. They met their healing in an act of obedience to Christ's command. The promise says, 'Sin shall not have dominion over you' (*Rom. 6:14*). So go ahead and make a valiant attempt against your lusts – and in doing your duty you will find God's performance of the promise.

The reason so many Christians complain about the power of their corruptions lies in one of two roots – either they try to overcome sin without acting on the promises, or else they only pretend to believe. They use faith as an eye but not as a hand; they look for victory to drop from heaven upon their heads but do not prayerfully fight to get it. To them, faith is mere fiction; for the man who believes that God will cause a thing to happen also believes that He will prosper the means which He appoints to bring it about.

Therefore, Christian, do not sit still and say your sin will fall. Be realistic and put on your armour; take up your arms to defeat it. God, who has promised you the victory, means to use your hands in the battle. 'Get thee up,' said God to Joshua, 'Wherefore liest thou thus upon thy face?' (*Josh. 7:10*). God received his prayer but before the Amorites could be defeated there was something else for Joshua to do besides pray and weep. And God has something else for you to do with your faith besides praying and expecting your lusts to disappear. Search your heart carefully to see if some sin is hiding there that will make you run before the face of every new temptation.

FIERY DARTS OF FEARFUL TEMPTATIONS

Leaving the first kind of fiery darts – attractive temptations – we now proceed to the second kind, those which fill the Christian with fear. It is only the power of faith that can quench fiery darts of this kind.

This particular kind of weapon is our enemy's tactic kept in reserve. When pleasing temptations prove unsuccessful, he opens his quiver and sends a shower of these arrows to set the soul on fire – if not with sin, then with fear. When he cannot carry a soul laughing to hell through the deception of pleasing temptations, he will try to make him go whining to heaven by his use of this different kind of attack.

Paradoxically, it is a sure sign that Satan is losing when he resorts to using temptations to produce fear in the Christian. An enemy who keeps a castle preserves it as long as it is his; but when he must retreat he destroys it to make it useless to those who come after him. While the strong man controls his own house he quenches those fireballs of conviction which the Spirit often shoots into the conscience; but when he hears mutinous whisperings of a full surrender to Christ, he sets the soul on fire by fearful temptations.

FAITH'S POWER TO QUENCH FEARFUL TEMPTATIONS

The devil must work even harder when Christ captures the castle and keeps it by the power of His grace. It is obvious that all the darts shot against Job were of this kind. When God let the devil practice his skill, why did he not tempt Job with some golden apple of profit or pleasure? Surely the high testimony God gave to His servant discouraged Satan from choosing this method; no doubt he had already tried Job's manhood and found him impenetrable. So he had no other way left but this. Now let us study three instances of this type of fiery dart and show how faith can quench them all – temptations to atheism, blasphemy, and despair.

I. THE FIERY DART OF ATHEISM

The first of Satan's fearful temptations is his dart of atheism, an arrow which he boldly aims at the being of God Himself. It is true that the devil, who cannot himself turn atheist, cannot make God's child an atheist either, for he has not only, in common with other men, an indelible stamp of deity in his conscience, but also such a sculpture of the divine nature in his heart as irresistibly demonstrates a holy God. It is impossible for a holy heart to be fully overcome with this temptation, because God's image within proves he has been created 'after God . . . in righteousness and true holiness' (*Eph. 4:24*).

[124]

The wicked are not cleared from atheism by their naked profession of God as long as their weak thoughts fail to produce obedience to Him. 'The transgression of the wicked saith within my heart, that there is no fear of God before his eyes' (*Ps. 36:1*). Thus David traces the wickedness of the sinner's life to the atheism in his heart. On the contrary, the holy life of a person saved by grace says that the fear of God is before his eyes and his belief in God is plain to see. Although a Christian can never be slain by the temptation of atheism, he may be haunted by it. Next I will show you how the Christian's faith may quench this fiery dart.

II. HOW FAITH QUENCHES THE FIERY DART OF ATHEISM

Why do we need faith for this? Will not reason stop the devil's lies in this issue? Can the eye of reason ever see God unless it looks through the lenses of faith?

Reason itself is a gift from God which is able to demonstrate His being. Even in places where Scripture has never been taught, the people still acknowledge a deity: 'For all people will walk every one in the name of his god' (*Mic. 4:5*). Yet during a furious assault of temptation it is faith alone that can quench the fire of this dart.

Reason is vague and does little more than show there is a God; it can never tell who or what this God is. Until Paul made the Athenians acquainted with the true God, they had very little light, although their city was the very eye of the world for learning. Scripture sets out God's plan for knowing Him, not by advanced culture and worldly knowledge but by truth: 'He that cometh to God must believe that he is' (*Heb. 11:6*). Faith fully counts on the credit of the Word and takes all on trust from its authority. He 'must believe that he is'; not just know there is a God, but know God to be God, a step which reason of itself can never take.

Our human nature is so blind that we have deformed

thoughts of God until with the eye of faith we see His face in the mirror of the Word. With the exception of Jesus, all men are atheists by nature because at the same time as they acknowledge a God they deny His power, presence, and justice. They allow Him to be only what pleases them: 'Thou thoughtest that I was altogether such an one as thyself' (*Ps. 50:21*).

Even if reason could demonstrate all that God is, it would be dangerous to dispute it with Satan. He has sharper reasoning than you. There is more difference between you and Satan than between the weakest idiot and the greatest theologian in the world. But in the Word there is a strong divine authority that builds a throne even in the conscience of the devil himself.

Although Christ was able to baffle the devil by reason, He chose to overthrow him in the way that we ourselves must use in skirmishes with Satan. He repelled him simply by lifting up the shield of the Word: 'It is written,' said Christ (*Matt. 4:4, 7, 10*). It is undeniable that Christ's quoted word had power to stun Satan; the shrewd enemy had no reply to Scripture but was stilled at the very mention of the Word.

If only Eve had stood by her first answer – 'God hath said' (*Gen. 3:3*) – she too could have silenced Satan. Thus the Christian must stand in the heat of temptation and place God's own Word between himself and Satan's blows: 'I believe that God is, though I cannot understand His nature; I believe the Word.' When this happens, Satan may trouble him but he cannot hurt him – and he probably cannot even bother him for very long. The devil hates the Word so much that he does not want to hear it. But if you throw down the shield of the Word and try to cut through temptation by the force of reason, you may soon be surrounded by your subtle enemy.

Among those few who claim to be atheists, most have neglected the Word and let the pride of their own understanding, coupled with the righteous judgment of God, drive them into atheism. They have turned their backs on God and His Word, digging into the secrets of nature so that they can be admired for their knowledge. But then, like those who carry a light into the mines of the earth until it fails them, God's secret judgments put out that light which at first they carried about with them. 'Where is the disputer of this world? hath not God made foolish the wisdom of this world?' (*1 Cor. 1:20*).

Certainly God's gift of reason can confirm His gift of truth. But if reason does not keep its place, it holds man still in his unbelief. Faith must not depend on reason, but reason on faith. I am not to believe what the Word says merely because it agrees with my reason; but I must believe my reason because it aligns with the Word. A carpenter lays his rule to the plank and sees it to be straight or crooked; yet it is not the eye but the rule that is the measure. He can always trust his rule to be right.

Therefore let the Word, like David's stone in the sling of faith, first lay low the temptation; and then, as he used Goliath's sword to cut off the giant's head, you can safely use your reason to finish the victory over Satan's atheistical attacks.

III. THE FIERY DART OF BLASPHEMY

Satan uses the fiery dart of blasphemy to annoy the Christian. In a general sense every sin is blasphemy. When a man does, speaks, or thinks anything against the holy nature or works of God with an intent to reproach Him, this is blasphemy. Job's wife was the devil's agent to provoke her husband to this sin: 'Curse God,' she said, 'and die' (*Job 2:9*).

The devil threatened Christ Himself with this sin by

inviting Him to fall down and worship him. But all he could do to God's Son was offend His holy ear by such impudence. Christ's holiness would not let him come an inch closer. But Satan has an easier time approaching the Christian. He shoots this fiery dart into the saint's imagination and stirs up unworthy thoughts of God, although these are normally as unwelcome to a Christian as the frogs which crept into Pharaoh's bedroom.

IV. HOW FAITH QUENCHES THE FIERY DART OF
  BLASPHEMY

Satan tries to defame God by aiming at the wicked man's natural tendency to blaspheme God. The devil was so sure Job was a hypocrite that he worked hard to make his lie come true: 'Put forth thine hand now and touch all that he hath, and he will curse thee to thy face' (*Job 1:11*). When the sinner is provoked, the inward frustration of his heart ignites crude thoughts about God, and together these appear in the obscenity of his tongue – 'This evil is of the Lord; what should I wait for the Lord any longer?' (*2 Kings 6:33*). It is loud blasphemy, the same seed of which is found in every unbeliever.

There is one spirit of wickedness in sinners, as there is one spirit of grace in saints. Every unbeliever has a bitter spirit against God and everything that carries His name. Let the lion out of his cage and he will soon show his bloody nature. An unbeliever has no more power to quench such a temptation than dry wood has to quench fire that is set to it. But let us see what faith can do to quench this dart.

(a) *Faith sets God within the sight and hearing of the*
  Christian

This keeps the soul in such awe that it does not harbor impure secret thoughts of God. David tells why the wicked are so bold: 'They have not set thee before them'

(*Ps. 86:14*). People who slander the names of others do it behind their backs. And sin seldom blasphemes God to His face; that is the language of hell. Atheism is mixed with blasphemy while sinners are on earth. They do with God as those terrorists did with Christ; they covered His face and then beat Him.

But faith sees God eyeing the soul to preserve it. 'Curse not the king,' says Solomon, 'no not in thy thought; and curse not the rich in thy bedchamber: for a bird of the air shall carry the voice, and that which hath wings shall tell the matter' (*Eccles. 10:20*). Faith warns, 'Do not blaspheme the God of heaven; you cannot even whisper softly enough for Him not to hear. For He is closer to you than you are to yourself.' Thus faith breaks the devil's snare. When God came to Job in His majesty, all Job's long speeches suddenly vanished and he covered his face with humility before the Lord: 'Now mine eye seeth thee. Wherefore I abhor myself, and repent in dust and ashes' (*Job 42:5–6*).

(b) *Faith accepts no report of God except from God's own mouth*

The person who gathers his understanding of God only from His Word cannot possibly have unholy thoughts of Him. It is the only true glass to see Him in, because it alone presents Him like Himself, in all the demonstration of His glory.

Faith conceives all its ideas of God by the Word, solves all cases of conscience, and interprets mysteries by this Word. But since Satan's skill cannot do this, he drives the person who is in a hard situation to entertain wrong thoughts of God. Thus he criticizes God's justice when blatant sinners have not been judged quickly; or he says he will not serve a God who permits His servants to wear ragged clothing. These are the broken glasses that Satan mirrors God in, so that he may distort His goodness to the doubting eye. And if we judge God to be what He appears in Satan's jagged pieces of deception, we might condemn the Holy One and be caught in a dangerous tornado of temptation.

(c) *Faith praises God in sad conditions*

Blessing and blasphemy are contrasting tunes. They cannot be played on the same instrument without changing all the strings. It is beyond Satan's skill to strike such a harsh stroke as blasphemy on a soul tuned for praise. 'My heart is fixed,' says David – there was his faith. And then he says, 'I will sing and give praise' (*Ps. 57:7*). It was faith that tuned his spirit and prepared his affections to praise.

Faith can praise God because it sees mercy even in the greatest affliction. Thus Job quenched this dart which Satan shot at him from his wife's tongue. 'Shall we receive good at the hand of God, and shall we not receive evil?' (*Job 2:10*). Will we let a few present troubles become a grave to bury the memory of all His past mercies? What God takes from us is less than we owe Him, but what He leaves us is more than He owes.

Faith has a good memory and can tell the Christian many stories of mercies; and when his present meal falls short, it entertains the soul with a dish of left-overs and does not complain. 'This is my infirmity: but I will remember the years of the right hand of the most High. I will remember the works of the Lord: surely I will remember thy wonders of old' (*Ps. 77:10–11*). Therefore, Christian, when you are in the depths of affliction and Satan tempts you to curse God as if He had forgotten you, do not let him finish his sentence: 'No, Satan, God has not forgotten my present needs; it is I who have forgotten His past mercies, else how could I question His fatherly care now?' Go, Christian, play over your old lessons. Praise

God for His past mercies and it will not be long before He gives you a new song.

As faith sees mercy in every affliction, it also keeps expecting more mercy. This confidence causes the believer to praise God as if the mercy were happening in the present. For example, when Daniel was in the very shadow of death, 'three times a day he prayed, and gave thanks before his God' (*Dan. 6:10*).

Mercy is in the promise as the apple is in the seed – faith sees it growing up and the mercy coming. A soul which expects deliverance will quickly scorn blasphemous thoughts. When relief is known to be on its way to a besieged garrison, this assurance raises their hopes. They refuse the temptation to become traitors. Yet when unbelief is the officer-in-charge, the soul doubts the intentions of God's heart and Satan finds a gate wide open.

Faith keeps the believer waiting but unbelief urges the sinner to blame God and man. And no one escapes the blasphemer's curse, not even God Himself. Examples of both extremes are found in the same Scripture passage. Faith can patiently wait on God even in the hard times: 'I will wait upon the Lord, that hideth his face from the house of Jacob, and I will look for him' (*Isa. 8:17*). But unbelief blasphemes the Creator just as enthusiastically: 'When they shall be hungry, they shall fret themselves, and curse their king and their God, and look upward' (*verse 21*).

(d) *Faith teaches the Christian to distinguish between Satan's temptations and personal sin*

Although Satan does not find a Christian able to take these blasphemous temptations in as his guests and give them a home for his sake, he knows it disturbs the soul's rest to have them continually knocking at his door. When he cannot demoralize the Christian by gaining his consent to these temptations, even then he hopes to accuse him of the sin which he refuses to commit. Satan wanted to play the leading role of defiler but must settle for two lesser parts — reviler and false accuser.

As the Jews forced Simon of Cyrene to carry Christ's cross, so Satan compels the tempted Christian to carry the guilt of his sin for him. And many times he so skillfully shifts it from himself to the Christian's back that the creature struggles under the baseness of his own heart. The humble Christian often fears the worst about himself even when he is not guilty. When the cup was found in Benjamin's sack the patriarchs took the blame even though they were innocent. The Christian's thoughts condemn him for sins that all belong to Satan.

When a person turns from his old sinful course to embrace Christ and declares for Him against sin and Satan, this is the time when these blasphemous suggestions usually begin to appear. They are sent from Satan out of revenge for the soul's rejection of him. The devil deals with the new Christian in the same way that his witches express spite against those who cross them. Sometimes they send lice or other tormenting pestilences. But faith can spotlight their spite, not the Christian's carelessness, as the breeding place of the problem.

In a word, does it not seem strange that when the Christian was an enemy to God he dared not venture into this sin because of its monstrous nature, yet now that he begins to love God these blasphemies, which were too big and horrible before, would fill his mouth?

The violent entry of these blasphemous temptations into the Christian's mind betrays their breeding place — Satan, not the person's own heart. They flash like lightning into the person's thoughts before he has time to decide what he is doing. Lust which overflows from the heart is, on the other hand, ordinarily more gradual in its persuasion.

Not only their sudden violence, but their incoherence with the Christian's former thoughts, heighten the probability that these temptations are darts shot from the devil's bow. Peter was known to be a member of Christ's company by his voice: 'Thy speech,' they say, 'agreeth thereto' (*Mark 14:70*). He talked like them and was judged to be one of them. On the contrary, we may say of these blasphemous thoughts, 'They are not the Christian's. Their language shows them to be the belching of a devil, not the voice of a saint. If they were woven by the soul, they would be something like the whole piece from which they are cut.' There is ordinarily a continuity in our thoughts, like a circle rising out of another circle in stirred water.

Sometimes as the Christian worships God, an intruding blasphemous thought barges in like a rude stranger. The tenant never ushers in a thief. If a holy thought surprises us when we are far from heavenly meditation, we may take it as a pure moving of Christ's Spirit. Who but He could appear so suddenly in the midst of the soul when the door is shut, even before the person can turn his thoughts to open it for Him?

Probably the blasphemies which rush toward your soul when you are praying and praising God are only the eruptions of the wicked one, sent to interrupt you in that work which he fears and hates the most.

(e) *Faith helps the Christian when blasphemous ideas are caused by his own sin*

Even when these blasphemous thoughts do originate in the person's heart, not in Satan's false accusations, faith assures the soul on solid scriptural authority that his sin is pardonable. 'All manner of sin and blasphemy shall be forgiven unto men, but the blasphemy against the Holy Ghost shall not be forgiven unto men' (*Matt. 12:31*). Pardon may be found in the court of mercy no matter how damaging the evidence may be. And if the creature believes this, Satan's dart is quenched; for his design is to make these temptations a trap-door through which he can shove your soul down into a bottomless pit of despair.

The blasphemy of blasphemies – I mean the sin against the Holy Ghost – will never touch a true believer. Although the Christian has no absolute protection or immunity from any sin short of that, yet the whole body of sin is weakened in every believer, and God's grace has dealt his corrupt nature a deadly wound which will ultimately cause its death.

A dying tree may bear a little more fruit, and a dying man may move his limbs, though not so strongly as when he was healthy. Thus sin in a saint will show its fruit, although it is unripe and of poor quality. But you have no reason to be discouraged when it stirs. Be thankful it cannot do much else! Even though Satan is ready to drop into his grave he still lifts up a hand against you to show his continuing hatred when his power fails to do what he wants it to.

Faith reveals clearly to the soul that Christians suffer more guilt from a few proud, covetous thoughts than from many blasphemous ones. The fiery darts of blasphemy may scare the Christian, but fiery lusts wound faster and more deeply. The warm sun makes the traveler undo his coat but the blustering wind makes him close it tightly. Temptations of pleasure entice the heart to receive them, whereas the horrifying nature of fearful temptations forces the Christian to resist them valiantly.

Lusts are like poison in sweet wine, swallowed before the person knows it and diffused to poison the Christian's spirits. But temptations of blasphemy are like extremely bitter poison; they are either spit out before they are down or vomited up by the Christian before they spread into his will. Sins are great or small by the share the will has in implementing them. And blasphemous thoughts, commonly having less of the Christian will in them than lusts, cannot be a greater sin.

Faith tells the soul there is a good reason for his suffering by these temptations; otherwise God would not allow Satan to send them. Possibly He sees some other sin as potentially a greater danger and lets Satan trouble you so that you will not be conquered by more serious temptations. It is better to tremble at the sight of blasphemous thoughts than to strut in pride at the display of your spiritual gifts. The first will make you think you are as vile as the devil himself, but the other will make you wicked and just like the devil in God's eyes.

Finally, faith assigns to the Christian some noble exploits for God which will disprove the devil's charge. This is the fullest revenge the Christian can take either on Satan for troubling him or on his own heart for spewing out such impure streams. When David in the cave preferred Saul's life above a kingdom – which one hearty blow might have secured for him – he proved that all his accusers were liars. So Christian, prefer the honor of God when it competes with sin and self, and you will stop the devil's mouth. Such heroic acts of zeal and self-denial will speak more for your holiness before God and your own conscience than these sudden blasphemous thoughts can do against you.

V. THE FIERY DART OF DESPAIR

Satan works overtime to bring souls down to the complexion of devils and damned sinners suffering under God's scorching wrath in hell because they become charred with black despair. Other sins are only introductory and make the person more vulnerable to such a temptation. As the wool takes a stain of some light color before it can be dyed with a darker shade, so Satan begins with his more pleasant sins so that he may later entangle the victim more hopelessly. But the devil is too clever to lay his net of despair in the bird's sight. Other sins are only the top cover, and once he flatters his prey into it, he has trapped him for eternity.

Despair, more than other sins, puts a man into a kind of possession of hell itself. As faith gives substance to the word of promise, so the cruelty of despair gives existence to the torments of hell in the conscience. This drains the spirit and makes the creature become his own executioner.

Despair puts a soul beyond all relief; the offer of pardon comes too late. Faith and hope can open a window to let out the smoke that offends the Christian in any circumstances. But the soul will be choked when it is fastened up within despairing thoughts of its own sins, and no crevice of hope is left for an outlet to the dread which smothers him.

VI. HOW FAITH QUENCHES THE FIERY DART OF DESPAIR

The chief of Satan's strengths is the greatness and the multitude of a person's sins, which he can use to bring a soul into such despair that he sees no way of escape from God's verdict against them. When the conscience is breached and waves of guilt pour in upon the soul they soon drown all the creature's efforts, as the great flood covered the tallest trees and highest mountains. And as nothing was visible then but sea and heaven, the despairing soul sees nothing except sin and hell. His sins stare him in the face as with the eyes of many devils, ready to drag him into the bottomless pit.

A mere fly dares to crawl over the sleeping lion, an animal whose awesome voice makes all beasts tremble when he is awake. Fools freely mock sin as soon as the eye of conscience is shut. But when God arms sin with guilt and lets this serpent sting the conscience, then the proudest sinner flees before it. Only faith handles sin in its fullest strength by giving the soul a glimpse of the great God.

FAITH OPPOSES SIN WITH A VIEW OF THE GREAT GOD

I. FAITH SEES GOD'S GREATNESS

The reason the presumptuous sinner fears so little and the despairing soul fears so much is that they fail to know God's greatness. But Scripture has healing for both of them: 'Be still, and know that I am God' (*Ps. 46:10*). Here the Father says, 'Know that I am God and that I am able to forgive the greatest sins; stop dishonouring Me by your unbelieving thoughts of Me.' Faith shows God to be God.

In order to know God for who He is we must conceive of His infinity – He is not only wise but *immeasurably* wise, not only mighty but *almighty*. Faith alone can establish this principle in a person's heart so that his actions will start agreeing with God's greatness.

Some say they believe in God's infinite mercy. But if they are still carriers of a hell flaming in their despairing hearts, they have not seen God in the greatness of His mercy. The creature's despair lies in saying that his sin is infinite but that God is not. He then becomes like the unbelieving Israelites: 'They remembered not the multitude of thy mercies; but provoked him at the sea, even at the Red sea' (*Ps. 106:7*). They could not see enough in God to help them in such a crisis. All they saw was a multitude of Egyptians to kill them and a multitude of waters to drown them. Thus despairing souls see a multitude of damning sins but no infinitude of divine mercy to save them.

Reason is short of stature, like Zaccheus, and cannot find mercy in a crowd of rushing sins. It is faith alone which climbs the promise; only then will the soul see

promise? Yet God's covenant with Jacob was always kept, although Jacob was not faithful on his part. Why? Because he was dealing with the holy God.

Another of God's attributes which kindles fear in the awakened sinner is His justice. The soul sees no way except hell for God to vindicate His justice. But faith empowers the soul to walk around in this fiery attribute with his comfort unsinged, even as the Hebrew children prospered in the flaming furnace (*Dan. 3*).

FAITH RELIEVES THE SOUL WHICH FEARS GOD'S JUSTICE

One might wonder whether or not God can be both just and righteous in pardoning a sinner. Faith shows that God may pardon sins, no matter how great, with safety to His justice. This question was settled at the council board of heaven by God Himself and He has expressed His decision in the form of a precious promise: 'I will betroth thee unto me for ever; yea, I will betroth thee unto me in righteousness, and in judgment' (*Hos. 2:19*).

Who is it that God intends to marry? One that has played the whore. And what does 'betroth' mean? God will forgive our sins and receive us into the arms of His love and peculiar personal favor. But how can such a righteous God betroth a whorish bride to Himself? He says He will do it in judgment and in righteousness. It is as if God admonishes, 'Do not try to clear My justice; I will do that Myself. It is My holy will to do it in this way.'

When Satan comes against the believer and questions how such a wretched man could ever find favor with God, faith can confidently reply: 'Yes, Satan, God can be as righteous in pardoning me as He is in damning you. He tells me it is "in judgment and in righteousness." I leave you to dispute this case with God, who is able to justify His own act.'

But still more evidence for the vindication of God's justice and righteousness in His pardoning act is found in the full satisfaction which Christ has given Him for all the believer's sins. It was the great purpose of Christ to bring justice to kiss mercy. Therefore before Christ pleads the sinner's cause with God, He sees to the satisfaction of God's justice by His sacrifice. He pays and then prays for what He has paid – presenting His petition for believing sinners written with His own blood so that justice can carefully read and accept it.

God provides for our salvation by this method so that even we weak ones might be able to justify Him, in justifying us, in the face of the most malicious devil in hell. 'Being justified freely by his grace through the redemption that is in Christ Jesus: whom God hath set forth to be a propitiation through faith in his blood, to declare his righteousness for the remission of sins that are past, through the forbearance of God; to declare, I say, at this time his righteousness: that he might be just, and the justifier of him which believeth in Jesus' (*Rom. 3:24–26*). Working expertly with the truths of this Scripture, faith builds a tower of absolute safety around the believer.

I. CHRIST'S PROPITIATION ALLUDES TO GOD'S MERCY

God promised to meet and speak with His people in such a way that no dread from His majesty would fall upon them. And just as the mercy seat fully covered God's holy law inside the ark, Christ's propitiation covers all the law which otherwise would accuse the believer. But not one threat now can arrest the believer, as long as this screen remains for faith to interpose between God's wrath and the soul. God cannot see the sinner for Christ who hides him, and justice cannot condemn the believer who keeps running to Christ and taking refuge in His satisfaction. The scarlet thread in Rahab's window kept the destroying sword out of her house; and by faith, the blood of Christ continually keeps the Christian out of wrath's reach. Christ's satisfaction worn by faith is the sign that distinguishes God's friends from His enemies.

II. GOD SEALS CHRIST'S ATONEMENT FOR SIN

Christ is the One 'whom God hath set forth to be a propitiation through faith in his blood' (*Rom. 3:25*). He is the One the Father has sealed and singled out from all others and set forth as the Person chosen to make atonement for sinners, as the lamb was taken out of the flock and set apart for the Passover.

Therefore when Satan lines up the believer's sins against him and confronts him with their severity, faith runs under the shelter of this Rock. 'Surely,' says faith, 'my Savior is infinitely greater than my greatest sins. I would be rejecting the wisdom of God's choice to doubt.' God knew what a heavy burden He had to lay upon Christ's shoulders but He was fully persuaded of His Son's strength to carry it. A weak faith may save but a weak Savior cannot. Faith has Christ to plead for it but Christ had none to plead for Him. Faith leans on Christ's arm, but Christ stood alone. If the burden of our sins had prevailed against Him, no one in heaven or on earth could have helped Him stand.

III. GOD'S MERCY DECLARES HIS RIGHTEOUSNESS

Everyone believes God is merciful to forgive; but it is harder to believe how He can be righteous in forgiving sinners. 'To declare, I say, at this time his righteousness: that he might be just, and the justifier of him which believeth in Jesus' (*Rom. 3:26*). God was saying, 'I know why it seems so incredible that I should pardon all your iniquities. You think because I am a righteous God that I would rather damn a thousand worlds of sinners than bring My name under the least suspicion of unrighteousness. I would indeed damn them over and over again, rather than stain the honor of My justice – which is Myself. But I command you and the greatest sinners on earth to believe it: I can be just and yet the justifier of those sinners who believe in Jesus.'

What more solid testimony of his justice can a judge give than to condemn his own son and acquit a stranger? When God did not spare His own Son, but delivered Him up for us all, He declared His highest hatred for sin and His most inflexible love for justice.

IV. CHRIST'S REDEMPTION FULLY PAYS SIN'S DEBT

If a man tried to pay for his own sin he would spend the rest of his life and eternity working in vain to cancel that debt. But God receives the whole payment from Christ in one sum, so that He could truly say, 'It is finished' (*John 19:30*). Jesus was saying, 'In just a few minutes the work of redemption will be finished. I have the whole amount now in my hand to pay God; and as soon as I bow My head, and the breath is out of My body, all will be finished.'

And the receipt for Christ's settlement with justice comes from the triumphant Word in God's own mouth: 'He is near that justifieth me; who will contend with me?' (*Isa. 50:8*). But Christ's atoning death did more than discharge our old debt. By the same blood He has made a new purchase for His saints. Thus God, who was the creditor, is now the debtor to His creature for no less than eternal life, which Christ has paid for and given every believer humble authority to claim in His name. So we see both the debt paid and the new purchase of life in one and the same Savior.

'But this man, after he had offered one sacrifice for sins for ever, sat down on the right hand of God; from henceforth expecting till his enemies be made his foot-stool. For by one offering he hath perfected for ever them that are sanctified' (*Heb. 10:12–14*). He not only crossed out the believers' debts but perfected them for ever. He made as certain provision for their perfection in glory as for their salvation from hell's punishment. From this refuge of His finished work He calls us to 'draw near . . . in full assurance of faith' (*Heb. 10:22*). This assurance comes from the attribute of God which we have feared in the past: His justice. But Scripture says, 'If we confess our sins, he is faithful and just to forgive us our sins, and to cleanse us from all unrighteousness' (*1 John 1:9*). He does not say 'merciful,' but 'just.' It is God's mercy which makes the promise but justice which performs what mercy has promised.

V. IN THE DAMNATION OF SINNERS, JUSTICE IS ONLY
PASSIVELY GLORIFIED

When Christ suffered, justice and mercy met. And justice is never more radiant in God or man than when it is in conjunction with mercy. Now in the Lord Christ's death they both shone in all their glory and mutually complemented each other. Here the white and the red – the roses and the lilies – flourished in such oneness that it is hard to say which presents the face of justice more beautifully, God's wrath upon Christ for us, or His mercy to us for His sake.

God forces His glory from devils and damned souls who do not willingly pay the debt. They acknowledge God to be just only because they must, but at the same time hate the One they vindicate.

But in the satisfaction which Christ gives, justice is actively glorified. Christ was not dragged to the cross but gave 'himself for us an offering and a sacrifice to God' (*Eph. 5:2*). He suffered as willingly for us as we ever sinned against Him. And believing souls now sing praises to the mercy and justice of Him who redeemed them, and will sing the same song for ever. Now how much better are the voluntary sufferings of Christ than the forced torments of the damned? And the melodious praises of saints in heaven than the forced acknowledgments of souls in hell?

FAITH FIGHTS SIN THROUGH THE GREATNESS OF GOD'S PROMISES

Only faith can see God in His greatness; and therefore nothing but faith can see the promises in their greatness because their value lies in the worth of Him who makes them. This is why promises have so little effect on an unbelieving heart, either to keep it from sinning or to comfort it because of sin's torment. Where there is faith to chase the promise, there the promise will give comfort and peace in abundance. It will be as sweet wine glowing with inward joy in the believer; but on an unbelieving heart the promise lies cold and ineffectual. It has no more effect on such a soul than medicine poured down a dead man's throat.

The promises do not comfort *actually* and formally, as fire has heat; if this were true we could be comforted merely by thinking about a promise. But the promises comfort *virtually*, as fire is in the flint, which requires labor and art to strike it out and draw it forth. Only faith can teach us this skill of drawing out the sweetness and virtue of the promise, and it does this in three ways.

FAITH TEACHES THE VIRTUE OF GOD'S PROMISES

I. FAITH GOES TO THE SOURCE OF THE PROMISES

Here the Christian can take advantage of the best view of

their precious qualities. We can understand very little about something unless we trace it to its source and see its beginnings. A soul knows his sins are great when he sees them flowing from an envenomed nature which teems with enmity against God. The sinner will tremble at the threatenings which roll like thunder over his head when he sees where they come from and the perfect hatred God has of sin.

It is just as true that the person will realize the intense value of the promises when he sees the fountain it flows from – the heart of God's free mercy. This is the origin of all promises. The covenant itself, which includes them all, is called 'mercy' because it is the product of mercy: 'To perform the mercy promised to our fathers, and to remember his holy covenant' (*Luke 1:72*).

Faith argues that if the promises flow from the sea of God's mercy, then they must be as infinite and boundless as His mercy is. So if you reject the promise, or question the sufficiency of God's provision of it just because of your sins, you dishonor mercy, the womb where the promise was conceived.

II. FAITH GOES TO THE END OF THE PROMISES

God's Word, the light which guides faith, discovers a double purpose of the promises – to exalt the riches of God's free grace and to comfort the believer.

(a) *Exaltation of God's free grace*

God Himself purposes to pardon and save a company of lost sinners for Christ's sake; and He does this through the promises of the gospel. God performs this mysterious design to gather His children and form one glorious choir to fill the heavens with triumphant hallelujahs for the mercy which forgave and saved them. When faith sees that God's aim is the praise of His mercy, it tells the struggling soul that it is impossible for the Father to reject a repenting sinner. For God must be true to His own thoughts and keep His eye on the finishing line which He Himself has drawn.

It is the exaltation of His mercy, says faith, which God has in His eye when He promises forgiveness to sinners. And which exalts His mercy more, to pardon little or weighty sins? Whose voice will sing the sweetest song of praise? Surely the man who has been forgiven the most. God is ready to pardon the vilest sinner who truly repents.

A physician will not send away those who desperately need his skill and treat only those with minor diseases. It is the great cures whose fame is spread abroad. When a terminally ill man is restored to health by the physician's care, this cure gladly commends his doctor to everyone who hears of it, and gains him more reputation than a year's work of ordinary cures.

Great revenues of praise are paid to God from those who have had great sins pardoned. Christ judges that the man who has been forgiven a five-hundred-dollar debt will love more than he whose debt was only fifty dollars. And where there is the most love there is likely to be the most praise. The voice of a Manasseh, a Magdalene, and a Paul will be heard above all the rest in heaven's concert.

Greatness of sin is so far from barring the forgiveness of a penitent sinner in God's thoughts that He pardons only those who confess that their sins are grievous. Therefore God uses the law to make way, by its convictions on the conscience, for His pardoning mercy to ascend the throne in the penitent sinner's heart: 'Where sin abounded, grace did much more abound' (*Rom. 5:20*). If we tremble at the greatness of our sins, we must triumph at the mercy which so far exceeds their greatness. The man who wonders at the height of some majestic mountain would much more marvel at the depth of the waters which could cover it from ever being seen again. But now let us examine the second purpose of the promise.

(b) *Comfort for the believer*

God's Word was written on purpose that 'we through patience and comfort of the scriptures might have hope' (*Rom. 15:4*). God gives sinners security concerning the reality of His mercy for the saving of those who would embrace Christ on the terms of the gospel. And He opens His heart and publishes the purposes of His love in many precious promises which run like veins throughout the whole body of Scripture.

In the design of His Word, God seals up all the comfort which His wisdom could find or the unbeliever could ever need, and makes a sanctuary in Jesus for those pursued by their clamoring sins. In so many words the New Testament guarantees the perfection of this refuge: 'That by two immutable things, in which it was impossible for God to lie, we might have a strong consolation, who have fled for refuge to lay hold upon the hope set before us' (*Heb. 6:18*).

Will you be perplexed with an argument drawn merely from the greatness of your sins, which is answered in almost every page in the Bible, in which safety-shelters are provided into which faith can retreat? Faith and fear are like the natural heat and moisture in the body, which is never healthy except when both are preserved. 'The Lord taketh pleasure in them that fear him, in those that hope in his mercy' (*Ps. 147:11*).

But let me warn you, Christian, not to expect favor from God in your distress if you plan to continue friendship with lust. Although mercy will be a sanctuary to the humbled sinner and shelter him from the curse of sin, it will not spread her wing over a bold sinner and his lust.

And do not sin just because the promises of mercy exceed your sins as far as God in His greatness surpasses the creature. It is as if your servant should find your cellar of strong wines and become drunk, when you keep them only to help those get well who are sick. Be careful not to misuse the holy vessels of the sanctuary of God's mercy. It is the sorrowing soul, not the sinning soul, which this wine of consolation belongs to.

III. FAITH PROVIDES WITNESSES TO WHOM GOD'S PROMISE HAS BEEN FULFILLED

God verifies His fulfilled promises by book-cases of the faithful cloud of witnesses. He would never have left the saints' great blots in the Scriptures open to the inspection of all succeeding generations if He had not intended to help tempted souls overcome this fearful temptation to doubt His promise of mercy.

Paul gives this very reason why such acts of pardoning mercy to great sinners are recorded. He shows first what filthy creatures he and other believers were before they were made partakers of gospel grace. 'Among whom also we all had our conversation in times past in the lusts of our flesh' (*Eph. 2:3*). Then he magnifies the rich mercy of God which rescued and took them out of that damned state. 'But God, who is rich in mercy, for his great love wherewith he loved us . . . hath quickened us together with Christ' (*verses 4–5*).

But God designed His plan of mercy to cover more generations than the contemporaries of Paul. 'That in the ages to come he might shew the exceeding riches of his grace in his kindness toward us through Christ Jesus' (*Eph. 2:7*). Wherever the gospel comes, even to the end of the world, the records of God's mercy will stop the mouth of unbelief. And this arrow on Satan's string will be made headless and harmless.

God commanded Joshua to take twelve stones out of the Jordan and set them up. His reason was 'that this may be a sign among you, that when your children ask their fathers in time to come, saying, What mean ye by these stones? Then ye shall answer them, That the waters of Jordan were cut off . . . : and these stones shall be for a memorial unto the children of Israel for ever' (*Josh. 4:6–7*). Thus God's pardoning mercy has taken some notorious sinners out of the very bottom of sin's hellish depths and set them up in His Word as a memorial of His faithfulness linked to their repentance. These examples are a sign that what He has done in the past, He still can and will do for you.

Are you afraid God does not have enough mercy for you? Look at the roll of pardoned sinners – a Manasseh, a Magdalene, a Saul, an Adam! These are landmarks that show what large boundaries mercy has drawn, and how far it goes to pardon the greatest sinners. It is a healthful walk for you to take this path and see the farthest stones of God's pardoning mercy.

But if after all this your sins still seem to exceed the proportion of anyone you can find pardoned in Scripture, faith shows you the way beyond all these examples for your soul's rescue. You can look to Christ, who never had sin of His own yet laid down His life to purchase and obtain pardon for all the elect.

Faith says, 'Suppose your sins *were* greater than any one saint's; are they as great as all sins of all the elect put together?' Cannot Christ procure your pardon, as He has for so many millions of His chosen ones? And even if your sins were as heavy as all theirs are, the sum would be the same; and God could forgive it if it lay in one heap. Christ is 'the Lamb of God, which taketh away the sin of the world' (*John 1:29*). See here the sins of the elect world tied into one bundle; God still carries it lightly away into the

[149]

land of forgetfulness! Faith tells you that the whole virtue and power of Christ's blood, by which the world was redeemed, is offered to you. And He personally brings it to you. Christ does not ration out His blood, some to one and some to another; but He gives His whole self to the faith of every believer. You belong to the Redeemer. And He is yours.

FAITH OPPOSES DESPAIR

The greatest command in the whole Bible is to believe. When the Jews asked our Lord Jesus, 'What shall we do, that we might work the works of God?' notice His reply: 'This is the work of God, that ye believe on him whom he hath sent' (*John 6:28–29*). It is as if He had said, 'Receive Me into your hearts by faith; do this, and you do it all.' This is the all in all. Everything you do is futile until this work is done; but when you have believed, God appreciates it as much as if you had kept the whole law. In fact, it is accepted in lieu of it: 'To him that worketh not, but believeth on him that justifieth the ungodly, his faith is counted for righteousness' (*Rom. 4:5*).

This man's faith in Christ is accepted for righteousness; that is, at the judgment he will escape the sentence as if he had never strayed a step from the path of the law. If faith is the work of God above all other, then unbelief is the work of the devil. He works harder to make men unbelievers than drunkards or murderers. And despair is unbelief at its worst. Unbelief among sins is as the plague among diseases, the most dangerous; but when it settles into despair, then it is like the plague which brings certain death with it. Unbelief is despair in the bud, but despair is unbelief at its full growth.

Every sin wounds the law and the name of God. But this wound is healed when the penitent sinner by faith comes to Christ and unites with Him. And through Christ God receives the sinner in the fullness of righteousness and vindicates His own name from the dishonor of the person's iniquities. It is a complete and glorious work done by God's forgiving mercy. But what would you think of a sinner who is not willing to have the law's wounds healed, who has dishonored God? The despairing person will not let Christ satisfy the wrongs which his sins have done toward God.

As the bloody Jews and Roman soldiers exercised their cruelty on every part of Christ's body – crowning His head with thorns, piercing His side with a spear, and fastening His hands and feet with nails – so the despairing sinner bruises the whole name of God. He puts a mock crown on the head of His wisdom and nails the hands of His almighty power while he thinks that his sins have put him out of reach and beyond the power of God to save him. This man pierces the tender mercy in a God who not only *has* mercy and love, but *is* mercy and love.

What is the sum of all this despair? Surely it represents the highest charge of the attempted murder of God Himself. For the fullness of God's love, wisdom, power, and mercy are more intrinsic to His being than blood is to the life of a man. Tremble and repent, for you are sinning as the dwellers in hell sin.

It is significant that despair clearly appears in the devil himself, who knows he cannot be pardoned and thus sins with a rage as high as heaven. And this sin has the same effects in men that it has in Satan. 'They said, There is no hope: but we will walk after our own devices' (*Jer. 18:12*). Sometimes a frustrated beggar starts cursing the owner of a house who does not answer his knocks upon the door. Similarly, despair teaches the sinner to swear profanely before the God of heaven. And once despair enters it is almost impossible to keep blasphemy out.

You who spend your life crying and sighing over your horrible crimes – why are you still fighting against God? Can you find any love in your heart toward Him, although you cannot at present find a breath of love coming from Him to you? Are you tender and afraid of sinning against Him even while you seem to have no hope for mercy from Him? If so, then be comforted; your faith may be weak, but you are far from being held down under the power of despair.

Judas was not damned merely for treason and murder; for others who had their hands in those sins were pardoned by faith in that blood which they had cruelly shed. But death began its eternal reign in him when despair and final unrepentance filled his heart. Despair being such, let us shrink from this damning gulf!

10: *Ninth Consideration: The Christian's Helmet*

And take the helmet of salvation (Eph. 6:17).

THESE words of Scripture present us with another piece in the Christian's armour – the helmet of salvation to cover his head in the day of battle. This helmet, together with most of the other pieces of armour, are defensive arms, to protect the Christian from sin but not to keep him from suffering.

Only one piece in the whole armour is for offense – the sword. Scripture hints that the Christian's war lies chiefly on the defense and therefore requires defensive arms to fight it. God has deposited a rich treasure of grace in every saint's heart, which the devil spitefully tries to rob the Christian of by waging a bloody war against him. And so the believer overcomes his enemy when he himself is not overcome. He wins the day when he does not lose his grace, his work being to keep what is his rather than to get what is the enemy's. Because the saint's war lies chiefly on the defense, we must instruct the Christian how to manage combat with both Satan and his weapons of war.

As a Christian soldier you must always stand in a defensive posture with your armour on, ready to defend the treasure God has given you to keep, and to repel Satan's assaults. But do not step outside the line of your calling which God has drawn about you. Let Satan be the assailant and come if he will to tempt you; but do not go out and tempt him to do it.

Even when the devil's instruments of war reproach the Christian, the gospel does not allow him to use the devil's weapons to return them stroke for stroke. 'Be pitiful, be courteous: not rendering evil for evil, or railing for railing: but contrariwise blessing' (*I Pet. 3:8–9*). You have a girdle and breastplate to defend you from their bullets – the comfort of your own sincerity and holy walk. With these you can repel the sordid arsenal thrown at you – but there is no weapon for self-revenge. A shield has been put into your hand to quench their fiery darts, but no darts of bitter words to retort against them. You are 'shod with peace' so that you may walk safely with the injuries they inflict, without any pain to your spirit – but also without pride to trample those who wrong you.

Most of the pieces of armour are to defend you in suffering, not to protect you from it. And you must prepare for even more suffering, because God has furnished you with sufficient armour to bear it. Armour is not to be worn by the fireside but in battle. How can the maker be praised if the metal of his arms is not tried? And where shall it be proved except amid swords and bullets? He who wants to live on an island of pleasure where the whole year is summer will never make a good Christian. Get ready for hardship or lay down your arms. Here is the reason why so few come at the beat of Christ's drum to lift His standard and why many who enlisted by a verbal profession drop out and leave Him. They do not want to suffer. Most men are more tender toward their skin than toward their conscience. They wish the gospel had provided armour to defend their bodies from danger and death rather than their souls from sin and Satan.

After we notice the linking word 'and' which clasps this helmet of salvation to the former piece of armour, showing the connection between the various pieces, we shall go on to observe three aspects of the helmet of salvation: first, the piece of armour itself; secondly, the use of the helmet; and thirdly, applications of the doctrine of the helmet of salvation.

THE CONNECTION OF THE HELMET WITH THE SHIELD AND WITH THE OTHER PIECES OF ARMOUR

Notice the linking word 'and': 'And take the helmet of salvation.' Every grace is lovingly joined to its companion. And all of them, though many pieces, make one suit; though many links, form a single chain. The sanctifying, saving graces of God's Spirit, then, are linked inseparably; they are connected to one another in their birth, growth, and decay.

I. THE CONNECTION OF THE SANCTIFYING GRACES IN THEIR BIRTH

Where there is one sanctifying grace, the others are present too. This is not true of common gifts and graces; these are handed out like the gifts Abraham bestowed on the children he had by his concubines (*Gen. 25:6*). They had various gifts but none had them all. But sanctifying graces are like the inheritance God gave Isaac; every true believer has them all. 'If any man be in Christ, he is a new creature: . . . behold, all things are become new' (*2 Cor. 5:17*).

As natural corruption is a universal principle of sin that sours man's nature, so sanctifying grace is also a universal principle which sweetens and renews the whole man at once, though not wholly. Grace comes into the soul as the soul comes into the body. It grows by steps but is born at once. The new creature has all his parts formed together, but not his degrees. One part of the world was discovered long after some others; yet all the world was made at the same time. Thus the Christian may notice one grace

[155]

stirring in his life before another. Now this connection of graces in their birth has a double purpose.

(a) *To relieve the sincere Christian in doubt*

Maybe you have been looking for faith but you cannot find it. Do not be discouraged; send out spies to search for some other grace, such as your love for Christ. Have you not seen your love for Him chasing away temptation with the same rebuttal Joseph gave his lewd mistress? 'How then can I do this great wickedness, and sin against God?' (*Gen. 39:9*).

Do you have a sincere desire to please Jesus or a deep sadness when you have done something that grieves Him? These are two veins full of the life-blood of love for Christ. Your love can tell you news of your faith. As Christ says, 'He that hath seen me hath seen the Father' (*John 14:9*). So if you have seen your love for Christ, you have also seen faith in the face of that love.

But what if your love for Christ is hidden in a cloud? Then see if you can find some repentance, despising yourself with the sight of your sins and rousing you to hate these sins as the enemies which have lured you into rebellion against God. For they are the bloody weapon which wounded God's name and murdered His Son. The grace you look for stands before you. What is love of God if not passion against sin as His enemy?

But sometimes you cannot see the love for the zeal or the fire for the flame. As by taking hold of one link you may draw up the rest of the chain which lies under water, so by discovering one grace, you may find them all. And while this sanctifying grace relieves the sincere Christian's doubt, it shames the hypocrite who grasps for one particular grace but shuns another.

(b) *To shame the hypocrite*

The Spirit of God does not come into a soul with half of

His sanctifying graces but with all of them. If your heart is set against one grace it proves that you are a stranger to the others. Love and hatred are of the whole kind; he who loves or hates one saint loves or hates every other saint. And the person who embraces one grace will find every grace dear; for they are as kin to each other as one beam of the sun is to another.

II. THE CONNECTION OF THE SANCTIFYING GRACES IN THEIR GROWTH AND DECAY

Increase one grace and you strengthen all; impair one and you will be a loser in all. The reason for this is that they are reciprocally helpful to each other. For instance, when love cools, obedience falters because it lacks the oil on its wheel that love used to drop. When obedience staggers, faith weakens. How can there be great faith where there is little faithfulness? In turn, weak faith makes hope waver; for it is the credit of faith's report which hope relies on to expect good from God. And as hope wavers, patience shatters and cannot keep its shop windows open any longer, because it trades with the stock hope lends it.

In the body there are many members, yet all form one body; and each member is so useful that the others depend on it. So in the Christian there are many graces but one new creature. The eye of knowledge cannot say to the hand of faith, 'I do not need you,' nor can the hand of faith say the same to the foot of obedience; but all are preserved by the mutual care they have of one another.

As a defeat of the whole city may stem from a tiny break in one part of its wall, and the soul may run out through a wound in a particular member of the body, so the ruin of all the graces may follow the ruin of any one of them. There is an even stronger bond of necessity among graces of our souls than there is among members of our body. For example, it is possible for a hand to be cut off without the death of the whole body, because not all its members are vital parts. But every grace is a vital part in the new creature and so essential to its very being that its absence cannot be supplied by substitution. In the body the other hand can do the work for the amputated hand, but faith cannot fill the office of love, nor love the work of obedience. The failure of one wheel spoils the motion of the whole clock.

INFERENCES DRAWN FROM THE CONNECTION OF GRACES

I. STRENGTH FOR WEAKENED GRACES

It is a careless man who jeopardizes the safety of his whole household by failure to repair one or two holes in the roof. Are you any less wrong to neglect the repair of one of your graces? When you are tempted to sin, do not look on it as a single sin, but as having all other sins in its womb. Think about what you are doing before you serve Satan in any one act; for by one sin you strengthen the whole body of sin. Give to one sin and that will send more beggars to your door; they will come with a stronger plea than the former. And while you may intend to entertain only one, all barge in with it. Your best way is to keep the door shut.

Even if it were possible to break this connection of sin and take off one link which pleases you most and not draw the whole chain after you, remember there is a connection of guilt also. 'Whosoever shall keep the whole law, and yet offend in one point, he is guilty of all' (*James 2:10*). A man cannot stab any part of the face without disfiguring the whole countenance and hurting the whole man. Thus the law is copulative; a wrong done to one causes the dishonor of all and so is resented by God, whose authority is equally in all.

II. COMFORT FOR TROUBLED THOUGHTS OF
   THE FUTURE

You may doubt whether your faith, patience, and other suffering graces will be strong enough to walk on turbulent waves without sinking. Christian, if the graces which God calls you to exercise now in your prosperous state are solid, you may trust that other suffering graces are standing unseen behind the curtain. And they too will step forward when God changes the scene of your affairs and calls them upon the stage to act out their part.

The more humble you are now with your abundance, the more patient you will certainly show yourself in seasons of need. As your heart is now above worldly enjoyments, even then you will stay above troubles and sorrows. Trees, they say, grow proportionately underground to what they do above ground. The earnest Christian will develop strong roots in regard to God's graces.

I. The Helmet of Salvation – What It Is

The apostle lends us a key to open our understanding of this piece of armour, the helmet of salvation: 'And for an helmet, the hope of salvation' (*1. Thess. 5:8*). There are three lamps in the entrance way to the various rooms of this grace: first, what hope is; secondly, why it is called the hope of salvation; and thirdly, why this hope is compared to a helmet.

THE NATURE OF THE HOPE THAT FORMS THE HELMET

Hope is a supernatural grace of God whereby the believer through Christ expects and waits for all those good things of the promise which he has not yet received, or not fully.

1. HOPE'S AUTHOR

He is called 'the God of all grace' (*1 Pet. 5:10*) – that is, the giver and worker of all grace, both of its seed and of its growth. It is impossible for a man to make one tiny blade of grass, or to make it grow. And it is just as impossible to produce the least seed of grace in the heart, or to add maturity to it. God is the Creator. And just as He is the Father of the rain which makes the herbs in the fields spring up, He also fathers the spiritual dews and influences which cause every grace to flourish.

God's hope is supernatural; and we distinguish it from the heathens' hope, which, with the rest of their moral virtues, if they contain any good, actually originate in God. Every man who comes into the world is indebted to God for all the light he has. This is only the remains of God's pure gift, as sometimes we see a broken turret or two standing in the midst of the ruins of some demolished palace. It serves only to help the spectator guess what fine buildings once stood there.

II. HOPE'S SUBJECT

True hope is a precious gem which no one can wear but Christ's bride, for Christless and hopeless are joined together (*Eph. 2:12*). Because hope and faith are inevitably kin, let us now look at their relationship. In regard to time, one does not come before the other; but in order of nature and operation, faith takes the precedency.

First, faith cleaves to the promise as a true and faithful word, and then hope lifts up the soul to wait for the performance of it. Who runs out to meet someone that he believes will not come? The promise is God's love-letter to His bride in which he opens His very heart and tells everything He will do for her. Faith reads and embraces it with joy, while hope looks out of the window with a longing expectation to see her husband's chariot coming toward her.

[160]

III. HOPE'S OBJECT

We run away from an evil thing; but if it is good we wait for it. Both hope and faith draw their lines from the same center of the promise, but there is one important difference between them. Faith believes evil as well as good; hope will not talk about anything but good. Hope without a promise is like an anchor without ground to hold by; it carries the promise on its name. David shows where he moors his ship and casts his anchor – 'I hope in thy word' (*Ps. 119:81*). And God's design fits the highest hope a Christian can have: 'No good thing will he withhold from them that walk uprightly' (*Ps. 84:11*).

Just as God has encircled all good in the promise, so He promises nothing but good. The object of hope is everything that the promise holds. God Himself is the highest good and His fullness is promised as the believer's highest joy. Therefore true hope aims at God and lifts the soul nearer Him, 'the hope of Israel' and 'the fountain of living waters' (*Jer. 17:13*).

Hope's object is aimed not only at the good of the promise, but at the performance of that promise at a future time. 'Hope that is seen is not hope: for what a man seeth, why doth he yet hope for?' (*Rom. 8:24*). The future is basic to hope's object and distinguishes it from faith, which gives a present being to the promise and is the substance of things hoped for (*Heb. 11:1*). Because of faith, the earnestness of the promise has its existence in a kind of interview with heaven; it brings the Christian and heaven together as if he were already there. Here by faith they embrace the promise (*Heb. 11:13*). Faith speaks in the present tense – 'We are conquerors, more than conquerors.' But hope is in the future – 'I shall.'

Hope reaches for the performance of the promise but when it holds the completed promise, it is swallowed up by joy and love. Either the full achievement of the promise, or the execution of the threatening, shuts out all hope. In heaven the promise is paid and hope dismissed because we have what we looked for; and in hell the threat is fully inflicted, and therefore no hope is left for release.

Hope is aided by Jesus Christ, for whose sake it expects to obtain the promise. It waits for all in and through Him. He is called 'our hope' (*1 Tim.* 1:1) because through Him we hope for what is promised, both as the purchaser, by whose death we freely expect good from God; and by whose Spirit we have the ability to hope. So then hope is ours because of the authority of Christ's blood and the infusion of His Spirit into us.

WHY THIS HOPE IS CALLED THE HOPE OF SALVATION

There are two obvious reasons why God has called the Christian's hope the 'hope of salvation.' Let us examine these now.

I. SALVATION TAKES IN THE WHOLE OBJECT OF THE HOPE

The word 'salvation' implies a state of bliss, where the mercies and enjoyments of all the promises meet. At the creation, light was first diffused through the firmament and then gathered into the sun. Add up the respective sums of all the good things promised in the covenant and the total is salvation. Salvation, then, is the ultimate object of the Christian's expectation, and that which comprehends the rest.

II. THE HOPE OF SALVATION DISTINGUISHES IT FROM THE WORLDLING'S HOPE

Natural men's hope is in the present life. They are so rooted in this world that their wish is that God will never take them out of it. Even when they say they hope to be saved, their consciences tell them they had rather stay here. They desire salvation more out of dread of hell than from hope of heaven. Of course they are not so insane as to prefer damnation in hell to life in heaven – but the truth is that they like the world better than either.

WHY HOPE IS COMPARED TO A HELMET

I. THE HELMET DEFENDS THE SOUL

As the helmet defends the head, a principal part of the body, so this 'hope of salvation' defends the soul, the principal part of man. The helmet protects the believer from dangerous or deadly impressions of sin or Satan. It defends the Christian because it is hard for temptations to snare a person who is satisfied with princely favor and who stands on the stairs of hope, expecting to be called at any time to the highest place a king can bestow.

On the other hand, weapons of rebellion are usually forged in discontent. When subjects think they are neglected by their prince, this feeling softens them to receive any impression of disloyalty that the king's enemy attempts to stamp upon them. Thus once the soul fears God has no inheritance for him he will commit any sin, great or small, at the sound of the tempter's trumpet.

II. THE HELMET MAKES THE HEART BOLD

As the helmet defends the soldier's head from wounds, so it also protects the Christian's heart from failing. Whoever wears this helmet need never be ashamed to boast in his holy God. For God Himself allows him to do this and confirms the rejoicing of his hope. 'Thou shalt know that I am the Lord: for they shall not be ashamed that wait for me' (*Isa. 49:23*). Confidence in God made David courageous in the midst of his enemies: 'Though an host should encamp against me, my heart shall not fear' (*Ps. 27:3*). He had his helmet of salvation on and therefore could declare,

'Now shall mine head be lifted up above mine enemies round about me' (*verse 6*).

A man cannot drown as long as his head is above water, and now it is the work of hope to do this for the Christian in dangerous places. 'When these things begin to come to pass, then look up, and lift up your heads; for your redemption draweth nigh' (*Luke 21:28*). Only Christ can tell His disciples to lift up their heads when they see other 'men's hearts failing them for fear, and for looking after those things which are coming on the earth' (*verse 26*). Yet their sun is rising when others' is setting and darkness is overtaking them. Two things make the head hang down – fear and shame. Hope delivers the Christian from both and forbids him to display any sign of a despondent mind by a dejected countenance.

This explanation of the meaning of the helmet of salvation brings us to the one general point of doctrine from which we draw our whole study on this piece of armour.

II. The Use of the Helmet

Hope is a grace which Christians will need continually, as long as our warfare with sin and Satan lasts. We are directed to take the helmet of salvation not for one particular occasion and then hang it up until another emergency calls us to use it again. But we must take it so as never to lay it down until God takes off this helmet to put a crown of glory in its place. Some war equipment is used only now and then; after it has served its purpose it is put aside and never missed. But the apostle Peter's counsel is 'Be sober, and hope to the end' (*I Pet. 1:13*).

The Christian is not beneath hope as long as he is above ground, nor above hope as long as he is beneath heaven. But once he enters the gates of that glorious city, he can say, 'Armour was for earth but robes are for heaven.'

Hope goes into the field and waits on the Christian until the last battle is fought. Then faith and hope together carry him into the hands of love and joy, which stand ready to take him into God's presence. But so that I may speak in more detail about hope's service to the Christian, I turn to five particular topics: first, hope and worthy achievements; secondly, hope and diligence in the smallest service; thirdly, hope and patience in sufferings; fourthly, influences of hope on Christians in affliction; and fifthly, hope and comfort when God delays performance of the promise.

HOPE AND WORTHY ACHIEVEMENTS

Hope of salvation moves the Christian to perform high and worthy services. It is a grace conceived for great action. As carnal hope stirs carnal men to achievements which gain them a reputation in the world, so this heavenly hope influences the saint's undertakings.

What makes the daring soldier rush into the mouth of death itself? He hopes to rescue honor from the jaws of death. Hope is the helmet and shield which make him calm in the face of every danger. What makes a man tear his hands and crawl up some craggy mountain which proves only a bleak, barren place to stand in? There he is wrapped up in clouds and can look over other men's heads and see a little farther than they. Now if these hopes – which borrow motives from human ambition and imagination – turn men toward accomplishments, how much more does the believer's hope of eternal life provoke him to noble exploits! Let us look at some examples.

1. HOPE FREES FROM LUST

When Moses came to give Israel the hope of God's approaching salvation, his people experienced a mighty change. Whereas they had cowered under Egyptian burdens and had not tried to shake off the oppressor's yoke, now they broke free and marched toward their promised rest. It did not seem to make any difference that Pharaoh chased them with raging determination – they were fortified with hope.

How helpless is the person who does not have this heavenly hope! Satan makes a slave of him and he becomes the footstool for every base lust to trample upon. He lets the devil ride him anywhere, at any time. No mud puddle is too filthy for Satan to lead him through with a twine thread. And the poor man follows because he does not know a better master, nor better wages than the sensual pleasures of his lusts.

But once this person hears the news of salvation and is enabled to see God's transcendent glory, with the offer of hope that he shall inherit it if he exchange Satan for Christ, he makes havoc among his lusts. Immediately he looks for ways of putting them to death. 'Every man that hath this hope in him purifieth himself, even as he is pure' (*1 John 3:3*). Like a captive prince, he sees his lusts as cruel kidnappers. If only he could escape he would enjoy his crown and kingdom; therefore he plots the utmost revenge against his captors.

Do you have a sin that refuses to bow? Has the lust for money snared you? Let your hope of heaven be strong enough to charm this devil! Can gold control you now when you hope to be an heir of that city where gold has no price? That place is paved with gold; God says we will walk on it. Will you let gold lie in your heart now when some day it will be under your feet?

II. HOPE CAUSES THE REJECTION OF WORLDLY PLEASURES

The world's system of materialism enslaves men and holds them as a prisoner is crippled by his chain. But when faith discovers the Christian's property in heaven and hope tells him how soon he will be leaving the earth, the worth of worldly possessions drops drastically. He can give up what he holds of the world's wealth when God tells him to do so, because his hope of heaven makes earthly possessions mean no more to him than the donkeys meant to anointed Saul.

Many who have seen the prospect of heaven's glory are ready for God to close their eyes in death. Simeon, for instance, did not want to live another day after his eyes had looked on the salvation of God. Abraham too had the hope of this salvation and therefore 'sojourned in the land of promise, as in a strange country . . . For he looked for a city which hath foundations, whose builder and maker is God' (*Heb. 11:9–10*). Canaan might have pleased him well enough if God had not told him of a heaven which He meant to give him. In comparison, Canaan seemed a barren land. The person who looks toward heaven takes his eyes off the world. 'Our conversation is in heaven; from whence also we look for the Saviour, the Lord Jesus Christ' (*Phil. 3:20*).

A man invests in the place where he hopes to receive the most profit. The publican sits at the receipt of custom. The courtier stands near his prince's throne. The merchant works in his warehouse. But the Christian's hope takes him past all these doors. 'My hope is not here,' he says, 'and so this is not my home. My hope is in heaven and I look for the Savior to come. My salvation is with Him. That is where I live, walk, and wait.'

Nothing but a steadfast hope of salvation can take the place of a man's worldly hope. Man cannot live without hope of some kind. If he has no hope for heaven, then he must borrow one from the earth. And what suits an earthly heart better than earthly hope? It is not easy for a man to part with his hope, no matter how meager it is. A drowning man will hold to a flimsy weed and die with it in his hand rather than let it go.

Felix is a good example. Paul preached a thundering sermon before him; and though the preacher was at the bar and Felix on the bench, God so armed the Word that he trembled to hear the prisoner speak of righteousness, temperance, and judgment to come. Yet even though Felix's conscience struggled with fear of judgment, he still looked for a bribe. But he missed his market; for as a sordid hope of a little money made him refuse to deliver Paul, so the blessed hope which Paul had for heaven made him refuse to purchase his own deliverance with a bribe.

III. HOPE MAKES THE SAINT BOLD

It is called 'a lively hope' (*1 Pet. 1:3*); and men who have it are bold. You may expect more from them than from many others. But why are other men stale and sluggish in God's service? It is because their hope is sluggish also. Hopeless and lifeless go together.

The man who thinks he works for a song will not sing at his work. A merchant serves his paying customer first and best. If we considered God in the same way, we would leave everything and do His business. This realization made Paul so devote himself to the gospel that he lost his worldly friends and laid down his own life 'for the hope of the promise' (*Acts 26:6*).

IV. HOPE BREEDS HOLY DESIRES

The higher our hopes of salvation rise the more our hearts will long for holy desires. 'Not only they, but ourselves also, which have the firstfruits of the Spirit, even we ourselves groan within ourselves, waiting for the adoption, to wit, the redemption of our body' (*Rom. 8:23*). Hope waits and will not let the soul sit down until the entire harvest standing in the field of the promise is reaped and gathered. The more partial payments the Christian receives the more his soul groans for the whole of his inheritance.

(a) *These foretastes acquaint the Christian with the joys of heaven*

As a believer's understanding of heaven increases, his desires are enlarged; and those desires break out into sad groans to think what sweet wine is drunk in full cups by glorified saints. And here he is allowed only a sip, just enough to kindle his thirst but not to satisfy it. It is harder now for him to live on this side of heaven than it was before he knew so much. He is like one who stands at the door and hears the sounds of a rich feast inside; through the keyhole he sees what a variety they enjoy. He smells the delicious food and samples the table scraps. None long for heaven more than those who enjoy most of heaven. Their continual cry is, 'Why is His chariot so long in coming?'

The Christian can never completely lose his hopes. He may have them nipped and set back by days of winter weather in the spring, which are more harmful because the warm sun has caused the flowers to bud. And so God's delays make the saddest impression upon those, above all others, whose expectations have advanced, to unfold into a kind of rejoicing through hope of glory. Waiting can be a deep trial to the soul.

(b) *Present grace and comfort urge the Christian to expect more*

David says, 'Because thou hast been my help, therefore in the shadow of thy wings will I rejoice' (*Ps. 63:7*). God's present grace makes him rejoice in the hope of what will come, and this hope makes him long for more: 'My soul followeth hard after thee' (*verse 8*). God gives his people their experiences with this very purpose engraved on them, to raise their expectations for more mercies at His hand. 'I will give her her vineyards from thence, and the valley of Achor for a door of hope' (*Hos. 2:15*). God tells us what blessings He will bestow upon the soul in covenant with Him and married to Christ. He alludes to His dealing with Israel, who came out of a desolate wilderness – where they had wandered and endured unspeakable hardship for forty years – into the pleasant, fruitful country where Achor was found.

Achor was a spot of ground of little worth; for God did not want the Israelites to delight in the land itself, but as the opening of a door through which He would lead them to possess their glorious heritage. And because Joshua believed God, he advanced Israel's banners with much courage against the proudest of enemies, knowing well that man could not shut that door which God had opened.

Thus every specific help God gives the Christian against any one corruption is intended to be an Achor – a door of hope from which he may expect the complete overthrow of that cursed seed in his heart. And when God adds the least degree of strength to His grace or comfort, He is giving us an Achor, or door of hope, that He will consummate both in glory.

Paul had many enemies at Ephesus, but having an effectual door opened to him for his encouragement, he kept serving God boldly. Once the gate of a besieged city flies open, the attackers press in with a shout, 'The city is ours!' Thus when, after much wrestling with God for pardon of sin or strength against sin, the door of the promise flies open, and God comes in with His comforting presence, hope takes heart and makes the soul press on to his reward with added zeal.

HOPE AND DILIGENCE IN THE SMALLEST SERVICE

God sets some men on the high places of the earth and

appoints them to exciting challenges. But He orders others to pitch their tents on lower ground and not be ashamed of their assignment, no matter how inferior it seems. Now to encourage every Christian to be faithful in his particular place, God has made promises which apply to them all. And His promises are like the beams of the sun: they shine as freely through the window of the poor man's cottage as through the prince's palace.

God's promises strengthen our hands and hearts against the discouragement that is most likely to weaken us in His service. They support and guard us against the furious opposition of an angry world: 'I will not fail thee, nor forsake thee. Be strong and of a good courage' (*Josh. 1:5–6*). This was a promise God gave to Israel's chief magistrate. And the minister's promise agrees with it, having generally the same trials, enemies, and discouragements: 'Go ye therefore, and teach all nations; . . . and, lo, I am with you alway, even unto the end of the world' (*Matt. 28:19–20*).

The temptation which usually troubles those in lower callings is envy to see themselves on the floor and their brothers elevated to higher service. Sometimes these temptations produce dejection when the believers feel like eunuchs who bring no glory to God, dry trees which are unprofitable in His kingdom.

To arm the Christian against discontent and discouragement, God promises as great a reward for faithfulness in the most menial service as He gives in more honorable service. Is anything more degrading than the role of a slave? Yet nothing less than heaven itself is promised to the faithful servant: 'Whatsoever ye do, do it heartily, as to the Lord, and not unto men; knowing that of the Lord ye shall receive the reward of the inheritance: for ye serve the Lord Christ' (*Col. 3:23–24*).

God honors the poor servant's drudgery in divine

service because he serves the Lord Christ. It is as if the Lord had said to him, 'Be not out of love with your coarse work, My child. Though your employment now is not the same as that of one in higher office, yet your acceptation is the same, and so shall your reward also be.'

Where hope is raised, the Christian cannot help but take sweet satisfaction from it. Jacob served in hope and expected his reward from a better master than Laban; this made him faithful to an unfaithful man. Joseph would not wrong his master, though his mistress urged him to. He chose to suffer his unjust anger rather than accept her impure love. The evidence of this grace in a servant is better security for his faithfulness than a thousand-dollar bond.

HOPE SUPPORTS THE CHRISTIAN IN THE GREATEST AFFLICTIONS

The hope of salvation supports the believer in the greatest afflictions. The Christian's patience is his back, where he carries his burdens; and some afflictions are so heavy that he needs a broad one to carry them. But if hope does not lay the pillow of the promise between his back and his burden, the least cross will prove too much. Therefore this promise is called the 'patience of hope in our Lord Jesus Christ' (*1 Thess. 1:3*).

Some men force themselves into a kind of quietness in their troubles because they cannot help it; they see no hope. I call this a desperate patience, and it may last for a while. But if despair were a cure for troubles, the damned could relax. Another patience very common in the world is stupid patience which, like Nabal's mirth, lasts no longer than his drunkenness. As soon as men realize their true situation their hearts die within them.

But the 'patience of hope' is a sober grace which abides

as long as hope lasts; when hope is healthy it floats and even dances on the waters of affliction, as a tight, sound ship sails in tempestuous seas. But when hope springs a leak, the waves break into the Christian's heart and he sinks until hope, with much work at the pump of the promise, clears the soul once again. This was David's case. 'Save me, O God; for the waters are come in unto my soul' (*Ps. 69:1*). And notice why this trouble rose, and where the waters came in: 'O God, thou knowest my foolishness; and my sins are not hid from thee' (*verse 5*). This man's guilt made him uncomfortable under his affliction because he saw his sin and tasted God's displeasure. But when he had humbled himself and confessed his sin, he could see the coast clear between himself and heaven. He could return to sing in the same affliction.

Now I want to show you even more specifically how powerfully hope influences the Christian who is in affliction.

INFLUENCES OF HOPE ON CHRISTIANS IN AFFLICTION

I. HOPE CALMS THE CHRISTIAN UNDER AFFLICTION

A hopeless soul cries out in anxiety, but hope keeps the King's peace in the heart. Hopelessness cannot rest very long because hope is not there to rock it to sleep. But hope stills a disturbed spirit when nothing else can, as the mother quietens her crying baby by laying it to the breast. When David's soul was uneasy because of affliction, he laid his soul to the breast of the promise: 'Why art thou cast down, O my soul? and why art thou disquieted within me? hope in God' (*Ps. 43:5*). And his soul sleeps as peacefully as a nourished child.

Moses' spirit was grieved when Aaron and Miriam vented their anger toward him in foul language. But he kept his peace and waited for God to prove his innocence. And no doubt his patience made God even more annoyed to see such a meek man wronged for His sake. Thus He moved quickly to wipe off the dirt they had thrown in his face before it could soak in to the prejudice of his good name in the thoughts of others. Waiting on God for deliverance during affliction is closely linked with holy silence. 'Truly my soul waiteth upon God: from him cometh my salvation' (*Ps. 62:1*). The Hebrew literally reads, 'My soul is silent.'

II. HOPE FILLS THE AFFLICTED SOUL WITH JOY

Hope brings such consolation that the afflicted soul can smile even when tears run down the face. This is called 'the rejoicing of the hope' (*Heb. 3:6*). And hope never produces more joy than in affliction. The sun paints the beautiful colors in the rainbow on a watery cloud. 'Rejoice in hope of the glory of God. And not only so, but we glory in tribulations' (*Rom. 5:2, 3*). Glorying is a rejoicing which the Christian cannot contain within himself; it comes forth in some outward expression to let others know what a feast he has inside. The springs of comfort lie high indeed when joy flows from the believer's mouth. And all the joy which sustains the suffering saint is sent in by hope at the cost of Christ, who has prepared unspeakable glory in heaven. Should we pity ourselves for the tribulations we go through on the way to Christ's glory?

While troubles attack with oppression, the gracious promises anoint with blessings. Hope breaks the alabaster box of the promises over the Christian's head and sends consolations abroad in the soul. And like a precious ointment these comforts exhilarate and refresh the spirit, heal the wounds, and remove the pain. Paul says, 'Hope maketh not ashamed; because the love of God is shed abroad in our hearts by the Holy Ghost which is given unto us' (*Rom. 5:5*).

Faith and hope are two graces which Christ uses above all others to fill the soul with joy, because these fetch all their wine of joy out of doors. Faith tells the soul what Christ has done and hope revives the soul with news of what He will do. But both draw sweet wine from the same source – Christ and His promise.

Other fountains of comfort tell the Christian how much he has suffered for Christ, rather than what He has done for him. But it is neither pleasing to Christ nor safe for the saint to drink his joy from this vessel. Would the servant wear the king's crown? Why cry hosanna to Christ's grace in us, when it is there only by God's mercy? Praise belongs to the One from whom we have our joy; so we are to 'rejoice in Christ Jesus, and have no confidence in the flesh' (*Phil. 3:3*). It is deceptive for us to have confidence in the flesh because of the instability of our hearts and the inconsistent behavior of our virtues, which ebb as often as they flow. Our human joy cannot be constant because our graces are not; as these natural springs are high or low, so their level would rise or fall. We would inevitably drink more water than wine – we would lack joy more often than have it.

But the Christian's cup need never be empty, because he draws his wine from an undrainable Fountain which never sends any soul away ashamed, as the brook of our inherent grace would certainly do sooner or later.

III. HOPE EXHILARATES THE AFFLICTED SPIRIT

Three ingredients of hope make this possible.

(a) *Hope's news of a happy issue heals the wounds of present suffering*

Sometimes when God comes to save His afflicted servants He surprises them before they look for Him. 'I know the thoughts that I think toward you, saith the Lord, thoughts of peace, and not of evil, to give you an expected end' (*Jer. 29:11*).

Hope is a prying grace; it can look beyond God's outward acts. With the help of the promise it is able to see into the very heart of God and read what purposes are written there concerning the Christian's particular circumstances. And it relays this message, encouraging him not to be troubled to hear God speaking roughly in the language of His providence. Hope assures, 'He intends your blessing, no matter how it appears otherwise. For as the law – which came hundreds of years after the promise to Abraham – could not annul it, neither can any intervening afflictions destroy those thoughts of love which for so long have been in His heart for your deliverance and salvation.'

In a storm the traveler can stand patiently under a tree while it rains, because he hopes it is only a shower, and he can see it clearing up in one part of the heavens while it is still dark in another. Providence is never too cloudy for hope to see fair weather coming from the promise. 'When these things begin to come to pass, then look up, and lift up your heads; for your redemption draweth nigh' (*Luke 21:28*).

When the Christian's affairs are most disconsolate, he may soon meet with a happy change. For the joy of that blessed day will come 'in a moment, in the twinkling of an eye'; and 'we shall be changed' (*1 Cor. 15:52*). One moment we are dressed in rags of mortal flesh; but in the twinkling of an eye we are arrayed with robes of immortality, embossed with a thousand times more glory than the sun's garment of light. 'It is but winking,' said a martyr to his fellow sufferer in the fire, 'and our pain and sorrow will be over.'

Hope is an ointment which heals from a distance. The saints' hope is laid up in heaven, and yet it heals all the wounds they receive on earth. But this is not all. As hope prophesies concerning the happy end of the Christian's afflictions, so it assures him he will be cared for while he endures them. If Christ sends His disciples to sea He will be with them when they need Him most. 'When thou passest through the waters, I will be with thee' (*Isa. 43:2*).

Hope is God's messenger that speaks to the person who has concluded he will never be able to outlive such a rough tide of affliction. Hope lifts his head above the surging waves and says, 'Go, for your God will be with you. Is not Christ your Husband? He can tell you how to suffer, for He was brought up in suffering from the cradle to the cross. Behold, He even comes out to meet you, glad to see your face, and ready to impart some of His suffering skill to you.' Because hope heals the heart, suffering is a harmless thing and not to be dreaded.

(b) *Hope assures the Christian that present sufferings*
bear no comparison to the coming joy of salvation
This assurance kept early Christians from despairing while the enemy spilled their blood. The scent of this hope revived their spirits: 'For which cause we faint not; but though our outward man perish, yet the inward man is renewed day by day' (*2 Cor. 4:16*). Is it not strange that their courage grew while they lost their blood? They welcomed the strong wine of hope: 'For our light affliction, which is but for a moment, worketh for us a far more exceeding and eternal weight of glory' (*verse 17*).

The man who buys the world's glittering hope at the expense of his conscience has paid too high a price. But we gain heaven cheaply, even if we lose all our carnal interests, even life itself. Who will grudge to give up the lease on a low-rent farm – which will expire in a few days (for such is our temporal life) – for an eternal inheritance of the saints in light? This hope has made God's faithful servants carry their lives in their hands, willing to lay them down, while they 'look not at the things which are seen, but at the things which are not seen: for the things which are seen are temporal; but the things which are not seen are eternal' (*2 Cor. 4:18*).

(c) *Hope teaches the necessity of suffering as we press on to salvation*

'Ought not Christ to have suffered these things, and to enter into his glory?' (*Luke 24:26*). It is as if Christ had said, 'Why do you mourn for your Master's death, as if all your hopes were smashed? Was there any other way He could get home and take possession of His glory that awaited Him in heaven?'

Truly the saint's way to salvation lies along the same road which Christ walked. 'If so be that we suffer with him, that we may be also glorified together' (*Rom. 8:17*). But this path would be impossible for us to tread if Christ had not gone before us to make the way. If we understand that afflictions are as necessary to carry us to glory as waters are to take a ship to port, we can reconcile ourselves to them and delight to travel that way.

Some philosophers say that God is blessing us when we live in the sunshine of prosperity and cursing us when our condition is overcast with adversity. But hope can see heaven on a cloudy day; it can expect good out of evil. The Jews open their windows when it thunders and lightens, expecting their Messiah to come. I am sure hope opens her window widest in a day of stormy tempest: 'I will also leave in the midst of thee an afflicted and poor people, and they shall trust in the name of the Lord' (*Zeph. 3:12*). 'Therefore I will look unto the Lord; I will wait for the God of my salvation: my God will hear me' (*Mic. 7:7*).

God does not take up the ax of His sovereignty into His

hand to make chips. When He has pruned severely and driven His ax the deepest, His people may expect some beautiful piece of work when all is finished.

It is sweet to meditate on Romans 8:28: 'We know that all things work together for good to them that love God.' If you should get up some morning and hear men on your house tearing off the tiles and taking down the roof with hammers and axes, you might think a gang of vicious enemies had come to destroy your home. But as soon as you understand that these workmen have been sent by your father to mend your house, you gladly endure the noise and trouble. Indeed, you thank your father for his care and expense. The very hope of the advantage that will come from the repairs makes you willing to dwell awhile in the inconvenient rubble of the old house.

The promise assures the believer that the heavenly Father intends no harm, only good, as He rebuilds the ruined frame of your soul into a glorious temple. And afflictions have a hand in the work. This insight frees you to pray, 'Lord, cut and shape me however You will, that at last I may be framed according to the pattern which Your love has drawn for me!' Some ignorant men fear the fuller's soap might spoil their clothing, but one who understands what refining means will not be afraid.

HOPE AND COMFORT WHEN GOD DELAYS THE PERFORMANCE OF THE PROMISE

Hope quietens the Christian's spirit when God waits a long time before He comes to perform promises. I have already told you that patience is the back where the Christian carries his burdens, and hope the pillow between the back and the burden. Now patience has two shoulders, one to bear the present evil and another to wait for the future good promised but not yet paid. And as hope makes the burden of the present cross light, it makes the longest delay of promised good seem short.

Where there is no hope there is no strength. 'And I said, My strength and my hope is perished from the Lord' (*Lam. 3:18*). God protected and provided for Israel in the wilderness, but as soon as they used up their Egyptian supplies they resented both Moses and God. Why? Their hope was grounded in human help.

Moses climbed the mountain and was out of the Israelites' sight for only a few days; yet they had to have a golden calf. They thought they would never see him again and gave him up for lost. God wants His servants to wait for what He means to give them, but few stay with Him because most are short-spirited.

You know what Naomi said to her daughters: 'If I should have an husband also to night, and should also bear sons; would ye tarry for them till they were grown? would ye stay for them from having husbands?' (*Ruth 1:12–13*). The promise has salvation in its womb; but will the unbeliever wait until the promise ripens and this happiness has grown up? No, he would rather mate with any base lust which pays him in some present pleasure than wait a long time, even if it is for heaven itself.

Tamar played the harlot because her promised husband was not given as soon as she wanted him (*Gen. 38*). And today many souls throw themselves into the embraces of the adulterous world because the comfort and joy of the promise is temporarily withheld, and God wants them to wait for their reward. 'Demas hath forsaken me, having loved this present world' (*2 Tim. 4:10*). Only the soul which has this divine hope will patiently wait for the good of the promise. Now, in handling this service of hope, I want to show you these three things – first, God often waits a long time before fulfilling a promise; secondly, it is our duty to wait; and thirdly, hope enables us to wait.

I. GOD OFTEN WAITS A LONG TIME BEFORE FULFILLING HIS PROMISE

To hope without a promise is to claim a debt that was never owed. The good things of the promise are not paid at once; if they were, there would be no use for the promises. God promised Abraham a son, but he waited many years for him after the bond of that promise. He promised Canaan to Abraham and his seed, yet hundreds of years intervened between the promise and the performance. All the patriarchs, who were the third generation after Abraham, died, 'not having received the promises' (*Heb. 11:13*). And Simeon had a promise 'he should not see death, before he had seen the Lord's Christ' (*Luke 2:26*); but this was not performed until he was almost ready to leave the world.

In a word, these promises, which are the portion of all the saints and may be claimed by all of them, have an exact date recorded in God's book of purposes. He does not express in His promise when He will perform it but instead vows to 'fulfil the desire of them that fear him' (*Ps. 145:19*). There often comes a long and sharp winter between the sowing time of prayer and the reaping of the promise. God hears us as soon as we pray. Prayers are not long on their journey to heaven, but long coming back in a full answer. Even today Christ in heaven does not have a full answer to some of those prayers He prayed on earth. He is still 'expecting till his enemies be made his footstool' (*Heb. 10:13*).

We have promises for subduing sin and Satan under our feet, but these enemies still hide within us; we have many scuffles with them before they are uprooted from our hearts. At times the Christian, who is an heir to all joy and comfort, can barely show a penny of this heavenly treasure in his pocket. And because they do not trust the ways of God, some are led into the temptation of questioning Him: 'Some saints may have His promises, but He does not give them to me. My prayers are not answered. Saints are conquerors over their lusts, but I am defeated by mine. There seems to be a heaven of comfort in the promise, but I am here in the belly of hell, swallowed up by fears.' All this trouble might be prevented if they had faith to believe this one principle of undoubted truth – that God does not perform His promises all at once, and that the fulfillment they desire may be seen on the way coming to them.

II. BELIEVERS MUST WAIT, AND SOMETIMES WAIT
LONG, FOR THE PERFORMANCE OF THE PROMISE

When God delays before He fulfills the promise it is the believer's duty to wait for it. 'Though it tarry, wait for it' (*Hab. 2:3*). God will perform it at the appointed time. It is hard work to wait when there is no sight of God's coming after days of prayer and nights of watching. To flesh and blood it is hard. Weak faith is out of breath and liable to turn back when it has gone a long way to meet God in returning mercy, and thus misses Him. This is why the apostle ushers in this duty with affectionate prayer: 'The Lord direct your hearts into the love of God, and into the patient waiting for Christ' (*2 Thess. 3:5*).

In the preceding chapter Paul had laid down a strong ground of consolation to Christians. They were 'chosen . . . to salvation' and 'called . . . by our gospel, to the obtaining of the glory of our Lord Jesus Christ' (*2 Thess. 2:13–14*). He assured them that God, who is 'faithful,' would 'stablish [them], and keep [them] from evil' (*2 Thess. 3:3*). Paul did not want believers to fall short of the promised glory, but at the same time they needed to realize what a difficult work it was for them amid their own weaknesses, the apostasies of others and the assaults of Satan, to hold fast the assurance of their hope to the end. It is as if he had said, 'It is a work you will never be able to do by yourselves – so wait patiently until Christ comes and brings the full reward of the promise with Him; the Lord direct your hearts into it.'

III. HOPE ENABLES THE SOUL TO WAIT

'It is good that a man should both hope and quietly wait for the salvation of the Lord' (*Lam. 3:26*). Hope groans but does not grumble when the promised mercy does not come straightaway. Hope's groans are sighed out from the spirit to God in prayer; these lighten the soul of its burden of fear. But the groans of a hopeless soul are vented in anger against God. They are like a loud wind to a fire – they make it rage even more.

But where there is hope, the heart is soon quieted. Hope is the handkerchief which God gently uses to wipe away the tears from the eyes of His people. 'Refrain thy voice from weeping, and thine eyes from tears: for thy work shall be rewarded, saith the Lord; and they shall come again from the land of the enemy. And there is hope in thine end' (*Jer. 31:16–17*). God's promises in a vision to Jeremiah filled the prophet's heart with joy and comforted him as much as a sick man after a night of welcome sleep: 'Upon this I awaked . . . and my sleep was sweet unto me' (*verse 26*).

When the promise seems to wait too long, however, hope helps the Christian with a threefold encouragement. First, hope assures the soul that even though God waits awhile before He performs the promise, yet He does not delay; secondly, that when He comes He will abundantly reward us for His long delay; and thirdly, that while He waits to perform one promise, He supplies us with the comfort of another.

ASSURANCE WHICH HOPE GIVES THE CHRISTIAN WHEN GOD DELAYS TO PERFORM HIS PROMISE

I. HOPE ASSURES THE SOUL THAT THOUGH GOD WAITS AWHILE BEFORE HE PERFORMS THE PROMISE, YET HE DOES NOT DELAY

'The vision is yet for an appointed time, but at the end it shall speak, and not lie: though it tarry, wait for it; because it will surely come, it will not tarry' (*Hab. 2:3*). How can we reconcile this tarrying and not tarrying? Though the promise tarries *until* the appointed time, yet it will not tarry *beyond* it! 'When the time of the promise drew nigh, which God had sworn to Abraham, the people grew and multiplied in Egypt' (*Acts 7:17*). Herbs and flowers sleep underground all winter in their roots but come up out of their beds, where they have lain unseen for so long, when spring approaches. And the promise will do this in its season.

Every promise is dated, but with a mysterious character; and because we cannot understand God's chronology, we think He must have forgotten us. It is as if a man should set his watch by his own hungry stomach rather than by the sun, and then say it is noon and complain because his lunch is not quite ready. We covet comfort and expect the promise to keep time with our impatient desires. But the sun will not move any faster if we set our watch forward, nor the promise come sooner if we antedate it.

It is most true, as someone has said, that 'though God seldom comes at our day, because we seldom reckon right, yet he never fails His own day.' The apostle exhorts the Thessalonian church not to 'be soon shaken in mind, or be troubled, . . . as that the day of Christ is at hand' (*2 Thess. 2:2*). But why did these saints need such an exhortation when they were looking for their greatest joy to come with that day? It was not the coming of that day which was so alarming, but the time in which some seducers would have persuaded them to expect it – before many prophecies had been fulfilled. 'For that day shall not come, except there come a falling away first, and that man of sin be revealed, the son of perdition' (*verse 3*). The promise waits only until those intermediate truths – which span a much shorter period – are fulfilled, and then nothing can possibly hold back the promise after that.

You may be bleeding from a wounded spirit and steeped in tears for your sin. The promise tells you that God is near to revive you – *you*, by name (*Isa. 57:15*). Yet you come from this prayer or that sermon with no glimpse of Him nor can you hear another word of security other than His promise. Be careful not to measure God's miles by your own scale; His 'near' may be your 'far'. God could easily have told His people the very time He meant to perform each promise. But He has concealed it to build our faith so that we may the more fully express our confidence in waiting to receive what He is ready to give.

Abraham's faith was strong enough to follow God even when He withheld the name of the place to which He was leading him. And so it requires great faith to rest satisfied with the promise when the time of payment is unknown. But if we consider whom we trust there is no reason to fear He will fail or delay a minute longer than the set time of the promise.

II. HOPE ASSURES THE SOUL THAT WHEN GOD DOES
    COME, HE WILL ABUNDANTLY RECOMPENSE HIS
    LONGEST DELAY

The wicked get nothing from God's forbearing to execute His threatenings except the storing up of more wrath. And the saints lose nothing by not having the promise presently paid, but rather, by their patience with God awhile longer, they treasure up more joy for the day when the promise will be performed. 'To them who by patient continuance in well doing seek for glory and honour and immortality, eternal life' (*Rom. 2:7*). It is not enough to do well, but to *continue* and to be *patient* while God delays.

Plowing is hungry work, yet because there is hope of reaping an abundance of food, the farmer does not give up. Hope says, 'Though you want lunch right now, hold out awhile and you will have lunch and dinner served together when evening comes.' And once the Christian sits down to enjoy the feast, he forgets the pain and weakness he felt in the field. 'Hope deferred maketh the heart sick: but when the desire cometh, it is a tree of life' (*Prov. 13:12*).

As there is a time which God has set for ripening the fruits of the earth, so there is a time set by Him for the good things of the promise, which we are to wait for and not unseasonably pick, like green apples off the tree. Many people who do not have faith or hope to quieten their spirits wrongfully snatch at that which would, in God's time, drop ripe into their bosoms. But what do these impulsive men get? Their harvest is thin and hard, like ears of corn reaped before they are mature. We have a duty to wait. 'Be patient therefore, brethren, unto the coming of the Lord' (*James 5:7*).

Wait on God as long as you have to, until He comes according to His promise and takes you out of your suffering. Do not be hasty to take yourself out of trouble. 'Behold, the husbandman waiteth for the precious fruit of the earth, and hath long patience for it, until he receive the early and latter rain. Be ye also patient; stablish your hearts: for the coming of the Lord draweth nigh' (*James 5:7–8*). Although the farmer wishes his corn were already in the barn, he waits for it to ripen in the ordinary course of God's providence. He is glad when the former rain comes, but he wants the latter rain too, and waits for it, though it is long in coming. And have we not all seen that a shower falling close to harvest time brings the ear to its completeness? The fullest mercies are the ones we wait for the longest. Jesus did not immediately supply wine at the marriage of Cana, as His mother had asked, but they had the more for waiting awhile.

III. HOPE ASSURES THE SOUL THAT WHILE GOD WAITS
TO PERFORM ONE PROMISE, HE SUPPLIES ANOTHER

This comfort is enough to quieten the heart of anyone who understands the sweetness of God's methods. There is not one minute when a believer's soul is left without comfort. There is always some promise standing ready to minister to the Christian until another one comes. A sick man does not complain if all his friends do not stay with him together, as long as they take turns and never leave him without someone to care for him.

We read of a tree of life which bears 'twelve manner of fruits, and yielded her fruit every month' (*Rev. 22:2*). What is this tree but Christ, who brings all manner of fruit in His promises and comfort for all times and all conditions? The believer can never come to Him without finding some promise to supply strength until another is ripe enough to be gathered.

When Jesus returned to heaven He gave His disciples the comfort that He would come again and carry them with Him into His Father's house, where He now lives in glory. This is precious indeed. But what would they do in the mean time to weather those many storms which would surely intervene between this promise and its performance? Our Savior considered this too, and told them He would not leave them comfortless but would give them another promise to keep house with in the meantime – a promise of His Spirit to be with them on earth until He took them to be with Him in heaven.

The Christian is never at such a loss that hope cannot relieve it. 'Blessed is the man that trusteth in the Lord, and whose hope the Lord is. For he shall be as a tree planted by the waters, and that spreadeth out her roots by the river, and shall not see when heat cometh, but her leaf shall be green; and shall not be careful in the year of drought, neither shall cease from yielding fruit' (*Jer.* 17:7–8). These waters are the promises from which the believer draws continual comfort. As a tree planted by the river flourishes, whatever the weather might bring, so does he. Possibly the Christian is afflicted and the promise for deliverance does not come. Then hope can support him at the cost of another promise. Though God does not deliver out of the affliction at present, yet He will nourish him in it.

If the Christian's grief will not let this promise free him of impatience and distrust, hope offers the mercy of God's forgiveness: 'I will spare them, as a man spareth his own son that serveth him' (*Mal.* 3:17). 'Who is a God like unto thee, that pardoneth iniquity, and passeth by the transgression of the remnant of his heritage? He retaineth not his anger for ever, because he delighteth in mercy' (*Mic.* 7:18). Certainly God would not have allowed so much impatience to break loose in Job had not His forgiving mercy been certain to endure to the full end of Job's affliction. And all the time, God had prepared a testimony of love to give Job before his unloving friends.

III. Applications of the Doctrine of the Christian Helmet

We have shown what the helmet of salvation is and several of its uses to the Christian. Now it is time to bring out how its doctrine applies to those who have it and to those who do not. Let me apply this doctrine in five areas: first, the metal of our helmet of hope; secondly, an exhortation to those who have this hope; thirdly, why we should strengthen our hope; fourthly, how we may do so; and fifthly, an exhortation to those who do not possess this helmet of hope.

THE METAL OF OUR HELMET OF HOPE

Most people are content with a cheap helmet which does no more good than a paper cap. Examine the metal of your own helmet and see what it is made of, because the one who tries to defend his own head – the serpent – aims to wound yours. No one but fools and children are naive enough to build their hopes on the sand. But wise men anchor their hopes for salvation as carefully as a prudent pilot moors his ship.

Nothing causes men more humiliation than to be disappointed in their hopes. 'They were confounded because they had hoped; they came thither, and were ashamed' (*Job 6:20*). But there is no shame like sinners' false hopes for eternal salvation; they will rise to shame everlasting (*Dan. 12:2*). They will awake from their graves to see, instead of the heaven they expected, a hell with a fiery mouth which expects them.

What will these dreamers do in the day of the Lord's anger when they see the whole world in flames around them and hear God – whose piercing eyes will see them through and through – calling them forth before men and angels to the judgment? Will they desperately wave their hope before the face of Christ? Surely their hearts will fail. In that day God will use their own tongues to show the folly of their ridiculous hope to all the world; none will be more harsh than their own consciences. Scripture foretells a time when the false prophets 'shall be ashamed every one of his vision, when he hath prophesied; neither shall they wear a rough garment to deceive: but he shall say, I am no prophet, I am an husbandman' (*Zech. 13:4–5*).

The most notorious false prophet in the world, and the one who deceives the most, is the vain hope which men take up for their salvation. It prophesies peace, pardon, and heaven as the portion of one who was never God's heir. But the day is coming, and soon, when this false prophet will be confounded. Then the hypocrite will confess he never had any real hope for salvation except an idol of his own imagination; and the religious man will throw off his profession, by which he deceived himself, and appear naked in his sinfulness. It is enough to make us carefully search our own hearts and find out what our hope is built upon.

Now hope of the right kind is well grounded. 'Be ready always to give an answer to every man that asketh you a reason of the hope that is in you' (*1 Pet. 3:15*). All Christians, no matter how weak, have grounded their hearts in Scripture for the hope they profess. What entitles you to inherit God's kingdom without a promise from Him? If someone should say that your house and land were his, would you give him your property just because he demanded it? Yet many hope to be saved who can give no better reason than this.

Just as a saint conquers fear by asking his soul why it is disquieted, the same question can throw the bold sinner from his prancing hopes. 'What reason do you find in the whole Bible for you to hope for salvation, when you live in the ignorance of God?' Certainly his soul would be as speechless as the man without the wedding garment was at Christ's question. This is why some dare not let themselves think about salvation – they know this thought would make a disturbance in their consciences that will not be stilled quickly. Or if they do ask, it would be like Pilate, who asked Christ what was truth but had no intention of waiting for His answer.

Perhaps you are ignorant and do not know who Christ is or how hope can fasten on to Him; or perhaps you just blindly hope that God is too good to send you to hell. But you have no reason to hope this and I cannot give you one. If He saves you the way you are now, in your hopeless and impenitent unbelief, He would have to make a new gospel for your sake; for the Bible damns you without hope or help. The gospel is 'hid to them that are lost' (*2 Cor. 4:3*).

You have plenty of knowledge. But many make no better use of their knowledge of the Scripture than thieves do of the understanding they have of the law. They research it only to become cunning enough to evade it, not to keep it. And many study the Word – especially those passages displaying God's mercy to sinners – and they stuff a pillow with these comforts to lay their heads on, when the cry of their abominations begins to break their rest. God deliver you from such a hope as this! Surely you mean to provide a better answer to give Christ at the judgment. Will your knowledge present as strong a plea for salvation as the sins which you wallow in testify against that knowledge? If there is hope for such as you, then Judas and Jezebel, even devils, will all join such good company as you call together.

But maybe you do have reformation as well as knowledge. You have put away your old life-style of corruption. Yet if you mean to be faithful to your own soul you must not rest in your neighbors' high opinion of your reputation. Do not judge your hopes for heaven by their survey of your outward behavior. You must look inward to ask what spring causes this new flow in the outward manner of life. This and this alone must decide the controversy and judge your hope, whether it be true or false.

It is not a new face which influences our behavior but a new principle which changes the heart within and proves hope to be genuine. 'Blessed be the God and Father of our Lord Jesus Christ, which according to his abundant mercy hath begotten us again unto a lively hope' (*1 Pet. 1:3*). New birth entitles us to new hope. If the soul is dead the hope cannot be alive. And the soul may be dead and yet put on very attractive reformation, as a dead body may be dressed in the finest clothing. A beggar's son in the clothes of a rich man's child may as well hope to be heir to the wealthy man's land as you hope to be God's heir in glory merely by outward reformation. A child's hopes come from his own father, not from a stranger.

What have you inherited from your father Adam except a sinful nature and fearful expectation of death? Hannah had a troubled spirit until she got a child from God; and have you not even more reason to be like that, until you get to be a child of God? It is a thousand times better to die childless than fatherless. It is far worse to have no father to give you an inheritance in heaven than to leave no child to inherit your estate on earth.

EXHORTATION TO THOSE WHO HAVE THIS HELMET OF HOPE

To those of you who do have the helmet of hope, let me emphasize these two duties: first, be thankful for this unspeakable gift; and secondly, live up to your hopes.

1. BE THANKFUL FOR THIS UNSPEAKABLE GIFT

I do not believe you have it if your heart is not thankful for it. 'Blessed be the God and Father of our Lord Jesus Christ, which according to his abundant mercy hath begotten us again unto a lively hope . . . to an inheritance incorruptible, and undefiled, and that fadeth not away' (*1 Pet. 1:3–4*). Do you have heaven in hope? It is more than if the whole world were in your hand. Earth's greatest king would be glad to change his crown for your helmet at his dying hour. His crown will not get him this helmet, but your helmet will bring you to a crown, a crown not of gold, but of glory, which once on will never be taken off.

Remember, Christian, it has not been long since you had only a fearful expectation of hell instead of a hope of salvation. But God took away the chains of guilt which weighed your soul down in despair and gave you favor in His celestial court. Of all men in the world, you are the most indebted to God's mercy. If you thank Him for crust and rags – food and clothing – how much more should you thank Him for your crown?

After you have praised Him with your spirit, you should collect the praises to God of your friends too – and then, in heaven, continue thanking Him throughout eternity for your helmet of salvation. It will be a debt you will never be able fully to pay.

II. LIVE UP TO YOUR HOPES

Let there be a suitable agreement between your principles and your practices – your hope of heaven and your walk on earth. As you look for salvation, walk the way your eye is looking. If the Christian fails to walk in the worthiness of his calling, he betrays God's hope for him. And the Word emphasizes the necessity of this walk. It stirs us up to act 'as becometh saints' (*Rom. 16:2*) and as 'it becometh the gospel of Christ' (*Phil. 1:27*).

When a man purposes to be laughed at as a clown, they put on him both king's robes and beggar's rags, that by this patchery of mock-majesty with sordid baseness he may appear the greater fool. And certainly it is the devil's design to cast the greatest shame on Christ and His gospel by persuading a man to profess a glorious hope of heaven but to live in utter unworthiness of such a royal inheritance. What would you think if you saw a man going into battle with a helmet of brass, with a wooden sword in one hand and a paper shield in the other? You would conclude that he could not harm his enemies unless they should split their sides with laughing at him.

How then should you live up to your hopes? Let us explore six specific ways.

(a) *In your company*

Man is made for fellowship. But with whom should you fellowship? Those who have the same hopes which you have! Saints are a society distinct from the world. 'Let ours also learn to maintain good works' (*Tit. 3:14*). 'Ours' – that is, of our fellowship. When Peter and John left prison they immediately 'went to their own company' (*Acts 4:23*). But when they had to be among the ungodly, they admitted that they were not in their own assembly and stayed no longer than necessary.

Surely there were many people in Canaan with whom Abraham might have associated; but he knew he was not to be linked intimately with them. Therefore 'he sojourned in the land of promise, as in a strange country, dwelling in tabernacles with Isaac and Jacob, the heirs with him of the same promise' (*Heb. 11:9*).

Consider where your hope will take you. Do not men look for companions on their way to heaven? Are the wicked going there with you? Until heaven's way and hell's way meet in one road this cannot be. And if your companion will not walk in the way to heaven, what will you do, walking with him? Will you compromise and walk his way? In a word, Christian, your hope points to heaven; and the one thing you hope for is to be delivered from all the presence of evil. Are you praying for that hope to be fulfilled? The object of your hope is the subject of your prayer. As often as you say 'Thy kingdom come,' you pray thus much. Are hoping and praying to be delivered from them consistent with keeping company with ungodly companions?

(b) *In your manner of life*

'What manner of persons ought ye to be in all holy conversation and godliness, looking for and hasting unto the coming of the day of God?' (*2 Pet. 3:11–12*). Every believing soul is Christ's spouse. The day of conversion is the day when she is betrothed by faith to Christ; and therefore she lives in hope for their marriage day when He will come and take her home to His Father's house – as Isaac took Rebecca into his mother's tent. And there they will live in His sweet embraces of love, world without end. When the bridegroom comes, does the bride want him to find her in dirty garments? 'Can a maid forget her ornaments, or a bride her attire?' (*Jer. 2:32*). Has a bride ever forgotten to have her wedding dress ready on her marriage day? Or does she forget to put it on when she expects her bridegroom's coming?

Holiness is the 'raiment of needlework' in which you will be 'brought unto the king,' your husband (*Ps. 45:14*). Why has this wedding day been put off for so many years? It has taken a long time for the bride's garment to be completed. But when its preparation is finished and you are dressed in it, then that joyful day will come: 'The marriage of the Lamb is come, and his wife hath made herself ready' (*Rev. 19:7*).

Christian, you have no more effective argument to defeat temptation than your hope. Of course it is good when temptation is defeated, no matter what the weapon is. Yet the Israelites used poor judgment when they borrowed the Philistines' grindstone to 'sharpen every man . . . his axe, and his mattock' (*1 Sam. 13:20*). So the

Christian's choice is inferior when he must use the wicked man's argument to cut through temptation. The saint has more purity of spirit than this. Hope's innocent argument will put you into a stronger tower against sin than all the sophisticated weapons of the uncircumcised world.

The sinner's lust rightly terrifies him with fire and brimstone, but your hope of heaven's glories keeps you out of lust's reach. Does a sin of sensual pleasure attack your castle? Then ask your soul, 'Shall my head lie now in a Delilah's lap, when before long it will be laid in Abraham's bosom? Should I yield to defile that body with lust when it is the very garment my soul hopes to wear in heaven? Be off, Satan! I will not have anything to do with you or with any of your offers which will make me unfit for that blessed place and holy state I wait for.'

(c) *In your affections toward heaven*

'Be sober, and hope to the end,' says the apostle (*1 Pet. 1:13*). You who look for so much in another world may very well be content with little in this one; nothing is more unbecoming to a heavenly hope than an earthly heart. Would you not think it inappropriate if a rich man with a vast estate picked up ears of corn left for the poor gleaners in the harvest field? Well, Christian, do not be angry if I tell you that you are doing a more disgraceful thing yourself if you follow this world's trash.

The higher the summer sun climbs above the horizon, the more intensely it clears the air and heats with its beams. And if your hope of salvation has mounted to any height in your soul, it will scatter the inordinate desires of this world and cause a warmer affection toward heaven.

Augustine, once relating a conversation he had with his mother about heaven, breaks forth: 'Lord, how contemptible this sorry world was in our eye in that day when our hearts were warmed with some sweet mention of that blessed place.' The nearer a man gets to heaven in his hopes, the further he moves away from earth in his desires. When he stands upon the heights of heaven he can look down upon the dunghill world as a little dust-heap, next to nothing.

(d) *In hope's mastery over your fear of death*

Why should you be afraid to die when you hope to live by dying? Is the runner afraid of coming to his goal too soon? Does the betrothed virgin grieve when her wedding day approaches? Death is all this to you and more. When it comes, your jubilee comes. You are free. Your race is run and the crown won – God will place it on your head as soon as the soul goes out of your body.

No matter how rough the voyage has been, it is finished; and death is your friend who uncovers and opens the ark of your body so that it may safely land your soul on the shore of eternity at the heavenly Father's door. In a word, your husband has come for you and knocks with death's hand at your door, to come forth to Him, that He may perform His promise which He made to you on your betrothal day. You do not love the Lord much if you are not willing to leave the place where you are and enjoy His blissful presence in His Father's royal palace of heaven, where such preparation has been made for you as you cannot know here.

Unbelievers have said that they do not think we Christians believe heaven to be as glorious a place as we profess; for if we did, we would not be so afraid to go there. All fear of death betrays strong unbelief and little hope. When we do not look upon death as we should, we are startled by it. If only faith could see through it and assure us of good, we should be as comfortable about the thought as we are now alarmed by it.

The horse enjoys that same hay in the barn which he

was afraid of when a little pile of it lay at a distance on the road. He did not recognize what it was then. Christian, if you can understand what message death brings, the fear of it will be over. It does snatch you from this world's familiar experiences but it leads you into joys which are incomparably better. At a formal dinner no one criticizes the servant who takes away the first course, after enough of it has been eaten, to make room for the main dish.

(e) *In your joy of hope*

A sad heart does not befit a lively hope. Only the servant with no hope of reward follows his master with a doleful countenance. Because this is not your fear, you wrong both yourself and God by your depressed spirit.

Christ no more wants to dwell in a sad heart than we want to live in a dark, melancholy house. 'Whose house are we, if we hold fast the confidence and the rejoicing of the hope firm unto the end' (*Heb. 3:6*). Open every window and let in the light which sheds its beams upon you from His promise. We do not entertain friends in a dark room or sit by them in a gloomy attitude; they would think we were bored by their company. Christ brings good news with Him and is worthy of a better welcome than your dejected spirit. If the slightest hope of salvation should be whispered to the damned, it would make a light in hell and cause rejoicing in the midst of torment. Be ashamed, you slouching saints, that a few thin clouds of some short afflictions should so wrap you up in darkness that the hope of heaven cannot turn your sorrow into joy and comfort.

(f) *In your fear of God*

'The Lord taketh pleasure in them that fear him, in those that hope in his mercy' (*Ps. 147:11*). Too often children forget to respect their parents once their inheritance is settled. And though the doctrine of assurance cannot rightly be accused of producing such bitter fruit, we are too prone to abuse it. Even the best of saints may be led far into temptation after the love of God with eternal life has been passed over to them under the seal of hope's assurance, and may fall into great sin.

God opened the depths of His heart and demonstrated His love to David and Solomon in great measure before both of them gave in to sin. A blot left on their history shows the somber shadows of their sin in the light of such divine love. And while their story leaves us examples of human frailty, it also portrays indelible assurance. Because this assurance spreads itself into highest rejoicing from the certainty of our expected glory, we must nourish a holy fear of God in our hearts.

The devil is delighted if he can cause saints to sin, but he glories most when he can lay them in the dirt in their Sunday clothes and make them defile their garments of salvation. If he succeeds, he tries to insult God by showing Him what a predicament His child is in and holds up the Christian's assurance for the world to laugh at. After Satan has thrown the Christian into some filthy sin he asks God, 'Is *this* the assurance You gave him of heaven – and *this* the garment of salvation You put on him? Look where he has laid it – and what a mess he has made of Your grace.' We tremble at the thought of putting such blasphemy of our living God into the devil's mouth!

God's beloved children must not loiter in the sunshine of divine love but keep moving their feet in the path of duty because God has been so kind as to make our walk most full of cheer. But we must not lose our reverential fear of God in His familiarity with us.

Moses is a good example. Did the Almighty ever treat a saint in flesh with more familiarity and condescension than this man, with whom He spoke mouth to mouth?

How did Moses handle this transcendent act of grace? Did he grow bold and forget the distance between himself and God when the divine Majesty stooped to speak with him in such a humble way? No, his heart was never more filled with the reverence of God than then. All God's goodness – especially His pardoning mercy – could not help but heighten his joy and overrun his soul with a sweet love to such a gracious God. Yet Moses' fear of God was not lost in the high tide of these precious affections: 'And Moses made haste, and bowed his head toward the earth, and worshipped' (*Exod. 34:8*). This favorite of heaven showed his fear of God most when God expressed His love to him most.

WHY WE SHOULD STRENGTHEN OUR HOPE

Just as there is a weak faith, there is a wavering hope. This we are to establish and consolidate by the diligent use of all means. Now hope is firm and solid when the Christian has no fear of its being opposed. By the anchor-hold that hope has on the promise the Christian is kept from the dejection and fears which swallow up men without hope.

The more pure gold is from dross and whatever is foreign to it, the more solid and valuable it becomes. So the more hope is refined from groundless presumption on the one hand and slavish fear and distrust on the other, the stronger it is. Scripture calls this the 'assurance of hope' (*Heb. 6:11*). Now to provoke you to a holy zeal in establishing this hope, consider these three arguments: first, it is your duty so to do; secondly, refusal to strengthen hope shows poor esteem of Christ and His salvation; and thirdly, your hope may be severely tested.

I. IT IS YOUR DUTY

Some say no one must labor for assurance. But whether we should believe God or them, let the Christian judge. For God's Spirit says, 'We desire that every one of you do shew the same diligence to the full assurance of hope unto the end: that ye be not slothful, but followers of them who through faith and patience inherit the promises' (*Heb. 6:11–12*).

God Himself exhorts the saint to seek 'the full assurance of hope.' Men with a weak hope sail with only a scant side-wind. But Paul prefers that Christians go before the wind and be carried with a full gale to heaven. This is done only when the soul, like a sail spread to the wind, is so filled with the truth and goodness of the promise that it rejoices in the certain expectation of what it will have when it comes to eternity's shore, though it is now weatherbeaten with a thousand temptations and trials on its passage.

Upon whom does the Spirit press this duty? Upon every Christian. It is sinful for a poor man to want the rich man's assets for his own and not be satisfied with less; but in the spiritual walk, it is highly acceptable for the Christian to covet all the riches of grace. Paul himself will not consider it wrong for you to work to have faith and steadfast hope as vigorous as he had. In fact, you should not be satisfied with less!

Finally, notice that Scripture imputes the saints' weak grace to their laziness. Thus Paul writes out his wish: 'that ye be not slothful' (*Heb. 6:12*). The diligent hand is the one that makes wealth in the world and the same is true of heavenly treasure.

II. A REFUSAL TO STRENGTHEN HOPE SHOWS POOR ESTEEM OF CHRIST AND HIS SALVATION

The more we prize something good the harder we work to have it. If a prince should lose a penny and one should bring him news that it has been found, it is such a petty thing that he would not care whether it were true or not. But if his kingdom lay at stake in battle and a report comes that his army has defeated the enemy, he would long to have this message confirmed.

Is heaven worth so little that you can be satisfied with a few probabilities and uncertain maybe's that you will ever get there? You must despise the blessed place if you are no more interested in your right to it than that. When Ahab advanced his army against Ramoth-gilead, Micaiah prophesied victory – 'Go, and prosper' (*1 Kings 22:15*). But the king had good reason to suspect that Micaiah's words were empty of truth and rebuked him: 'And the king said unto him, How many times shall I adjure thee that thou tell me nothing but that which is true in the name of the Lord?' (*1 Kings 22:16*).

If you have some hope of heaven, and you believe that your eternal happiness or misery depends on it, you must search your heart by the light of God's Word. And after an impartial review of what you read there, command your conscience to tell you the naked truth – what your spiritual standing is and whether or not you may hope that salvation is yours.

When Peter heard about Christ's resurrection he did not fully believe; but he ran as fast as he could and looked into the sepulchre, proving how dearly he loved his Lord. Thus, Christian, even if the promise of eternal life has not yet produced such an assurance of hope that you can enjoy it without doubting, you can show your appreciation of it by trying to strengthen your hope and put away all doubt of it.

III. YOUR HOPE MAY BE SEVERELY TESTED

The wise sailor prepares his ship for the worst. He anticipates bad weather and cross-winds which might make trouble for him later. The voyage may be pleasant after all but he knows it is easier to carry provision to sea than to get it when at sea. Protection in adversity is not usually found unless it has been sought in time of peace. God Himself tells us we have 'need of patience' – and He means stored-up patience – 'that, after ye have done the will of God, ye might receive the promise' (*Heb. 10:36*). And if this is true of patience it is also true of hope, because patience bears everything on hope's back.

Now because we never know how much affliction and temptation God intends to lay on us we must never stop trying to strengthen our hope. There are hard duties to be performed and strong trials to be endured which require a proportionate hope. We are to 'hold fast the rejoicing of the hope firm unto the end' (*Heb. 3:6*).

Can the Christian with weak hope rejoice? No, he is like a leaky ship with rich cargo; the fear of sinking takes away the owner's joy in the treasure it carries. If you tell this man to rejoice in his inheritance that is laid up in heaven for him, he will tell you he might not ever get that far.

Waiting patiently a long time for God's mercy is a hard duty. 'It is good that a man should both hope and quietly wait for the salvation of the Lord' (*Lam. 3:26*). Weak hope is short of breath and cannot wait long with any quietness. Impatient people are commonly the hardest ones to please – they complain if they do not get exactly what they want when they want it.

When David's faith and hope were weak he quarreled with everyone. Even the prophet who brought him news of the kingdom did not escape his censure – and all because the promise came later than expected. 'I said in my haste, All men are liars' (*Ps. 116:11*). The promise was not a day past its due time, but David missed the true fulfillment of it because of his impatience. But look at the psalmist when his faith and hope were strong. Then he was not so hasty to call for mercy at God's hands but realized his victory was as safe in God's hands as if it were already in his own. 'Praise waiteth for thee, O God' (*Ps. 65:1*). It is as if he had said, 'Lord, I quietly wait for a time to praise You. My soul is not disturbed because You delay. I am not murmuring but stringing my harp and tuning my instrument with confidence so I will be ready to sing when the news of my deliverance comes.'

It is not easy for a child to be patient until dinner when he sees preparations for a great feast; but a mature person waits quietly when the meal is a little later than usual. Our childishness and weakness of grace – especially of hope – make us lose patience as we wait for God's timing. Strengthen your hope, and patience will grow along with it.

In a word, Christian, you have many trials and strong temptations to conquer before you enter heaven's gate and are clothed with your garments of salvation. Defend your hope now and it will defend you in times of trouble; strengthen hope and it will carry you through them. Every member of the body is careful to protect the head from getting hurt. The hands ward off the blows and the feet run to take the head away from danger. The mouth readily receives medication to cure a headache. Salvation is to the soul what the head is to the body – the principal thing that should be kept secure. And hope is to our salvation what the helmet is to the head. Now if a man is unwise enough to risk his head under a weak helmet in the midst of bullets, he is even more foolish to hazard his salvation with a weak hope. Christian, the outcome of the battle with the enemy depends on your hope; if that fails, you have lost.

Your hope is in conflict with temptations and suffering as a prince is in the midst of his army. He puts life into his men while he looks on and encourages them to fight. But if a report of the king's death comes, their courage falters. This is why Ahab insisted on being propped up in his chariot to conceal his fatal wounds from his soldiers.

Satan aims his arrows straight at your hope. And if these darts hit their mark your spirit bleeds profusely and questions pour out of the wound: 'Can sins as horrible as mine really be forgiven? Such old, festered sores of lust – can they ever be cured? These afflictions I have had for so long, can they possibly be removed or endured any longer?' Fight as for your life by holding up your wounded hope in the chariot of promise, and do not bow to despair and let the devil trample on your soul. As soon as your hope gives up, this cursed fiend will take his full revenge and your soul will be defenseless. This defeat will so crush you that you will desperately ask, 'Why should I think of praying, hearing, and meditating, when there is no hope anyway?'

Should we call the doctor after our friend has died? What good will rubbing the body do when the head is severed from it? The army broke up as soon as everyone knew Ahab was dead. And so you will abandon all thought of gaining any ground against sin and Satan when your hope is gone. You will then fall either into Cain's atheism or into Judas' horror of conscience and bury the thoughts of your desperate condition in a heap of worldly projects.

I come now to counsel you how to strengthen your hope: first, study the Word of God diligently; secondly, keep a pure conscience; thirdly, ask God for a stronger hope; fourthly, increase your love; fifthly, exercise your hope; and sixthly, recall past mercies.

HOW TO STRENGTHEN HOPE

I. STUDY GOD'S WORD DILIGENTLY

The Christian is bred by the Word and he must be fed by it or his grace will shrivel up and die. The growing baby feeds often at the breast. As God has provided food in His Word to nourish every grace, so the Scriptures provide nutrients for the saint's strong and solid hope. 'That we through patience and comfort of the scriptures might have hope' (*Rom. 15:4*). The devil knows this so well that he works hard to deprive the Christian of the help stored in the Word. And he is right, for as long as this river remains unblocked which makes glad the City of God, with comfort brought in on the stream of its precious promises, he can never besiege the City.

The devil deprives some people of this scriptural relief by mere laziness. They complain about doubts and fears like sluggards crying out of their poverty as they lie in bed. But they will not get up and search the Word for the satisfaction of their need. Of all others, these sell their comfort most cheaply. Who pities the starving man who has bread before him but refuses to move his hand to take it?

To some Christians, Satan presents false applications of the Word and thereby troubles their spirits. The devil is an exceptionally bright student in theology and makes no other use of his Scripture knowledge than to lure the saint into sin – or into despair for having sinned. He is like a dishonest lawyer who attains legal skill merely to force an honest man into serious problems by the tangled suit he brings against him.

Now if Satan so proficiently manipulates the Word to weaken your hope and deprive you of your inheritance, you should develop a holy skill to maintain the right and defend your hope. In your study of the Word, then, you must closely pursue two goals – and pursue them until they are yours.

(a) *Understand from the Word the conditions of salvation and of life in heaven*

Some conditions do exist, or salvation would be free for all, no matter whether the person believes or not. If God had set no bounds at Sinai and specified who should come up, then anyone and everyone could have gone with Moses. If God sets no conditions, then the most abominable sinner as well as the humble saint may touch God's holy mount. Concerning salvation, the Word holds forth two conditions according to the two different covenants.

(i) *The covenant of nature or the law covenant.* God made this covenant with Adam and the condition was perfect obedience. This is not required now, and the man who stands groping at this door in the hope of entering into life will find it nailed up. At the same time he deprives himself of that true door which stands open to him. 'Whosoever of you are justified by the law; ye are fallen from grace' (*Gal. 5:4*). Therefore you must inquire what the other covenant is.

(ii) *The covenant of grace.* The condition of this new covenant is repentance and faith. It makes God and men friends again, as if God had preserved His friends from ever leaving Him in the first place. Strive therefore to believe these promises and hold to the truth as an irreversible principle, that whoever sincerely repents of his sins and, with 'faith unfeigned,' receives Christ as Lord and Savior has the Word and oath of God for the pardon of his sins and the salvation of his soul.

The weight of the Christian's whole building rests so completely on repentance and faith that the Spirit of God has put away all doubt concerning their certainty: '*Surely he hath borne our griefs*' (*Isa. 53:4*). There is no question – it was our debt He paid. Why else would God's Son have suffered unto death? Was it to give us a pattern of patience? This is true but not the entire reason, for some of our fellow saints have been admirable examples of this. Surely there was more. He 'carried our sorrows' and 'was wounded for our transgressions' (*Isa. 53:4–5*). This undertaking was so mighty that no saint could do this for us – only the Son of God. 'This is a faithful saying, and worthy of all acceptation, that Christ Jesus came into the world to save sinners' (*1 Tim. 1:15*).

'If we confess our sins, he is faithful and just to forgive us our sins' (*1 John 1:9*). What can the repentant person fear? 'Wherein God, willing more abundantly to shew unto the heirs of promise the immutability of his counsel, confirmed it by an oath' (*Heb. 6:17*). We could not ask for more security than our faithful God gives of His own accord. The Roman government did not require its magistrates to take oaths – it assumed their honor was bond enough to make them righteous. Surely then God's Word deserves the fullest credit, for He stooped to give an oath that would sink into our minds as an indisputable truth.

(b) *Make sure you are a repenting and believing sinner*
We read in the Bible of a threefold assurance: first, assurance *of understanding* (*Col. 2:2*); secondly, assurance *of faith* (*Heb. 10:22*); and thirdly, assurance *of hope* (*Heb. 6:11*). Knowledge forms the proposition, faith makes the assumption, and hope draws the conclusion.

Thus the Christian can say, 'I know from the Word that the repentant, believing sinner will be saved; my conscience shows me that *I* repent and believe. And although I am unworthy, I can firmly hope that I shall be saved.' And as forcefully as the Christian agrees with God's truth and repents, so his hope will be – strong or weak. If his assent to the truth of the promise is weak, or his evidence of faith and repentance is uncertain, his hope that is born of these will inherit its parent's infirmities.

II. KEEP A PURE CONSCIENCE
Living godly in this present world and 'looking for that blessed hope' are joined together (*Tit. 2:12–13*). Thus a soul void of godliness must be destitute of all true hope,

and the godly person who is careless in his holy walk will soon find his hope faltering.

All sin brings trembling fears and shakings of heart to the person who tampers with it. But sins which are deliberately committed are to the Christian's hope as poison is to his body, which eventually drinks it up. Sins produce a lifeless Christian and make thoughts of God dreadful to him: 'I remembered God, and was troubled' (*Ps. 77:3*). They make the man afraid to look on the God of judgment. After all, does the servant want his master to come home and find him drunk?

When Calvin's friends tried to persuade him to give up his night studies, he asked if they wanted his Lord to come and find him idle. God forbid that death should find you lying in the puddle of some sin unconfessed and unrepented of! Can your hope then carry you to eternity with joy? Can a bird fly with a broken wing? Faith and a good conscience are the two wings of hope. If you have wounded your conscience by sin, renew your repentance so that you may act in faith for the forgiveness of it and redeem your hope.

If a Jew pawned his bedclothes God mercifully provided that they should be restored to him before night: 'For that is his covering only . . . : wherein shall he sleep?' (*Exod. 22:27*). Hope is the saint's covering which wraps the person who lays his body down to sleep in the grave. 'My flesh,' says David, 'shall rest in hope' (*Ps. 16:9*). Christian, redeem your hope before the sun of your temporal life goes down, or else you are sure to lie down in sorrow. A man who has no hope of resurrection to life has a sad time going to the bed of the grave.

III. ASK GOD FOR A STRONGER HOPE

This is how Paul encouraged the saints at Rome: 'Now the God of hope fill you with all joy and peace in believing,

[209]

that ye may abound in hope, through the power of the Holy Ghost' (*Rom. 15:13*). God is the God of hope; not only of the first seed but also of the whole growth and harvest of it in us. He does not give a saint the first grace of conversion and then leave the completion of it wholly to his human skill.

Be sure you humbly acknowledge God by constantly waiting on Him for your spiritual growth. 'The young lions' are said to 'seek their meat from God' (*Ps. 104:21*). God has taught them to express their wants when they are hungry; and by this they have learned that their Maker is also their Supplier. At first a baby expresses his needs only by crying; but as soon as he knows who his mother is, he directs his cries to her.

The Father can always find you, Christian. He knows what you want but He waits to supply you until you cry to Him. Does God care for the beasts in the field? Then surely He will care for you, His child in His house. You might pray for more riches and be denied; but a prayer for more grace is sure to be answered quickly.

IV. INCREASE YOUR LOVE

Love has a secret yet powerful influence on hope. Moses befriended the Israelite when he killed the Egyptian who had fought with him. And love kills slavish fear – one of the worst enemies hope has – and thereby strengthens hope's hand. Whoever pulls up the weeds helps the corn to grow. It is fear that oppresses the Christian's spirit so that he cannot act or hope strongly. 'Perfect love casteth out fear' (*1 John 4:18*). The freewoman will cast out the bond-woman. Fear is one of Hagar's breed – an affection that keeps everyone in bondage who partakes of it.

Love cannot tolerate fear. The loving soul asks, 'Can I fear that the One who loves me most will ever hurt me? Fear and doubt, away with you! There is no room for you in my heart.' Charity 'thinketh no evil' (*1 Cor. 13:5*).

The more you love Christ, the more strongly you will hope in Him and comfortably wait for Him. These two graces are often mated in Scripture. 'The Lord direct your hearts into the love of God, and into the patient waiting for Christ' (*2 Thess. 3:5*). Love Him and you will wait for Him. 'Keep yourselves in the love of God, looking for the mercy of our Lord Jesus Christ unto eternal life' (*Jude 21*).

V. EXERCISE YOUR HOPE

Repeated acts strengthen habits. You have no more money in your chest at home at the year's end than when you deposited it. Of course it is good that it has not decreased, but you could have invested it and made a profit. 'Thou oughtest therefore to have put my money to the exchangers, and then at my coming I should have received mine own with usury,' Christ told the slothful servant (*Matt. 25:27*).

God's promises are hope's substance to act upon. A man can as well live without air as faith and hope can live without a promise, and without taking in refreshment from that promise frequently. Therefore, set some time apart to meditate on what God has said. If you appreciate your health, do not be satisfied with the air that comes to you as you work in your house or office, but walk out into the fields once in a while to take in air that is fresh and full. And if you are a wise Christian you will not be satisfied merely to think about God's promises now and then while you are preoccupied but will find a place apart and enjoy meditating on them.

Sometimes, however, when the Christian recalls past sins his hope is crushed by the memories staring at his conscience with grim looks. This is the best time to pick out a promise where he can see hope triumphing over the problem. David did this when he was in a painful situation: 'If thou, Lord, shouldest mark iniquities, O

Lord, who shall stand?' (*Ps. 130:3*). But then he put his soul out of this fear by laying down his conclusion as an unalterable truth: 'But there is forgiveness with thee, that thou mayest be feared' (*verse 4*). That is, 'there is forgiveness in Your very nature, Lord; because You carry a pardoning heart in Your bosom, there is forgiveness in Your promise. Not only does Your mercy draw You to forgiving thoughts, but Your faithful promise binds You to give it to all who humbly reach out for it.' David laid his foundation in God's mercy and faithfulness and then began building hope on it again. 'I wait for the Lord, my soul doth wait, and in his word do I hope' (*verse 5*). He was saying, 'Lord, I take You at Your Word and by Your grace I will wait at this door of promise and never leave until forgiveness of my sins has been sent out to meet me.' This taste of God's goodness was so sweet that David hesitated to eat it alone but invited other godly persons to share it with him: 'Let Israel hope in the Lord: for with the Lord there is mercy, and with him is plenteous redemption. And he shall redeem Israel from all his iniquities' (*verses 7–8*). Because he had learned to hope in God's faithfulness, David fought despair until it surrendered.

When Satan comes to rob us of our hope, strong doubt often comes with him because of the greatness of the things we hope for. Thus our soul becomes so overwhelmed that it cries out: 'Does a rebel like me really have a right to hope God will make me His son and heir? Can I have His forgiveness and His favor too? Could He actually be making me a robe of glory in heaven, where I will minister to Him, before I have served Him any more effectively than this on earth? This is too good to be true.' There we stand as amazed as the disciples when the first announcement of the Lord's resurrection surprised them.

Now, Christian, to equip you to stride over this

stumbling-block, observe the prints of God's greatness stamped upon His promise. Sometimes He expresses these on purpose to free our thoughts and help us believe more easily. For example, when God promised what great things He would do for Abraham, He added, 'I am the Almighty God' (*Gen. 17:1*). And to the prophet He spoke, 'Let the wicked forsake his way, and the unrighteous man his thoughts: and let him return unto the Lord, and he will have mercy upon him; and to our God, for he will abundantly pardon' (*Isa. 55:7*).

How can such great mercy come to such unworthy children? God has His own way of forgiving sins, a way that no man can follow Him in; for it is as far above our ways as the heavens are above the earth. If you grasp this understanding it will be a key to unlock the greatest promises in the Bible and let you enter into their untold treasures.

When you read any promise remember the One who has made it – it is *God's* Word. And when you think of Him, do not confine Him to your finite apprehensions; but always conceive of Him as an infinite Being whose center is everywhere and circumference is nowhere! When you have raised your thoughts to the highest, then know you are farther from reaching His glory and immensity than a man is from touching the sun with his hand when he is upon a hill or mountain. This is what it means to ascribe greatness to God.

Suppose a king should promise to adopt a poor cripple and make him heir to his crown. The message might seem incredible to the man when he considers the distance from his beggar's cottage to the king's palace. He could more easily believe it if the ruler had authorized a private hospital room or an adequate pension for him. Yet recognition of the king's great creating power required to raise him from nothingness to the highest honor helps the man realize that this strange accident might not be altogether impossible.

If we spend all our thoughts on our unworthiness of heaven we shall never realize we are among the chosen ones who will enjoy it. But when we believe the pleasure God takes in demonstrating His greatness – making miserable creatures happy instead of allowing their misery to continue in eternal damnation – and the cost He paid for His mercy to reach us, we see Him as the Most High God! When we weigh and meditate on these truths they open our hearts, though fastened with a thousand bolts, to believe without question all that He has said.

VI. RECALL PAST MERCIES

When the strong Christian's spiritual rest is broken by very great fears for the future, he can read the history of God's gracious dealings with him. Thus he endures his night of affliction with comfort and hope. But those who have not penned in their memories the remarkable instances of God's loving favor to them miss comfort's sweet companionship.

Sometimes little scraps of writing found on a man's desk help save his estate, for without these records he would have spent the rest of his life in prison. And often it is one experience remembered which frees the soul from despair – a prison where the devil longs to trap the Christian. God's dealings with David were often the subject of his meditation and of his songs; and when his hope faltered, he regained it by recalling God's goodness to him: 'I said, This is my infirmity: but I will remember the years of the right hand of the most High' (*Ps. 77:10*).

When a hound has lost the scent, he hunts backward to recover it and pursues his game with a louder cry of confidence than before. Thus Christian, when your hope is at a loss and you question your salvation in another world, look backward to see what God has done for you in this one.

We receive payment of some promises here; but we must wait until heaven to receive others. God fulfills some promises as an earnest to our faith that the others will also be paid when their time comes. And every judgment inflicted on the wicked is deposited as a down-payment of the full sum of wrath God will release in hell. But He has promised that 'sin shall not have dominion over you' (*Rom. 6:14*) – not even in this life. Look over your receipts.

Has the power of sin been broken in your life? Has the prince of this world, whom you once willingly obeyed, been dethroned in your heart and affections? Then let this assure you that you will have full dominion over sin in heaven before long, since it has begun to lose its power over you here on earth.

Notice how David raised his hope to expect heaven's perfect holiness from his sanctification begun on earth. First he declared his belief in God and then his expectation from Him: 'As for me, I will behold thy face in righteousness: I shall be satisfied, when I awake, with thy likeness' (*Ps. 17:15*).

Have you felt God's supporting hand keeping you from sinking under your temptations and troubles? David knew this and fed his hope for eternal salvation with acknowledgment of God's support: 'Thou hast holden me by my right hand' (*Ps. 73:23*). Thus hope led him closer and closer to his desire: 'Thou shalt guide me with thy counsel, and afterward receive me to glory' (*verse 24*).

Just as memories of God's goodness strengthen the Christian's hope of salvation, they also lift his head above life's hardest battles. Surely David would have been more terrorized by the big looks and bragging conduct of Goliath if remembrance of the slain bear and lion had not held them down. Figuratively David had already killed this uncircumcised giant when he tore those unclean beasts into pieces. And therefore when he marched toward Goliath, this was the shield he lifted up as a covering: 'The Lord that delivered me out of the paw of the lion, and out of the paw of the bear, he will deliver me out of the hand of this Philistine' (*1 Sam. 17:37*).

Past experiences with God are a sure foundation for hope in future hardships and also a powerful argument in prayer. Saints use these experiences to tell the Father what He has already done for them and to expect His continued care. 'Save me from the lion's mouth: for thou hast heard me from the horns of the unicorns' (*Ps. 22:21*). A Christian can pray in faith from past experience and expect a favorable answer when former mercies are the plea for what he wants at present.

God intends more comfort in every mercy than the mercy by itself amounts to. For instance, suppose you prayed for God to heal you and He answered by snatching you out of the very jaws of death at a time when you were going down its throat. The comfort of this particular mercy, good as it is, is the very least God has for you. For He wants you to make it a support when your faith and hope are shaken by any future crisis. 'Thou brakest the heads of the leviathan in pieces, and gavest him to be meat to the people inhabiting the wilderness' (*Ps. 74:14*). In His mercy at the Red Sea God was thinking about what Israel would need to live on for forty years in the wilderness. He wanted them not only to feast on the joy of this present mercy but also to hold it firmly in their memories. Thus their faith would not lack a meal in the hungry wilderness all the time they would be in it. Sometimes a Christian has nothing else on his table but the promise and his experience; and anyone who cannot make a soul-refreshing meal with these two dishes deserves to stay hungry.

God compares His promise to 'the rain' which makes the earth 'bring forth and bud, that it may give seed to the sower, and bread to the eater' (*Isa. 55:10*). Why should you want only half the benefit of God's mercy? When He performs His promise and delivers you out of trouble you are comforted and your heart bursts with thankfulness. Here is 'bread for the eater' – something which satisfies you right now. But where is the 'seed for the sower'? The farmer never spends all the corn that he reaps but saves some for seed to bring him another crop. So you should not only feast with the joy of mercy but save the remembrance of it as hope-seed, to strengthen you to wait on God for further mercy and help in time of need.

You have seen God bare His arm to help you. So unless you think He has lost the strength or use of it, hope still has an object to act upon, to lift your head above the water. No person ever drowns in despair unless he loses his hold on the power of God.

Another way to let God rescue you from despair is to remember how often He has proved your unbelief to be a false prophet. Has He not knocked at your door with inward comfort and outward deliverance after you had already put out the candle of hope and given up looking for Him? He came to Hezekiah after he had concluded that his case was beyond hope and help (*Isa. 38.10–11*). Have you ever been left alone with fear as if an everlasting night had come and there would never be another morning? Yet even then God proved those despairing thoughts all liars by an unlooked-for surprise of sweet mercy which He crept in and gently brought to you. Why then are you frightened again and again by your distrustful thoughts, which God has so often proved liars? Stop feeding your hopes on the corpses of slain fears!

Remember too how even when you have been impatient and despairing in your afflictions, nevertheless God's mercy has been at work all the while to deliver you from them. David is an instance of this: 'I said in my haste, All men are liars. What shall I render unto the Lord for all his benefits toward me?' (*Ps. 116:11–12*); 'I said in my haste, I am cut off from before thine eyes: nevertheless thou heardest the voice of my supplications when I cried unto thee' (*Ps. 31:22*). He was saying, 'I prayed with so little faith that I unprayed my own prayer! I assumed my dilemma was hopeless but God forgave my hasty spirit and gave me the mercy which I had hardly any faith to expect.' And with his experience, David raises every saint's troubled hope: 'Be of good courage, and he shall strengthen your heart, all ye that hope in the Lord' (*verse 24*).

EXHORTATION TO THOSE WHO HAVE NOT GOT THE HELMET OF HOPE

If you still do not have the helmet of salvation it should be the first thing you set about to obtain if you have any sense at all. Begin your search by making room for these three considerations in your thoughts: first, hopelessness is a matter of great sadness; secondly, it is possible to obtain a hope of salvation; and thirdly, consider the cruelty of pulling down eternal destruction on yourself.

I. HOPELESSNESS IS A MATTER OF GREAT SADNESS

Paul says that the man without God is without hope – 'having no hope, and without God in the world' (*Eph. 2:12*). 'The heart of the wicked is little worth,' says Solomon (*Prov. 10:20*). Why? It does not have God to make it valuable. If God, who is light, is not in your understanding, you are blind. If God is not in your conscience to comfort it, you must be a raging devil or a stupid atheist. If God is not in you, the devil is; for a man's heart is a house that will not stand empty.

You cannot afford to be without hope in life or in death. It is a sad legacy that shuts out the rebellious child from all claim to his inheritance. But even if you do have wealth, it is *all* you have. Does it not make your heart ache to think that your reward is all paid here, and will be spent by the time the saints start receiving theirs?

Yet it is far worse to be without this hope when death comes. The condemned prisoner had rather stay in his cell than accept deliverance at the executioner's hand. The hopeless soul has more reason to prefer to spend his eternity in earth's worst dungeon than to be eased of his pain with hell's torment. Here is the sad confusion in the thoughts of guilty men when their souls leave their bodies. If the sobs of mourning friends in the room of a dying man make his passage harder, how much more will the horror of the sinner's own conscience frighten him when he sees the flaming inevitability of his approaching destination?

Are you cutting your short life into chips by wasting time on trivia when your salvation still has not been worked out? Are you pampering and decorating your body while your soul is slipping into hell? This is like painting your door when the house is on fire. It would be far more becoming for you to call upon God and lie in repentant tears for your sins at His feet than to wallow in your sensual pleasures and let your sleeping conscience temporarily ease the dread thought of your approaching punishment.

II. IT IS POSSIBLE TO OBTAIN A HOPE OF SALVATION

I do not mean the way you are now, for it is as impossible for you to get to heaven without salvation as it is for God to lie. If any devil in hell had a thousand worlds at his disposal, he would give them all for this hope and count it a bargain.

But you have many specific promises from God's faithful mouth that if you seek Him in His time and way, as surely as God is in heaven today, you will live there with Him in glory. 'Your heart shall live that seek God' (*Ps. 69:32*). There are millions of blessed people now in heaven experiencing the truth of this Word who once had no more right to heaven than you have now. That place is not crowded too full for God to make room for you also, if you have a mind to go there.

One prayer which Christ made on earth will keep heaven's gate open for all who believe on Him until the end of the world: 'Neither pray I for these alone, but for them also which shall believe on me through their word' (*John 17:20*). This should make your soul leap within your breast while you hear invitations of the gospel as the baby once did in Elisabeth's womb when the virgin Mary spoke her greeting.

Sinner, do not ever say that ministers ask you to climb an impossible hill or attack an unconquerable city. It is Satan and your own unbelieving heart that tell you this. And as long as you listen to them you are likely to do what they suggest. But whatever they say, know this – if you miss heaven, the Lord can wash His hands of your blood; damnation will be laid at your own door.

What God has offered He is willing to give; but you voluntarily turned away from eternal life. And whatever your lips might argue to the contrary, your heart would not accept His terms. Thus when the heavenly jury asks how your murdered soul came to such a miserable end, you will be found guilty of your own damnation. No one loses God except the man who is willing to part with Him.

III. CONSIDER THE HORROR OF PULLING DOWN ETERNAL DESTRUCTION ON YOURSELF

What a sad epitaph for a man's tombstone: 'Here lies one

who cut his own throat, who destroyed himself! This is the man, that is the woman, who would not be reclaimed.' They saw hell in front of them and yet jumped into it, ignoring the invitations of Christ by His Spirit and by ministers of the gospel.

It would be a cruel person who could watch his horse starve in his stable when he had plenty to feed him; it would be even more heartless to hear his servant crying for bread and deny it. And what if this were done to a child or wife? But because nature cries loudest for self-preservation, the greatest violence that can possibly be done to the law of nature is to forget the responsibility we owe to our own life. It is the epitome of cruelty for the sinner to starve his own soul by rejecting Christ, 'the bread of life.'

Only a few deranged people commit physical suicide, but spiritual suicide is common. You can hardly go into a house on any day of the week and not find people attempting to murder their souls. They carry around the very knife – their beloved sins, I mean – to stab themselves. Some are willing to spend all they have on doctors when their physical lives are threatened, yet they are so cruel to their dying souls that they turn away Christ the great Physician when He has come to heal them freely.

In a word, people employ an abundance of wisdom and discretion in ordering their worldly affairs; yet when it comes to the business of heaven and the salvation of their souls, they are not like the same men. It is like a man who provides food for all his servants but they in turn refuse to let him eat; he then remains the only starving person in the house. Men provide for their back and belly, house and family; but they themselves starve in the meantime. The power of some lust keeps them from using their understanding and reasoning to search for salvation. How then can their souls ever hope to survive or prosper?

And the sword of the Spirit, which is the word of God (Eph. 6:17).

Here we have the sixth and last piece in the Christian's armour brought to our hand – the sword of the Spirit. Throughout the ages the sword has been a most necessary part of the soldier's equipment and has been used more than any other weapon. A pilot without his chart, a student without his book, a soldier without his sword – all are ridiculous. But above these, it is absurd to think of being a Christian without knowledge of God's Word and some skill to use this weapon.

The usual name in Scripture for war is 'the sword.' 'I will call for a sword upon all the inhabitants of the earth' (*Jer. 25:29*); that is, 'I will send war.' Now such a weapon is the Word of God in the Christian's hand. By the edge of this sword his enemies fall and all his great exploits are done: 'They overcame him by the blood of the Lamb, and by the word of their testimony' (*Rev. 12:11*). But before we enter into a detailed discussion of the sword of the Spirit, let us notice the kind of arms here presented for the Christian's use and the place and order in which it stands.

THE KIND OF ARMS FOR THE CHRISTIAN'S USE
This weapon is both defensive and offensive. The rest of the apostle's armour are defensive arms – girdle, breast-

plate, shield, and helmet. But the sword both defends the Christian and wounds his enemy.

I. IT IS FOR DEFENSE

No matter how glorious the Christian's other pieces of armour, he would easily be disarmed without a sword in his hand. And surely the believer would be stripped of all his graces if he did not have this sword to defend them and himself too against Satan's fury. 'Unless thy law had been my delights, I should then have perished in mine affliction' (*Ps. 119:92*).

This is like God's flaming sword which kept Adam out of paradise. The saint is often compared to Christ's garden and orchard; and with the sword of the Word he keeps his orchard from being robbed of God's sweet comforts and graces by Satan's constant invasions. The Word of God is a terror to Satan; he cannot overcome the dread of it. Let Christ simply say 'It is written,' and the fiend runs with confusion and terror. And saints have found that the most successful instrument to defend themselves against Satan's fiercest temptations is that phrase which came from Christ's own blessed lips.

Ask David which weapon he used to ward off his enemy's blows and he will tell you it was the Word of God. 'Concerning the works of men, by the word of thy lips I have kept me from the paths of the destroyer' (*Ps. 17:4*). That is, 'By the help of Your Word I have preserved myself from those wicked works which destroy those without this weapon.'

II. IT IS FOR OFFENSE

As the sword defends the soldier it offends his enemy. Thus God's Word is a killing sword as well as a keeping sword. Not only does it keep the believer from surrendering to external temptation but it kills his inward lusts and completes the victory. A man may escape his enemy one day and be overcome by him the next. And some may evade the world's pollution temporarily but ultimately they are slain by the secret enemy of lust which was never destroyed by the power of the Word.

THE ORDER AND PLACE OF THIS PIECE OF ARMOUR

The apostle gives the Christian all the other pieces of armour and then fastens on this sword last. Although God's Spirit does not always bind Himself to methods, let me give a double significance to the place and order the sword stands in.

I. THE GRACES OF GOD'S SPIRIT ARE NECESSARY TO THE RIGHT USE OF THE WORD

Nothing is more abused than the Word because men come to it with unsanctified hearts. The heretic quotes it to prove false doctrine, but how can he father his monstrous births on the pure and chaste Word of God? Surely it is because he comes to the Word without the girdle of sincerity – and God lets him miss truth.

Another man reads the Word and is more hardened in his lusts than ever before. He takes false security from the imperfections of some saints and presumptuously continues wallowing in his own sins. This impudent man comes to the Word with an unholy heart but expects the breastplate of righteousness to defend him from dangerous temptations.

Still others, without faith to give existence to the truth and the warnings in their conscience, run boldly upon the point of this sword and dare God to strike them with it: 'Where is the word of the Lord? let it come now' (*Jer. 17:15*). Their mockery plays with this sacred sword and defiantly cries, 'Your fearful threats say God's judgments are coming. Let us see them. Is

God's sword rusty that it takes Him so long to get it out of the scabbard?'

And the despairing soul, without a helmet of hope, fares no better. Instead of lifting up the Word to defend himself against the fears of a guilty conscience, he falls upon the weapon given him to slay his enemy with and destroys his own soul. This is why the apostle first put on the other pieces and then delivered the sword to them to use for their good. A sword in a madman's hand, and the Word of God in a wicked man's mouth, are used to hurt only themselves and their closest friends.

II. THE CHRISTIAN CANNOT BE SAFE WITHOUT THE WORD

Even after the Christian is girded with his plate of righteousness on his breast, the shield of faith in his hand, and the helmet of hope covering his head, he must still take the sword of the Spirit, which is the Word of God. This is not a book to be read by the slowest students in Christ's school only but by the brightest scholars fit for heaven's academy. It is like the architect's rule – as necessary to lay the top stone of the building at the end of his life as the foundation at his conversion. Only a foolish builder throws away his plumb-line before the house is finished.

I come now to take up the weapon laid before us – 'and the sword of the Spirit, which is the word of God.' Observe three parts in this text: first, the weapon itself; secondly, why the Word of God is called the sword of the Spirit; and thirdly, how to use this sword.

I. The Weapon Itself

I begin with the weapon itself – 'the sword of the Spirit, which is the word of God.' At first I hold forth this naked sword and then put it into its sheath again, to handle it under the metaphor of a sword. Here we see the twofold

Word of God – first, the eternal Son of God; and secondly, the declarative Word of God, differing according to the various ways He reveals His mind.

WHAT IS MEANT BY THE WORD OF GOD

I. THE ETERNAL SON OF GOD

'The Word was with God, and the Word was God' (*John 1:1*). 'And he was clothed with a vesture dipped in blood: and his name is called The Word of God' (*Rev. 19:13*). This speaks of a person, and He is no other than Jesus Christ the Son of God. But Christ is not the Word of God referred to in this text. The Spirit is Christ's sword, rather than Christ the sword of the Spirit: 'Out of his mouth goeth a sharp sword, that with it he should smite the nations' (*Rev. 19:15*).

II. GOD'S DECLARATIVE WORD, ACCORDING TO THE DIFFERENT WAYS HE REVEALS HIS MIND

When the earth had only a few people, and they lived a long time, God declared His mind by dreams and visions and by immediate revelations to faithful witnesses, who in turn instructed others. They lived so long that three holy men were able to preserve the purity of religion by tradition from Adam's death until the time just prior to the Israelites going down to Egypt. Thus God delayed committing His will to writing because it was safely kept by a few trustworthy men.

But after the age of man's life was shortened and the population multiplied, God wrote the Ten Commandments with His own finger on tables of stone to keep His people from idolatry and corrupt worship. Later He commanded Moses to write the other words he had heard from Him on the mount; and all the while God continued to demonstrate His will by supernatural revelations.

Finally, it pleased God for His sacred Word to be

finished by Christ the great Teacher of the church, and by the apostles, His public notaries, for saints to use until the end of time. A curse from Christ's own mouth belongs to anyone who adds to or takes away from God's written Word: 'If any man shall add unto these things, God shall add unto him the plagues that are written in this book: and if any man shall take away from the words of the book of this prophecy, God shall take away his part out of the book of life, and out of the holy city, and from the things which are written in this book' (*Rev. 22:18–19*).

This one book of Scripture records all the ways God has directly revealed Himself to man, and we are to receive it as the undoubted Word of God. It contains a perfect way of faith and life. The 'last days' are so called because we are not to expect any other revelation of His mind to us. 'God, who at sundry times and in divers manners spake in time past unto the fathers by the prophets, hath in these last days spoken unto us by his Son' (*Heb. 1:1*).

THE HOLY SCRIPTURES ARE THE UNDOUBTED WORD OF GOD

By the Scriptures I mean the Old and New Testaments contained in the Bible. Both are that one foundation upon which our faith is built: 'Built upon the foundation of the apostles and prophets' (*Eph. 2:20*). And it came as truly and immediately from the unerring mind and heart of God as our breath comes from within our bodies: 'All Scripture is given by inspiration of God' (*2 Tim. 3:16*) – breathed by Him.

Both matter and words were breathed by God; for the things which they spoke were 'not in the words which man's wisdom teacheth, but which the Holy Ghost teacheth' (*1 Cor. 2:13*). God did not give a theme in Scripture to be enlarged upon but confined it to what He

[227]

said. This is why no Scripture is to be understood by our personal interpretation; we must take the meaning of it from itself. One place in it enlightens another, because it did not come from the spirit of any man, 'but holy men of God spake as they were moved,' or carried, 'by the Holy Ghost' (*2 Pet. 1:21*).

Men need arguments to prove their words are true; but the Word of God is a sufficient witness to itself. What pure truth says must be a free testimony. Christ thought it derogatory to borrow from man's testimony but referred to Himself according to what Scripture said about Him; and He was more than willing to stand or fall in the opinion of His enemies in the light of that written testimony.

The Spirit of God lifts the heart to believe God's Word by putting His own weight to the persuasions written in it. He then leaves the imprint of these truths sealed on the soul. Thus I want to share some of the arguments in Scripture which prove its parentage is divine. The two general topics of my demonstration are these – first, the subject matter of the Scriptures; and secondly, the supernatural effects produced by them.

DIVINITY OF SCRIPTURE: ITS SUBJECT MATTER

The matter contained in the holy Scriptures demonstrates their heavenly descent; it cannot be the product of man. Let us now search to see whether or not these all bear the image of God upon them. Here are the parts of the Scripture for us to examine – first, historical; secondly, prophetical; thirdly, doctrinal; and fourthly, preceptive.

I. HISTORICAL

In this section let us consider: first, the antiquity of the matter; and secondly, the simplicity and sincerity of the penmen.

(a) *The antiquity of the matter*

What resource could man possibly have in his reading and learning to enable him to write the history of the creation? Heathens, by inquiry of natural reason, have discovered that the world had a beginning and that it could be the workmanship of no one but God. But how does their discovery compare to the compiling of a distinct history of how God worked to produce the world, the order in which every creature was made, and the time involved? To be qualified for such a task a man would have to be pre-existent to the whole world and an eyewitness to each day's work. And man, who was himself created on the last day, cannot do this.

Yet there is history even more ancient than the creation in Scripture, where we find what was done in heaven before the world began. Who could bring us reports of the ever-lasting decrees then resolved on, and the Father's promises to the Son of eternal life for His elect at the given time?

(b) *The simplicity and sincerity of holy penmen*

Some human authors accurately preserve the history of others, reflecting their faults and weaknesses as well as their accomplishments. But where are the men who objectively record the blemishes of their own house? At this point the pens often refuse to ink the whole truth. They can make a blot in their history but not on their own names; and even if they should mention any scars these will be found in extremely fine print.

But none of this self-love appears in the history of Scripture. The penmen are free to expose their own shame and nakedness to the world. Thus Moses impartially branded his own tribe for their bloody murder on Shechem. Nothing escaped his pen – he chronicled the proud behavior of his sister and God's severe chastisement of her, and even the incest of his own parents (*Exod. 6:20*).

Moses was no more protective of his personal honor than that of his family but recorded his own flaws one after the other: reluctance to obey God; impatience and murmuring at the troubles which came with His call to service; and unbelief after miraculous confirmations of God's promise. His pen was guided by a Spirit more than human.

II. PROPHETIC

Such wonderful predictions could flow from no pen but one moved by a divine hand, because all of them took place in God's exact timing. Where else could these come from except Him? 'The secret things belong unto the Lord our God' (*Deut. 29:29*). This is an incommunicable prerogative of the only true God, who stands on the hill of eternity and from there has the full perspective of all things; and to whose infinite understanding they are all present tense.

Because Satan is ambitious and wants people to think he too can prophesy, he has assigned false prophets in every age to dictate abuse to the ignorant world. But his predictions are no more real prophecies than his miracles are true miracles. For these forecasts are dark and cleverly packed like a picture in folds. They carry two faces under one hood, and in these folds the subtle serpent wraps himself to save face whichever way the event may turn out. With this in mind, we can easily identify several characteristics of Satan's false prophecies.

(a) *Natural causes are labeled supernatural*

If a man tells you that a friend will die within a few months, and then the friend does die, you might think at first it was a valid prophecy. But after you realize that the man who told you this was a doctor and had diagnosed your friend's serious illness, you would no longer think of him as a prophet, but admire him as a skillful physician. Thus when we consider Satan's many years of experience in studying natural knowledge, we will not accept his predictions as prophecies but see him as a learned naturalist with a short and dark text of natural causes.

(b) *Moral and political causes are called miraculous*
What the devil told Saul would happen to his army and kingdom was nothing but what he rationally concluded from the premises which lay before him; in that God had rejected Saul and anointed another man to be king, together with the full measure of Saul's sins – culminating in his going to a witch for counsel – and a great Philistine army gathered against him. Coupled with his burning conscience, all these made it appear that the devil, without a gift of prophecy, had accurately envisioned Saul's doom.

(c) *God may reveal future events to Satan as His instrument*
The hangman is not a prophet. He cannot tell a man when he will be executed until he gets a warrant from the king appointing him to carry out his orders. Satan could have told Job beforehand what afflictions would come to his estate, servants, children, and his own body because God had allowed him to be the instrument to bring all these trials upon Job. But neither Satan nor any other creatures is able to foretell events which do not arise from natural causes nor follow moral and political probabilities.

Prophecies in Scripture are locked up in the cabinet of the divine will to prove their heavenly extraction. They must come from God, who can tell us what only He knows. Who else but God, for example, could have told Abraham where his heirs would be and what would happen to them four hundred years after his death?

Finally, how wonderful are the prophecies of Christ the Messiah! His person, birth, life, and death are as specifically set down many ages before His coming as if recorded by those who were with Him and saw with their own eyes all that happened.

Some things foretold of Christ seem too small to deserve a place in sacred prophecy. For instance, our Savior's riding on a colt; the thirty pieces of silver; and the preserving of His bones whole, when those who suffered with Him had theirs broken – these apparently unimportant passages have helped to strengthen our weak faith in the belief of the prophecy. A great weight of the argument proving the truth and divinity of prophecy moves upon these little hinges; because the less these are in themselves, the more piercing the strong eye that could see such small things at so great a distance. None but an infinite understanding could have seen this!

These prophecies have been openly read and known for so long that it is impossible for the devil to remain ignorant of them and not do his best to block their coming to light. Nevertheless, not even all his lies and persistent attacks could keep each one from happening in the fullness of its time. Here the wisdom and power of God break out with such a strong beam of light that no dark enemy of Scripture can prevail against its force.

III. DOCTRINAL

I mean only those grounds and principles of faith laid down in Scripture to be believed and embraced by all who desire eternal life. A few examples will suffice.

First, God Himself, who is the prime object of our faith. Who but God could tell us who and what His nature is? Natural reason has found that there is a God, and His power is taught in the school of nature. But how do uneducated men learn the true knowledge of God, when profound philosophers continually grope like dunces after endless theories but never find the door? The apostle answers: 'The world by wisdom knew not God' (*1 Cor. 1:21*).

God Himself must reveal the trinity of Persons in the

Godhead, for the heart of man can never aim high enough to find such truth. And the same can be said of all the gospel – Jesus Christ, God-man, justification by faith in His blood, and the whole method of grace and salvation through Him. These truths could never enter the heart of the wisest man in the world; yet a little child, under the preaching of the gospel, believes these mysteries which even Plato and Aristotle overlooked.

Once these mysteries are revealed by divine communication our reason stares at them as strangers to the natural mind. It is as if the owl were to declare the sun has no light because her weak eyes cannot bear to look at it. Thus we must believe these truths upon the trust of Him who relates them, and not accept or reject them as they agree with, or differ from, our reasoning. Anyone who tries to handle this doctrine with his reason rather than his faith is like a blacksmith who lifts a red-hot iron with his hand instead of with his tongs. What can he expect but burned fingers?

IV. PRECEPTIVE

The preceptive part of Scripture contains commands and precepts. It carries the mark of divinity on its forehead, which is clearly seen if we consider, first, the vast extent of Scripture commands; and secondly, their purity.

(a) *The vast extent of Scripture commands*

Does a prince issue royal laws to all mankind without respect of people and nations within his circle of power? Of all the empires the world ever had, the Roman was the greatest; yet when the Roman eagle's wings were fully grown they could not overspread more than a comparatively small part of it. How vain it would have been for the emperor to make laws for those nations which did not even know him!

But Scripture carries laws for all mankind, wherever

they live – even in places where the Bible has never been seen. Their sound is gone into all the earth and their words to the end of the world. Many of these written laws are only a second edition of what was found written in the consciences of men and women before the Scripture ever came forth. So if the laws indelibly imprinted in men's consciences are of God, then Scripture must come from Him also.

As the Scripture lays its precepts on everyone, rich and poor, so its commands bind the whole man: the heart with its most inward thoughts, as well as the outward man, is enclosed in these chains. Those Scriptures containing our duty to God require that we do everything with the heart and soul. If we pray it must be 'in spirit' (*John 4:23*). And in the realm of human relationships, the heart is deeply involved: 'Thou shalt not hate thy brother in thine heart' (*Lev. 19:17*).

Just as veins follow arteries in a man's body, the promises and chastenings accompanying the commands of Scripture are suitable to the spiritual nature of those commands. The rewards and punishments coincide with the spiritual performance or neglect of them: 'Blessed are the pure in heart: for they shall see God' (*Matt. 5:8*) – not 'Blessed are they who have clean hands and an unwashed heart'.

'Cursed be the deceiver, which hath in his flock a male, and voweth, and sacrificeth unto the Lord a corrupt thing' (*Mal. 1:14*). The deceiver is a hypocrite who gives God the skin for the sacrifice, the shell of duty for the substance, and outward obedience instead of obedience of the heart. The main object that God's laws are leveled at and against is the obedience or disobedience of the heart. And the soul and spirit is the vessel where blessings or curses are poured, depending on obedience or disobedience: 'They

[234]

shall praise the Lord that seek him: your heart shall live for ever' (*Ps. 22:26*); or, 'give them sorrow of heart, thy curse unto them' (*Lam. 3:65*).

Who could form laws to guide men's hearts or prepare rewards to reach their souls and consciences? An earthly king would be ridiculed if he made a law that his subjects love him or confess their unfaithful thoughts. And further, what mortal ruler could ever assume that he could keep the hearts and thoughts of men within his jurisdiction?

Throughout the years men have schemed to plan acts of murder but were attacked by their own consciences before anyone could accuse them. Their surrender came about not because of a law but because they dreaded the arrest of their conscience for violating God's law. For this law not only restrains hands from killing but also binds hearts from cursing. It rules in the consciences of vile men like a bit that God rides the most stubborn sinners with, and curbs them so they can never completely shake it out of their mouths.

(b) *The purity of Scripture commands*
God is 'the Holy One' (*Isa. 43:3*). He alone is perfectly holy: 'The heavens are not clean in his sight' (*Job 15:15*). And as God is the only holy Person, so the Scripture is the only holy book. Dregs appear in even the holiest writings of the sincerest men when they have stood awhile under the observation of a critical eye. Scripture too has been exposed to the view of all sorts of men yet can never have the least impurity. It is so pure that it makes filthy souls clean: 'Sanctify them through thy truth: thy word is truth' (*John 17:17*). There is nothing in Scripture to feed the flesh or afford fuel to any lust. It puts every sin to the sword and strikes through the loins of all sinners, affluent or penniless: 'To be carnally

minded is death; but to be spiritually minded is life and peace' (*Rom. 8:6*).

Athenagoras well said, 'No man can be wicked that is a Christian, unless he be a hypocrite.' The Scripture which he professes to be his rule of faith and life will not allow him to embrace a false doctrine or unholy practice. Christianity alone can glory in this, for heathens were led into many sensual abominations by their false and drunken gods. But the Christian cannot blame his sins on God, who does not tempt anyone to do evil but hates both the work and the worker of sin. Neither can the Christian blame his Bible, which damns every sin to the pit of hell, and all who live in it: 'Tribulation and anguish, upon every soul of man that doeth evil, of the Jew first, and also of the Gentile; but glory, honour, and peace, to every man that worketh good, to the Jew first, and also to the Gentile' (*Rom. 2:9*).

Who could be author of this blessed book but the blessed God? If any creature made it, he had to be either wicked or holy.

(i) *No wicked creature could author Scripture*. Surely the wicked would never have taken such pains to pull down their own kingdom of darkness, the great plot running through the Bible from start to finish. And certainly no unclean spirit or evil man would exalt holiness. Even though Satan is bold, he would never be so impudent as to claim such a heavenly work. And even if he could, the glorious beauty of holiness that shines on the face of God's Word would forbid any man in his right mind to believe that a black fiend had fathered it. Every creature begets like creatures. And what likeness is there between light and darkness?

(ii) *No holy creature could author Scripture*. Could any creature with the least spark of love for God dare counterfeit and blaspheme His authorship by prefixing

'Thus saith the Lord' with his own name? Surely the earth which swallowed up Korah for pretending to be an authority from God would not have spared Moses himself if he had spoken something in God's name which he had not received from Him. So then no one owns the authorship of Scripture but God; and He has claimed this with enough miracles to convince a hardened atheist of their divinity.

DIVINITY OF SCRIPTURE: ITS SUPERNATURAL EFFECTS

Nothing can be the cause of an effect higher than itself. If we find such effects – above the capability of any creature – to be the product of Scriptures, it is evident that Scripture itself is supernatural. What the psalmist said of thunder, we may apply to the Almighty speaking from heaven: 'The voice of the Lord is full of majesty'; it 'breaketh the cedars' – kings and kingdoms; it 'divideth the flames of fire' (*Ps. 29:4, 5, 7*). With one bucket of this spiritual water, martyrs quenched the flames of the furious fires where their enemies threw them. It 'shaketh the wilderness' of the wild world, making the proudest sinners tremble like leaves in the wind (*verse 8*). It 'discovereth the forests' (*verse 9*) and hunts sinners out of their thickets of lies, where they run to hide from the cry of divine vengeance.

But to speak more specifically, there are four powerful effects which the Word has on the hearts of men, and each will prove its divine origin. First, it has a heart-searching power; secondly, it exercises a power to convict the conscience; thirdly, it has power to comfort a dejected spirit; and fourthly, it has the power of conversion.

I. POWER TO SEARCH THE HEART

God's Word looks into our secrets and tells us what we do in our most private places and times. It comes where no officer can search – I mean the heart. Christ came to His disciples 'when the doors were shut . . . and stood in the midst' (*John 20:19*). Thus the Word comes into the sinner's heart without asking permission and stands there in the middle of his hidden thoughts. Often the sinner's motives are revealed by the preached Word as if the minister had looked through his window. Because God Himself is the Word, and can come between the joints and marrow, only He can claim this incommunicable attribute: 'I the Lord search the heart' (*Jer. 17:10*).

Now if only God can search the heart, then the Word which does the same thing can come from no other but God Himself. Who can make a key to this lock of the heart but the One who made the lock also? Suppose you locked up some money and no one but you knew the secret place where you hid the key. If you should find the key removed and the box opened, you would soon conclude who had done this. Thus your heart has been exposed and its secret thoughts laid open to you in the Word. God is in it. He made the key. But now let us look at two secrets which the Word reveals.

(a) *What only the person knows*

Christ told the woman of Samaria what even her closest neighbors did not know. And because of His revelation she concluded He was a prophet, a man of God. We too can know that Scripture is the Word of God when it does the same thing today.

(b) *What the person himself does not know*

God is 'greater than our heart, and knoweth all things' (*1 John 3:20*). He knows more about us than we do ourselves. His Word dives to the bottom of the heart and brings up filth which the eye of the conscience never saw before. 'I had not known lust, except the law had said, Thou shalt not covet' (*Rom. 7:7*).

If the Word finds out something which escapes the

examination of a man's own conscience, does this not prove a Deity is in it? The apostle persuades us to know the power of the preached Word to lay open the heart: 'And thus are the secrets of his heart made manifest; and so falling down on his face, he will worship God, and report that God is in you of a truth' (*1 Cor. 14:25*).

II. POWER TO CONVICT THE CONSCIENCE

Conscience is a castle safe from attack unless God carries on the fight. No power can direct it to stoop but that which heaven and earth must obey. He who disarms the strong man must be stronger than he is. And He who masters the conscience must be greater than it is. Now the Word is able to shatter this power of the soul which refuses to bow to anyone except God.

As long as Job was untouched by God's hand he enjoyed his prosperity and assumed that his spiritual wealth matched his material worth. But when the law charged him with sin, it stripped his conscience as naked as his outward condition would later become. For the first time he saw how empty of all holiness he really was. The Word had such power upon him that it laid him, with his fair skin of pharisaical strictness, trembling over the bottomless pit of his own unrighteousness.

What can move like the arm of the Word? When a prisoner preached to Felix the judge he shuddered under its convicting power. Who but God could make those men who were guilty of shedding the blood of Christ and scorned His doctrine so terrified that they cried out in the middle of Peter's sermon, 'Men and brethren, what shall we do?' (*Acts 2:37*). Does not this evidence carry as visible a print of a Deity as the moment when Moses split the rock with a small rod in his hand?

III. POWER TO COMFORT

Conscience is God's prison in the person's own heart, and

no one can release him except the one who put him there. Only a weak king has no place to fasten up offenders but a prison another can break open. But when God puts a sinner in the chains of conviction no one else can set him free. 'A wounded spirit who can bear?' asked Solomon (*Prov. 18:14*).

The pain of a wounded conscience comes from the somber sense of God's wrath for sin. And no one can heal this except the One who can assure the soul of pardoning mercy. This power lies so deep in God's heart that He alone can be the messenger to bring such news. Therefore the Word which does this can come only from Him.

Not only does the Word assure us of God's forgiveness but fills the soul with 'joy unspeakable and full of glory' (*1 Pet. 1:8*). We do not need to wait for further confirmation from heaven; the Spirit that first brought the Word has sealed it in the hearts of innumerable believers.

All saints acknowledge that their comfort and peace are drawn from these wells of salvation. 'In the multitude of my thoughts within me thy comforts delight my soul' (*Ps. 94:19*). But 'fools because of their transgression . . . are afflicted' (*Ps. 107:17*). And what can ease them? There is no relief except through prayers and tears: 'Then they cry unto the Lord in their trouble, and he saveth them out of their distresses' (*verse 19*). And notice the key God uses to open their prison door: 'He sent his word, and healed them' (*verse 20*).

Great and mighty things are done by Scripture. God's Word puts out the very flames of hell. Its light of joy is so pure and powerful in the saint's heart that it quenches carnal joy with its beams, as the sun does fire on the hearth. The Word treads on scorpions and serpents and they have no power to hurt those who believe. It conquers the fear of death. Devils know the Word and run before it, quitting their strongholds and leaving consciences for the Word to enter with sweet comforts and strong consolations. Scripture makes the soul that was bound by despair and thrown into the fiery furnace of God's wrath to walk unsinged. The Word brings heaven down to earth and gives the believing soul as clear a prospect of the heavenly Jerusalem as if he were already walking in its blessed streets. And finally, the Word satisfies the believer with the same feast which glorified saints feed on.

IV. POWER OF CONVERSION

When John's disciples asked whether or not Christ was really the Messiah, He did not tell them directly but let them take their answer from the marvelous works He did. 'Go,' said Jesus, 'and shew John again those things which ye do hear and see: the blind receive their sight, and the lame walk, the lepers are cleansed, and the deaf hear, the dead are raised up, and the poor have the gospel preached to them' (*Matt. 11:4–5*). Man is transformed into the very nature of the gospel and regenerated by the Spirit which breathes through it.

We have saved the Word's converting power until last in this discussion because it is the greatest wonder of them all. When souls are converted, the blind receive their sight. You were darkness but now you are light in the Lord. And the lame walk – the soul's feet are set free to run after God.

The Word makes a new mold for the heart and so changes a person that he is as unlike his former self as a lamb is to a wolf. One is meek and the other fierce – this must be from God. How many men were once prisoners of their lusts, possessed with as many devils as sins and driven by them, who heard one gospel sermon and then sat at Jesus' feet, free and in their right mind? I hope you can say what the apostle said: 'We ourselves also were sometimes foolish, disobedient, deceived, serving divers lusts and pleasures . . . But after that the kindness and love of God our Saviour toward man appeared, . . . he saved us, by the washing of regeneration, and renewing of the Holy Ghost' (*Tit. 3:3–5*).

You who are the letter of Christ, written not with ink but with the Spirit of the living God, can you doubt that the Word which is able to bring you home to God has come from Him? Long may a man sit at the feet of a philosopher without giving up his old lustful heart and finding it replaced with a new and holy one!

But even the best philosopher of them all has sins – such as wrong attitudes – which are acted out behind the closed doors of the most private room of the inner man. Men could never find out about these sins; but the Word treads on the high places of spiritual wickedness and does not leave any stronghold untaken. It chases sin and Satan to their hiding places and digs lusts out of their holes where they have earthed themselves. The heart itself is no safe sanctuary for sin. The Word will take it – as it took Joab from the horns of the altar – in order to slay it.

I cannot give a better example of the Word's converting power than its miraculous conquests when the apostles were first sent out to preach the grace of Christ. Wherever they went the world was up in arms against them and the devil at the head of their troops to resist this ministry of the Word. Yet they turned the world upside down without drawing any other sword but the 'everlasting gospel.' Nothing less than the arm of the Almighty could have achieved such triumphs – sinners renounced idolatries which had deceived them all their lives; and most important of all, sinners received a new Lord, the crucified Jesus. But now let us consider three unique circumstances to emphasize the truth of conversion by God's Word.

(a) *The lowliness of the men who preached conversion*

Christ's followers were as simple in their intellect as they were in worldly sophistication. But this was what confounded their enemies, who recognized that these poor men could personally contribute no more to the success that followed them than the blowing of rams' horns did to the flattening of Jericho's walls or the sounding of Jehoshaphat's musical instruments to the routing of formidable enemies. There is only one explanation – the breath of God caused them to sound the trumpet of the gospel; and His sweet Spirit humbled the hearts of their hearers.

(b) *The nature of the doctrine they commended to the world*

Their message was not only strange and new, but contrary to man's corrupt nature. It contained nothing to please the sinner's lust. Christianity is easily embraced if it is presented in a whore's dress, with its purity adulterated. But the doctrine of Christianity in its own native excellency lays the axe to the root of every sin and defies all who participate in wickedness.

This may make us step aside – as Moses did at the burning bush – to see a doctrine believed and embraced that is pure nonsense to carnal reason, teaching us to be saved by another's righteousness. Indeed reason brings a wide gulf of objection against the doctrine of trusting Christ to deliver from sin and Satan; yet multitudes of believers through the ages have come and offered themselves to it under baptism, even as soldiers seal their enlistment with an oath.

(c) *The meager worldly encouragement the Word gave its disciples*

If the Word had promised favor of kings or places of honor we would not be surprised to see so many turn to Christianity. But the gospel which the disciples preached did not come with a single bribe in its hand; no golden apples were thrown along the path to entice sinners. Christ tells His disciples not to stoop or take up crowns for their heads but a cross for their backs: 'If any man will come after me, let him deny himself, and take up his cross, and follow me' (*Matt. 16:24*). The Savior's words which the apostles taught did not lead to palaces but to prisons. These men did not dream of getting the world's treasure but prepared themselves to part with what they had.

When believers can forget all their earthly interests – property, children, and wives – and welcome the bloodiest deaths their enemies can imagine, a heavenly power must be resting on the altar of the doctrine where they are willing to be sacrificed. The disciples did not aim for fame in history nor to purchase heaven's glory by martyrdom. The doctrine they preached allowed neither but taught them that when they had done their best and suffered the wrath of evil men for God's sake, they were to renounce all glory and consider themselves only servants. All these considerations twisted together make a strong cord to draw you, even with your doubts, into a firm belief of the divine parentage of the Scriptures.

II. Why 'the Word of God' is called 'the Sword of the Spirit'

The first part of the text presented the weapon itself which has been commended to the Christian's use – the Word of God. The second part describes this weapon as the sword of the Spirit. Two important questions, then, deserve the focus of our study: first, why is the Word of God compared to a sword? and secondly, why does this sword carry the Spirit's name?

WHY GOD'S WORD IS COMPARED TO A SWORD

The sword is the weapon continually used by soldiers to

defend themselves and to rout their enemies. Thus it illustrates the most excellent use of God's Word, by which the believer both defends himself and cuts down his enemies.

WHY THIS SWORD IS ATTRIBUTED TO THE SPIRIT

'The weapons of our warfare are not carnal, but mighty' (*2 Cor. 10:4*). Because Satan is a spirit we must fight him with spiritual arms. And the Word is a spiritual sword. Let us now consider three reasons why the written Word is known as the sword of the Spirit.

I. GOD IS THE AUTHOR

His hand alone formed and fashioned this weapon; it did not come from any creature's forge. But 'holy men of God spake as they were moved by the Holy Ghost' (*2 Pet. 1:21*).

II. THE SPIRIT IS THE ONLY TRUE INTERPRETER OF THE WORD

The Scriptures must be read and understood by that Spirit who made them. Only He who designed the lock can help us find the key to open it. 'No prophecy of the scripture is of any private interpretation' (*2 Pet. 1:20*). And why not? Because it did not come from any private spirit. 'For the prophecy came not in old time by the will of man' (*verse 21*). Who knows the mind of God as well as the Spirit?

III. ONLY GOD'S SPIRIT CAN GIVE THE WORD POWER IN THE SOUL

Unless the Holy Spirit lays His weight upon the truths we read and hear, and engraves their image in our minds and hearts, they leave no more impression than a seal set upon a stone would do. It was not the disciples' rowing, but Christ's coming, that calmed the storm and brought them to shore. Our study of the Word cannot convince the mind or satisfy the heart until the Spirit of God comes to enforce it.

'Do ye now believe?' Christ asked His disciples (*John 16:31*). That same question had often knocked at their door but it could never be received until the Spirit stretched out His hand to turn the key!

THE WRITTEN WORD IS THE SWORD BY WHICH CHRISTIANS OVERCOME ENEMIES

The Spirit will do nothing for believers without the Word, and they in turn can do nothing without Him. The Word is the sword and the Spirit of Christ the arm which wields it for the saints. All the great conquests which Christ and His followers achieve in the world are accomplished with this sword. When He comes against His enemies this sword is girded on His thigh: 'Gird thy sword upon thy thigh, O most mighty' (*Ps. 45:3*). His victory over them is also ascribed to it: 'And in thy majesty ride prosperously because of truth' – that is, the Word of God (*verse 4*).

In Revelation 1:16 we find Christ holding 'in his right hand seven stars,' indicating the personal way He cares for His chosen ones. And how does He protect them? 'Out of his mouth went a sharp two-edged sword.' This is the wonderful privilege which the covenant of grace gives the poorest believer. Adam did not have such a benefit in the first covenant; when he fell, a flaming sword kept him out of paradise. But there was no sword to keep him from sinning when he was innocent; he had to be his own lifeguard.

But now the Word of God stands between saints and all danger. This truth will be even more clear if we single out the Christian's chief enemies and show how they must all receive their fatal blow and fall before the Word.

GOD'S WORD OVERCOMES PERSECUTORS

Christians will face persecution as long as the devil has children in the world to inherit their father's kingdom of darkness. And these cruel adversaries are not afraid to trample upon those stars of heaven whose light shows men of the world their hideous sins.

Thus the fires of martyrdom have been kindled and massacres of the saints conceived so that innocent believers would linger in the painful jaws of death long enough to 'feel themselves die.' What ladders does God use to scale such mountains of satanic pride? And where are the weapons for God's people to resist and overcome these monster-like men who openly defy the Lord?

We find mighty weapons in David's tower – the Word of God. Here are shields and bucklers, the sword and darts by which Christians of every age have defended themselves against raging persecutors and triumphed over their strongest powers. God's army overcomes every enemy by one of two ways – conversion or destruction. The Word of God is the sword which effects both – it has two edges.

I. CONVERSION

Sometimes God's elect, through ignorance and prejudice, are joined with the saints' enemies. But the sword of the Spirit is a sacrificing knife to rip open their hearts and empty the hot blood of their sins which turned them away from the church, and to prepare them as an offering acceptable to Him.

Thus the murderers of our blessed Lord heard just one sermon and at a single prick of the sword of the Spirit in Peter's hand began vomiting up the blood of Jesus. They were sick of their sins and immediately threw down their persecuting arms and entered their names in God's roll.

Christ never had a more furious enemy in the world than Paul, whose heart was so inflamed with hatred against the church that he breathed out slaughter like a hot furnace. Yet what arms did Jesus need besides the Word of God to capture the castle of Paul's heart? He preached such a thundering sermon from His heavenly pulpit that it dismounted this proud rider and left him a humble prisoner. Then the Spirit began His work of conversion.

Thus the riotous enemy of the saints was tamed by the terrors of the law and renewed by the gentle mercy of the gospel. Now Paul was more ready to lay down his own life for the defense of the gospel than ever he had been to take away the lives of those who professed it.

II. DESTRUCTION

If God's enemies continue to harden themselves against the truth by refusing to repent, destruction is all they can look forward to. They are like animals 'made to be taken and destroyed' (*2 Pet. 2:12*). And they may know before-hand what will destroy them – the Word of God: 'If any man will hurt them, fire proceedeth out of their mouth, and devoureth their enemies: and if any man will hurt them, he must in this manner be killed' (*Rev. 11:5*). These men freely butchered and burned the saints, yet the Word the saints preached will destroy their enemies. It lives on to avenge the saints on their enemies. God's Word will give them the fatal stroke.

The sword of the Word has a long reach; it is at the breast of every enemy God has. And although they feel secure and powerful, sooner or later God will open one door or another to let destruction come upon them. The prophet expressed the impending ruin of the Philistines by announcing: 'Woe unto the inhabitants of the sea coast, . . . the word of the Lord is against you' (*Zeph. 2:5*); as if he was saying, 'You are a lost people and the whole world cannot save you now, because the Word of the Lord is against you.' Like lightning, the curse of the Word burns to the very root of sin. All seven nations of Canaan fell into the mouth of Israel as ripe fruit falls into the mouth of the one who shakes the tree. The Word of the Lord had gone before them and the fate of their foes was certain.

Too often we look upon governments as the forces that control the earth's affairs, yet these are no more than a fly on the wheel. It is the Word of God which decides all that is done on the world's stage. 'I have this day set thee over the nations and over the kingdoms, to root out, and to pull down, and to destroy, . . . to build, and to plant' (*Jer. 1:10*). The whole earth is God's; and who has power to build on His ground, or pull down, but Himself? In His Word He has already spoken His mind – exactly what He will do to His enemies and for His saints.

GOD'S WORD OVERCOMES HERETICS

The persecutor kills only the body but the seducer poisons the soul. It is better to be slain outright by his sword than to be taken alive, as the apostle puts it, in 'the snare of the devil' (*1 Tim. 3:7*).

When Paul fell into the chains of the persecutor he rejoiced that he had escaped the snare: 'I have fought a good fight, I have finished my course, I have kept the faith: henceforth there is laid up for me a crown of righteousness' (*2 Tim. 4:7–8*). He triumphed as if the battle were over and he had won, when actually he was about to lay his head on the block under the hand of Nero's headsman: 'I am now ready to be offered' (*verse 6*).

How could Paul shout victory when in that desperate position? This made him triumph: he had kept the faith. If he had left it by cowardice or sacrificed it for a false doctrine he would have lost his soul. But because he chose to keep the faith, he parted with his life to receive a better one at God's hands than was taken from him by man's.

Though the sword of war in the hand of a barbarous enemy is heavy judgment, the propagation of error is much worse. This is the sting in the tail of that judgment. Many godly ones might fall by the sword of their enemy but only those who are not among God's sealed ones feel the sting of being poisoned with error. Therefore they alone are said to be 'hurt.' We may be cut off by an enemy's sword and not be hurt; but we cannot drink one drop of their doctrine and still say that.

When Paul warned Timothy to stand in defense against seducers he sent him to the Scripture and told him to shut himself up in it: 'But continue thou in the things which thou hast learned and hast been assured of' (*2 Tim. 3:14*). We can load ourselves down with other arms by stumbling over many authors; but whoever has the sword of the Spirit has all he needs to encounter the fiercest champion of error the devil can train up and command. Persons in error can no more stand before us holding this sword than a child with a wooden dagger could stand against a giant armed with deadly weapons.

All error dreads the light of the Word and is more afraid of being examined by it than a thief dreads a strict judge. To expose the doctrines of heretics is to overcome them. When they come face to face with the Word they must hang their heads like Cain; they are put to shame. This is the only way to test suspicious teachings – if they can walk upon this fiery law unhurt and unreproved, they may safely pass for truths.

Paul tells us that some 'will not endure sound doctrine' (*2 Tim. 4:3*). These want a doctrine which will suit their own preferences, and the Word will not do this. 'He who is his own teacher,' said Bernard, 'is sure to have a fool for a master.' And God spoke the same warning through Solomon: 'The way of a fool is right in his own eyes: but he that hearkeneth unto counsel is wise' (*Prov. 12:15*). He is truly wise who makes the Word of God the man of his counsel.

GOD'S WORD OVERCOMES CORRUPTIONS AND LUSTS

These two enemies are more formidable than the former ones because they are within – lusts which rise up against us and confer with the devil himself to cause trouble with our flesh. The spark of lust is ours but the flame is Satan's, because his temptations are the gusts which spread it. And when fire meets with such strong winds to carry it on wings, where will it take us?

A whole legion of devils can be cast out of the body more quickly than one lust from the soul. Satan likes his lodging better in the heart than in the house. He went willingly out of the Gadarene into the swine because by coming out of his body and contenting himself awhile with a lesser house, he hoped for a way to get fuller possession of the souls of men.

God's Word is the believer's only weapon. Like Goliath's sword, it hews down and cuts off man's stubborn lusts. It can master our lusts when they rise up in their pride. If lust ever rages more at one time than at another, it is when youthful blood is hot and impetuous. The young man's sun is still climbing higher and he assumes it is a long time until night. So it must be a strong arm that brings an impulsive youth off his lusts when his appetite is determined to taste every sensual pleasure that sin affords.

But let the Word of God meet this headstrong young man in all his boldness, with his feast of sensual delights before him, and notice what happens. Whisper a few syllables of gospel in his ear, pricking his conscience with the point of its sword, and watch him take to flight as fast as he can! David has the prescription to cure this young man of his lusts – not just one, but all of them. How can a young man cleanse himself by washing in this Jordan? 'By taking heed thereto according to [God's] word' (*Ps. 119:9*). The Word is more than enough, for it is called 'the rod of [God's] strength' (*Ps. 110:2*).

With this rod in Moses' hand God worked great miracles to plague the Egyptians and save the Israelites. He tamed proud Pharaoh, making him and his people loose their hold on Israel. In fact, they were glad to see them go! By this rod He divided the sea for Israel's escape and drowned the Egyptians. And by this rod of His Word God still touches men's consciences, cleaves the rocks of their hard hearts, divides the waves of their lusts, and brings sinners from under the power of sin and Satan.

Augustine could never get free from his lusts until he heard a voice saying, 'Take, read!' He opened the Bible at Romans chapter 13 and what he read caused a mighty earthquake in his soul. The prison doors of his heart immediately flew open and the chains of lusts which his own efforts could never file off now dropped away. He confessed that he had been a slave to these lusts and tied to them with unbreakable chains of pleasure linked with guilt. He had rolled around in his filthy lusts with as much amusement as if he had been resting on a bed of spices, anointing himself with precious ointments. Yet this one word came with such a commanding power that it tore every one of them out of his heart and turned his love into a defiant hatred of them.

As the Word is the weapon by which God brings sinners out of the devil's power into freedom, He also uses it to defend His saints from temptations which would draw them back into sin. Satan, now thrown out of his kingdom, tries diligently to reclaim the forgiven sinner.

But those kingdoms that we win by the sword we must keep by the sword. David tells how he stood his ground and guarded it against the enemy: 'Concerning the works of men, by the word of thy lips I have kept me from the paths of the destroyer' (*Ps. 17:4*). It is as if he had said, 'Would you like to know how I escape the ungodly things that most men like to do? The answer is God's Word, which keeps me safe from the temptations which carry men off to be slowly destroyed.'

Can we go against sin and Satan with a better weapon than the one Christ used to fight the tempter? Of course He could easily have laid the devil at His feet with one beam shot from His deity if He had wanted to fight that way. Yet He chose to conceal the majesty of His divinity and let Satan come close to Him so that He could conquer him with the Word and demonstrate the value of that sword which He would leave with His followers to fight the same enemy.

God promises to punish the 'leviathan' – Satan – by His 'great and strong sword' (*Isa. 27:1*). This Old Testament passage refers to the whale, the great devourer, who does not fear any fish in the sea except the swordfish, by whom he is often killed. For, receiving one thrust of his sword, the whale hastens to the shore and beats himself against it until he dies.

Thus the devil, the great devourer of souls, sports himself in the sea of this world, as the leviathan does in the ocean – and swallows the majority of mankind with no power to resist. Yet when he confronts an armed saint who knows how to use God's Word he has met his match.

GOD'S WORD OVERCOMES AFFLICTIONS

Another enemy invading the Christian is an army made up of relentless bands of afflictions. Sometimes an outward affliction attacks and then an inward affliction follows closely; at other times a whole host pour their shot together at the believer. This is what happened to Paul when he said 'without were fightings, within were fears' (*2 Cor. 7:5*). He endured an overwhelming struggle of external afflictions and conflicts within his own heart all at once. It is awful when a city burns from the inside while the enemy attacks her outer walls. Yet even the most godly saints sometimes have both the rod on their backs and God's rebukes in their spirit at the same time. 'When thou with rebukes dost correct man for iniquity, thou makest his beauty to consume away like a moth' (*Ps. 39:11*).

Sometimes God corrects His children with outward crosses, but smiles with inward manifestations of grace; He chastises with a fragrant rosemary rod. The one sweetens and softens the other. But at other times He may send a cross with a frown in it. He whips with outward affliction and, as an angry father, tells His child, 'This lash is for that wrong – and that for this one.' And when the Christian comes under the hand of an afflicting God, Satan will not be far away, anxious to throw his salt and vinegar into the believer's wounded spirit to lead him even further into temptation.

God often sends so many troops of various afflictions to a Christian that it is hard for him to endure them all; yet God's Word brings fresh supplies of faith and patience to keep his spirit from being blinded by despair. The Word of God brings the Christian warrior all needful supplies; it is his counselor and comforter both on and off the battlefield.

David plainly affirms that his heart would have died if it had not been for the Word: 'Unless thy law had been my delights, I should then have perished in mine affliction' (*Ps. 119:92*). The Word was his spiritual Abishag which kept his soul warm in seasons of severest testings. All the

[254]

world's enjoyments heaped on him would have left his heart cold if the Word had not lain in his bosom to bring inward peace: 'This is my comfort in my affliction: for thy word hath quickened me' (*verse 50*). A word of promise is more necessary to a soul shivering in affliction than warm clothing is to the body in freezing winter.

When Adam was thrown out of paradise naked into the coldness of the world – with his guilty conscience within and crosses without – God gave him a word of promise to sustain his soul before He taught him to make coats for his body. The Lord knew full well how necessary this word was to keep him from becoming prey a second time to the devil and from being swallowed up by the miseries and sorrows which he had thrown himself into. God would not let him lie open to their assaults even one day, but put the sword of a promise into his hand to defend and comfort his heart during all his troubles.

One believer said he would rather do without food and drink, light, air, and life than be without God's sweet words which opened the dungeon of his troubled soul and brought him into the light of inward joy: 'Come unto me, all ye that labour and are heavy laden, and I will give you rest' (*Matt. 11:28*). Now if a single promise, like an ear of corn rubbed in the palm of faith, and applied by the Spirit of Christ, can afford such a satisfying meal of joy to a hungry soul, what price can we put on the whole field of Scripture, which stands thick with promises as precious as this one!

Beyond the comforting value of God's promises, moreover, we see them as the granary of *all* spiritual provision whereby our Joseph, the dear Lord Jesus, nourishes and preserves His brothers during a time of famine. They are the hive of sweetness where the believing soul stays warm in the winter of affliction and lives abundantly on stored-up mercies. They are the safe havens to which the tempted soul steers his weatherbeaten ship and here stays secure until the heavens clear and the storm is over which the world, sin, and Satan bring upon him.

Even when death itself approaches and the devil has one last skirmish to win or lose the victory for ever, faith in the promise carries the Christian's soul out of the garrison of his body – where he has endured such a hard siege – with colors flying and joy triumphing, to heaven, leaving only his flesh behind in the hands of death. But on his flight the believer takes along an assured hope that his body will be redeemed before much longer at the day of resurrection.

THE PRESUMPTION OF ANY RELIGIOUS SYSTEM IN DISARMING PEOPLE OF THIS SPIRITUAL SWORD

Is the Word the sword of the Spirit with which the Christian can vanquish his enemies? Then we must charge with cruelty any religious system which disarms people of the only weapon which can defend them against enemies which seek their eternal death. It is true, these leaders have a few fig leaves to hide this shameful tradition, making the world believe they are merciful not to want their parishioners to wound themselves with this weapon. They even subpoena Peter's testimony to witness in their defense, for he once said there are 'some things hard to be understood, which they that are unlearned and unstable wrest, as they do also the other scriptures, unto their own destruction' (2 Pet. 3:16).

But did Peter forbid people to read the Word, just because some unstable men twisted the Scripture? Exactly the contrary is true. For in other verses he counsels Christians not to be led away with the error of the wicked but to 'grow in grace, and in the knowledge of our Lord and Saviour Jesus Christ' (*verse 18*).

Light is the chariot which carries the influence of the sun. So the knowledge of Christ brings with it the influences of His grace into the heart. And how did Peter expect people to grow in the knowledge of Christ unless they read Scripture, the only book where it can be found? How wrong for teachers to want the people to learn this knowledge solely from their preaching, and not from the Bible! How can a congregation be sure they are hearing *truth* unless they have Scripture, the only touchstone to try the purity of the doctrine? God Himself directs His Word not to any one honored group – not to a select few – but to *every* man (*Rom. 1:7; 2 Cor. 1:1*). Why are laws made if they cannot be declared? And why was Scripture ever written if not to be read and known of all men? By the same authority with which the apostle wrote his epistles, he commanded them to be read in the church. Did ministers of the early church hide God's Word from the people instead of encouraging them to hide it in their heart?

It is true that some men do wrest Scripture to their own destruction, just as occasionally somebody chokes on a piece of bread if he is not careful when he eats. But must everyone starve for fear of getting choked? Some hurt themselves with sharp weapons; must the whole army then be disarmed, and only a few officers be allowed to wear the sword? If this argument were enough to seal up the Bible, we must deny it to intellectuals as well as to common men; for it is a known fact that the grossest heresies have bred in the finest minds. Whenever proud men insist on being wiser than God, their foolish minds get darker and darker until they become so accustomed to the blackness that they can no longer see His sovereignty.

THE SUFFICIENCY OF SCRIPTURE

Can there be a greater blasphemy to our God than to imply His Word fails to contain everything necessary for salvation? Would God send His people into battle and put such a dull sword into their hand that it could not defend them and cut their way through their enemies' powers to heaven, whither He commands them to march? Why would the Father give arms that are not fit to oppose any enemy that comes, since He knows how to furnish us with the best weapons? Would He give us weak and insufficient weapons for defense and then warn us to use nothing else? He would be sending His unknowing sheep to the slaughter to have their throats cut by the enemy.

God Himself highly commended this sword of Scripture to His people when He told Timothy it was 'able to make thee,' as a Christian, 'wise unto salvation' and, as a 'man of God' or minister of the gospel, 'perfect' and 'thoroughly furnished unto all good works' (2 Tim. 3:15, 17). And does He not forbid us to use any other weapon than that which Scripture supplies? He sees it as renouncing allegiance to Him to go anywhere else for counsel or protection except to His Word. Scripture is sufficient for God's purposes, and is able to furnish every true Christian in the world with wisdom enough to find salvation for his soul.

THE WICKEDNESS OF USING THE SWORD TO DEFEND SIN

The heretic picks up God's Word to justify his corrupt ways, forcing it to lie against itself. Many profane men dare to protect their ungodly life-styles by using the Word – which they know in their minds only – to ward off much-needed reproofs. For instance, if you tell a sensual person his choices are wrong he will counter that Solomon said 'a man hath no better thing under the sun, than to eat, and to drink, and to be merry' (*Eccles. 8:15*). As if God Himself, who directed Solomon's pen, must be a friend of gluttons and drunks too! In truth, 'to eat, and to drink, and to be merry' in this particular context amounts to no more than serving God with gladness in the abundance of the good things He gives us to enjoy.

Man's heart is desperately wicked when he steals such sweet portions of Scripture to disguise his lusts. Verses declaring God's free grace, given to melt sinners' hearts and draw them to Christ, are often used as a wedge to keep a hard heart from bowing before the Savior. God gave examples of holy men's downfalls to encourage us to fear and to stand, and to take hope in His mercy. Yet many choose to wallow like animals in their own wasted lives. They insist that everything will be all right because some very important saints had a dreadful fall and yet had their sins forgiven and their souls saved.

Satan madly uses the few instances of late repentance in Scripture to beg time of the sinner and make him stay just a little longer in the Sodom of his sin. 'The eleventh hour,' he persuades, 'has not come yet. Why repent before you have to?' Because Satan lies so skillfully, the story of the penitent thief who went to heaven from the cross has – against God's will – been used to lead many sinners to a place of execution in another world.

Sinners, is it not enough for you to have your lusts, but must you also cite Scripture for your encouragement, forging God's hand-writing to support your sin? The devil abused Scripture like this when he tried to make Christ agree to his cursed offer in the desert. Why are you walking in the deceiver's steps? By this you make one sin two.

No sin is small, but the least sin amounts to blasphemy

when you commit it on a pretense of Scripture. The devil cannot think of anything he had rather glory in than to wound God's name with His own sword. He coaxes man to sin and then brags that God made him do it. If God ever singles out a man on the face of the earth for His utmost wrath, it will surely be the person who shelters his sin under the wing of holy Scripture.

THANKFULNESS FOR THE WORD

Instead of letting Satan wrest Scripture from us by his wily stratagems, let us be excited to bless God for the sword He has furnished us with out of His grace. If a man possesses a kingdom but has no sword to keep his crown he cannot expect to enjoy it very long. We live in a world where our lives are not safe unless we are fully armed. There is no other way for us to reach heaven without traveling through the enemies' territory. What are the hopes, then, of an unarmed soul ever reaching heaven at last?

When Israel marched out of Egypt toward the promised land, few or none would trust them to travel through their country without rising up in arms against them. And the Christian will find his march to heaven even more dangerous, for Satan has not become more meek than he used to be, nor the wicked world kinder to the people of God. What mercy God showed when He gave us a sword to take us out of danger of them all! This weapon is in your hand right now, Christian, as the rod was in Moses'. Even if an army of devils is behind you and a sea of sins before you, with this sword, wielded by your faith, you can cut your way through them. Truly Scripture is a mercy incomparably greater than the sun in the heavens. In fact, we can more easily spare the sun's warm beams of light than give up God's Word for the church. If the sun were gone we would lose our physical life; but if Scripture were eclipsed our souls would stumble into hell. Specifically, then, we must bless God for three particular mercies concerning His Word.

I. BLESS GOD FOR THE TRANSLATION OF SCRIPTURE

The translated Word is our sword taken out of its scabbard. How much good would it do a Christian who understood only his mother tongue if this sword were sheathed in Hebrew or Greek? Like John, he might weep at the sight of the sealed book which he could not read. So let us bless God who sent not angels but men, equipped by God's anointing on their work, with the ability to roll away the stone from the mouth of the fountain!

Now Christian, when you must stay at home because of afflictions, you have God's Word to keep you company in your loneliness. And though you cannot sit with your brothers and sisters at the Father's communion table, you do not have to miss a nourishing meal. Even if you cannot carve the main servings as well as your minister can, still you are able to pick up comfort as the Holy Spirit helps you reach for it. God has made the most necessary truths hang on the lower limbs of this tree of life, well within the grasp of afflicted Christians who are of an ordinary stature in knowledge.

II. BLESS GOD FOR THE MINISTRY OF THE WORD

Think about the times when persecutors drew bloody swords to keep God's people from coming close to this tree and you will have a clear channel for thanksgiving to flow. And look back to all the years of spiritual ignorance when this cellar of living water was locked up in the original tongues and there was not a key anywhere in the city. Surely we can bless God for bringing His Word all the way to our understanding.

God has opened a public school for His children to learn to use their weapon. If a man thinks he no longer needs to attend the Spirit's school, he takes the surest path to depriving himself of the Spirit's teaching at home. 'Quench not the Spirit. Despise not prophesyings' (*1 Thess. 5:19–20*). The two are joined; if you despise one you lose both. And if you are too proud to learn from a layman you are unworthy to be taught by the minister.

But you Christians who sit at Jesus' feet in your right mind – is it always worth your effort? Are you paid well for this investment of time? If you are a Christian you will keep yourself in God's Word at home, feeding on many sweet refreshments in the secret places where you go to meditate. Has He ever failed to satisfy you?

Surely David knew how to spend his solitary hours beneficially, yet in his solitude he was hungry for the assembly of saints. And he took God's Word with him into each wilderness: 'My soul thirsteth for thee, my flesh longeth for thee in a dry and thirsty land, where no water is' (*Ps. 63:1*). Why, David? How can you call this 'a dry and thirsty land, where no water is'? Can you not just let down your empty pail and draw up water from the well of the Word? It was the sanctuary that David's heart longed for – 'to see thy power and thy glory, so as I have seen thee in the sanctuary' (*verse 2*).

God threatens to bring a famine 'of hearing the words of the Lord' (*Amos 8:11*) – not a famine of reading the Word, but of hearing it. Even though we have the Bible to read at home we are in a famine unless the Word is preached. And we must call it that! 'The word of the Lord was precious in those days; there was no open vision' (*1 Sam. 3:1*). Without public ministry of the Word, even the strongest Christians will in time experience emptiness.

Suppose a town, well laid up with corn, were besieged by the enemy. When each family is forced to grind with private handmills all they need, what difficulties will they soon be in. And so the most mature saints, when they have no more of the Word for their souls to live on than what they grind with their own private meditations, will miss the minister and realize God's mercy in putting him in a place to grind and divide up the Word all week for them.

Now if strong Christians cannot do without the ministry of the Word, what about weaker saints who need the minister to divide the Word? To leave them to do the best they can would be like setting a whole loaf of bread and a sharp knife in a nursery and telling infants to help themselves. Surely most of them would cut their fingers rather than fill their hungry mouths with bread.

III. BLESS GOD FOR THE POWER OF SCRIPTURE IN YOUR SOUL

Has this sword ever cut your heart open to separate a lust from your life? Praise God for the pain He caused during this operation of faith. Solomon says, 'Faithful are the wounds of a friend; but the kisses of an enemy are deceitful' (*Prov. 27:6*). God's wounds cure but sin's kisses kill. Italians say that 'play, wine, and women consume a man laughing.' It is true – as sin kills the sinner laughing, God saves souls bleeding from the wounds which His Word inflicts. Be glad if you have been enabled to get free of the luring lusts which would have kissed you to death and caused you to fall into the hands of an angry God. The blood He draws from you now will save the life of your soul for ever.

There is not another sword like this in all the world that can cure with cutting; not another arm could use this sword to do this much with it, besides the Spirit of God. And no one else can pierce the conscience, wound the spirit, and cut down lusts which grow such strong roots but God Himself. But do not think He does this for everyone who reads the Bible; here is where you should praise His sweet mercy. There were many widows in Israel when God sent His prophet to the woman of Zarephath. So why did He come to her? Was there never a time when a drunkard or liar sat next to you in church at the moment that God armed His Word to strike *you* down and stab *your* heart with conviction? Then cry out your thankfulness for His distinguishing mercy: 'Lord, why have you chosen to show Yourself to *me*?'

THE IMPORTANCE OF STUDYING GOD'S WORD

God has left only one book to the church, and can we refuse to study it? There is an immense treasure in a nearby mine but too often we remain paupers because we will not put on work clothes to dig it out. The rust of our gold and silver, which we earn by much harder work, will rise up in judgment and say: 'You worked overtime for pay-checks that turned into rust and dust; but you walked right over the field of the Word, where an incorruptible treasure was to be found, and yet were too lazy to do anything about it.'

What has happened to the hunger of saints to study the Scripture? In years past they gave all they had – even the blood out of their veins – to purchase a few pages of it. Either these people were fools to pay so high a price for this knowledge or you are greater fools to refuse it when it is so readily obtainable. But so that you will not think I am persuading you to consider a work which is optional, you must understand the indispensable double necessity of knowing Scripture – a necessity of command and a necessity of means.

I. THE COMMAND

'Search the scriptures' (*John 5:39*) – the command could not be any plainer. But even if God had not expressed this duty so explicitly, the very penning of His Word would unmistakably convey His purpose. The passage of a law is enough to make subjects obey it. And it does not do any good for us to plead ignorance; the publication of law carries with it an obligation for us to find out exactly what it means and how it applies to us.

Christ fastens condemnation on the ignorance of men when He Himself has provided knowledge: 'This is the condemnation, that light is come into the world, and men loved darkness' (*John 3:19*). Many people avoid the light because they do not intend to walk in it. Now if ignorance of the Word is condemned where light shines, surely God commands us to open our eyes to take in the knowledge it sheds forth; for a law must be broken before a condemning sentence is pronounced. Because you live within the sound of this gospel, you will be judged by it whether you know it or not.

The Jews once had the Word deposited right into their hands: 'Unto them were committed the oracles of God' (*Rom. 3:2*). These Scriptures were given to them, and now to us, as a dying father leaves his will to his son, not for him to throw it aside among waste papers, but for him to study it so as to perform everything written in it.

God's Word is called 'the faith which was once delivered unto the saints' (*Jude 3*) – delivered to their study and care. If we had lived when Christ was here in the flesh, and He left us one last special thing to take care of, would we not have abandoned everything else to perform the will of our dying Savior? It is for His sake that we keep and transmit this faith from one generation to the next as long as this world lasts.

II. THE MEANS

The Word contains the whole counsel of God for bringing sinners to eternal life. But if you refuse to search the Scripture and sit at the feet of the Spirit – who prepares

His disciples for heaven by this one book – where will you meet another master who has the words of eternal life?

Scripture is the way of God that leads us to Him. In other journeys we might miss some streets and take a few wrong turns, and still arrive at the right place eventually; but there is no other way to God except by His Word. And how can we walk that way if we are ignorant of it? Even if you fail in everything else you do, study the Bible. After all, what is important? You can read volumes of philosophers and still miss God. He has allowed these men, wise in their own wisdom, to shape a religion to themselves so He can prove them wrong. He wants the whole world to learn this lesson in another school, the ministry of the gospel – which comes only from hearing and doing the Word. 'After that in the wisdom of God the world by wisdom knew not God, it pleased God by the foolishness of preaching to save them that believe' (*1 Cor. 1:21*).

Do you want to come to the true knowledge of sin? Scripture alone dissects the whole body of sin and gives us a perfect anatomy lecture on its most secret parts. It discovers the ulcers of our wicked hearts which cause death to thousands who through ignorance of Scripture never know what their disease is. For instance, if lust does not break out in open sores philosophers pronounce the victim a healthy person. The plague of the heart, though an old ailment, has never been diagnosed properly or treated effectively except by this sacred book. But Scripture does more than diagnose sin; it tells us where we got the infection in the first place – from Adam. And which of the world's most recognized thinkers would ever admit such genealogy? Without Scripture, the pitifully brilliant scholar will ultimately lie in the pit of sin and never know who has thrown him in.

The question is, Do you want to get out of this pit? Your own rope is too short to reach and too weak to draw you up. Unless you take hold of the cord of love which God lets down to you, there is no way out. Life and death are before you; I leave you to your choice. Let me warn you, though – if you are determined to reject the Almighty and launch out into eternity without His Word to direct you, then prepare to run aground on the shores of hell. Prepare to harden your heart, if you can, against the endless flames kindled for all those 'that know not God, and that obey not the gospel of our Lord Jesus Christ' (*2 Thess. 1:8*). And know to your terror that in spite of your preferred and professed ignorance, one day you will understand Scripture perfectly. And that understanding will only make the tormenting fire burn hotter.

Hell moves from below to meet you when you are headed toward it. It will stir up the dead for you and its prisoners will close in with taunting reproaches: 'We are heathens but we do not have any reason to blame God for this punishment, though we never heard of such a thing as the gospel. We damned our own souls by rebelling against every tiny ray of light God sent. But you – you rejected God's Word and had to break through every one of His promises to get to this place!'

GOD IS ABLE TO INTERPRET HIS WORD

No one can enter into the knowledge of God's Word unless His Spirit unlocks the door. Even if you were a confirmed genius you would still be like the blind Sodomites around Lot's house, groping but not able to find the way into true saving knowledge. The person with the wrong key is as far from entering the house as the man with no key at all, if not further. At least the one without a key might call out to the person inside, while the other keeps trusting to his false key. The Pharisees, for instance, were full of head knowledge of the Word but stumbled fatally over the whole truth of Christ which both Moses and the prophets taught.

At the same time, many people who these Pharisees considered ignorant began to see the Messiah. Make no mistake – no one is too smart for God to blind; but on the other hand, no one is too blind and ignorant for His Spirit to open his eyes. God moved on the waters at creation and changed a rude mass into the beauty we now enjoy; and His same power can move on your dark soul and enlighten it to look at Him. 'The entrance of thy words giveth light; it giveth understanding unto the simple' (*Ps. 119:130*).

As soon as you enter the Spirit's school you begin to show progress. Then He commands us to encourage those who are in the habit of discouraging themselves: 'Strengthen ye the weak hands, and confirm the feeble knees' (*Isa. 35:3*). Why? 'The eyes of the blind shall be opened, and the ears of the deaf shall be unstopped' (*verse 5*). 'A highway shall be there, and a way, and it shall be called The way of holiness; the unclean shall not pass over it; but it shall be for those: the wayfaring men, though fools, shall not err therein' (*verse 8*).

Now the more aware you are of your weakness, the more fit you are for the Spirit to shape you into the likeness of Christ; for a proud student and a humble teacher will never agree. 'God resisteth the proud, and giveth grace to the humble' (*1 Pet. 5:5*). He has no pleasure in the arrogant person, but He has patience with the humble and diligent. Remember – Jesus never became impatient with His disciples but was willing to teach them the same lesson over and over again, until finally they said, 'Lo, now speakest thou plainly' (*John 16:29*).

III. How to Use the Sword of the Word

You may be saying, 'You have said enough to let us know how necessary this weapon is to defend a Christian in combat with God's enemies, but do not stop now. What good will a sword by our sides do, a Bible in our hands or in our mouths, unless we know how to use it?' I will arrange my answers accordingly and show you how to handle the different kinds of enemies that will surely come against you.

HOW TO USE THE SWORD AGAINST PERSECUTORS

Christians do not have to surrender to this enemy's bloody flag when he breathes out slaughter and launches furious assaults against Christ's flock. We must not let him trample upon our glory by defiling our consciences and causing us to renounce our faith at his commands. But just as this decision is not always easy, neither is it automatic. It involves three distinct acts of the Christian's own will.

I. TAKE A STAND ON SCRIPTURAL PRINCIPLES AND PRACTICES

It is important for a man to know that Christianity is not a problem-free walk. Even the most valiant soldier loses courage when he must fight in a mist and cannot tell the difference between friends and enemies. But it is even more urgent for the Christian to know which principles he suffers for.

First, ignore the indictment of accusations which the persecutor brings against you – it is nothing but a façade for his deeper motives to destroy your peace. It always has been and ever will be Satan's strategy to disfigure the lovely face of truths for which Christians are persecuted so that he can paint on a harsh and heavy make-up of justice and make the world believe that God's children suffer as evil-doers.

Now you will not be able to stand up under these heavy charges unless you are fully persuaded in your own conscience that you are suffering for righteousness' sake. What other people think or say does not matter. One reproof from our own thoughts wounds far more deeply than the reproaches of all the rest of the world put together. The gospel, for example, came to the Thessalonians 'in much assurance'; only then could they open their door 'with joy' to receive it, though affliction and persecutions came along with it (*1 Thess. 1:5–6*).

II. LET SCRIPTURE TEACH YOU MORE FEAR OF GOD
AND LESS FEAR OF MAN

Every man dreads falling into the hands which he fears most. So if God has gained the supremacy over your fear, you will rather run into the hottest flames the persecutor kindles than make Him your enemy.

'Princes have persecuted me without a cause: but my heart standeth in awe of thy word' (*Ps. 119:161*). David weighed man's anger and found God's hand to be heavier. Thus Scripture so clearly reveals the frailty of man's threatening rage compared with God's power that he no longer fears the worst which man can do to him. 'Cease ye from man, whose breath is in his nostrils: for wherein is he to be accounted of?' (*Isa. 2:22*). 'Fear not them which kill the body, but are not able to kill the soul: but rather fear him which is able to destroy both soul and body in hell' (*Matt. 10:28*).

Children are afraid of imaginary monsters that cannot possibly hurt them, but play with fire that will burn them. It is no less childish to be frightened by the threats of an enemy who has no more power than we give him, but to play with a very real hell-fire, into which God can cast a person for ever. What did John Huss lose when his enemies put a fool's cap on his head? They could not take off the helmet of hope he wore underneath it. Or how much nearer did this martyr come to hell because his persecutors committed his soul to the devil? No closer than some of their own cruel crew are to heaven for being sainted in the Pope's calendar.

Melanchthon said Luther and other faithful servants were doubly cursed because the Pope had cursed them. But what does the psalmist say? 'Let them curse, but bless thou' (*Ps. 109:28*). If you have God's good Word, you do not have to fear the world's bad words. A dog can bark all night long but the moon will never change color because of the noise he makes. And the saint need not change his countenance because of his persecutors' abuse.

III. SURRENDER YOUR LUSTS TO THE SWORD OF THE SPIRIT

The person who cannot endure the edge of the Spirit's sword to mortify his lusts will not be free of his flesh for Christ's sake when persecution comes. Can you be willing to lay down your life for Christ and still lodge an enemy in your heart that tries to take away His life at every turn?

Persecutors tempt as well as torture; they promise honor as well as threaten hardship and devouring fire. And if your love of the world has not already been laid down, it is easy to predict what choice you will make when trouble comes – you will embrace the present world and leave Christ outside your chamber door.

But it is entirely possible to die for Christ and yet not be His martyr. Even if you give your body to be burned but harbor a lust, you have offered up an unclean sacrifice. The only Christian who is truly Christ's martyr suffers for Christ as He Himself suffered: 'If, when ye do well, and suffer for it, ye take it patiently, this is acceptable with God. For even hereunto were ye called: because Christ also suffered for us, leaving us an example, that ye should follow his steps: . . . who, when he was reviled, reviled not again; when he suffered, he threatened not' (*1 Pet. 2:20–21, 23*).

It is hard work to keep the spirit cool in the fire, free of anger and revenge toward those who so unmercifully opened the door to the furnace. But because of grace, the person who can stay calm in this situation becomes a glorious overcomer. Flesh and blood would prompt an ordinary man to call down fire from heaven, rather than mercy and forgiveness on his persecutors.

He who forgives wins the battle, for the enemy's blows only bruise his flesh; but wounds of love pierce the soul and conscience. Saul confessed that David, whom he had so furiously persecuted, was the better man: 'Thou art more righteous than I' (*1 Sam. 24:17*).

When two opposites are in contest the winner is the one which preserves its own nature and turns the other into the likeness of itself. Fire, for instance, transfuses its heat into water and forces the liquid to yield to it. Thus when a sufferer loves his enemy his forgiveness may not change the latter's hatred to love but it does turn the enemy's conscience against himself and forces him to justify the person whom he wrongfully persecutes.

IV. STRENGTHEN YOUR FAITH IN GOD'S PROMISES
    CONCERNING PERSECUTION

Faith is the saints' victory over the world. Thus when Saul drove David from the court into a cave, the psalmist's faith triumphed and he sang as pleasantly as a meadowlark: 'My heart is fixed, O God, my heart is fixed: I will sing and give praise' (*Ps. 57:7*). Saul apparently was winning but his heart could not sing to David's tune. A thousand fears pressed in upon him, while David himself lived free of worry as his enemies tried to take his life.

Faith in the promise, then, like the widow's oil, not only cancels your indebtedness to worldly cares but also affords you plenty of substance for unspeakable joy. Even so, we should not ignore the sorrows which try to rob Christians of this joy in times of suffering.

SCRIPTURAL PROMISES FOR BELIEVERS' SORROWS

I. PERSONAL PROBLEMS

God's promises are many, and fitted exactly to each particular personal problem; but it requires diligent study to gather them all in. God has purposely scattered these promises throughout His Word rather than clustered them in one place, so we must search every corner of Scripture – and then rejoice at what we have found!

Do not be deceived by the peace of the church you see at present. In the summer time a pharmacist gathers ingredients for vital medication which he may not need until winter. How soon great persecution may come against the church, we cannot tell. Sometimes winter breaks in upon us before we expect it; and who is the man in the most trouble then? Surely the one who received the Word in prosperous seasons but made no provision for bad weather.

What are you afraid of? Is it terror of prison or torture by fire? Then be comforted. If your strength is too weak to carry you through them you will never be called to walk that way. God's written guarantee says He 'will not suffer you to be tempted above that ye are able' (*1 Cor. 10:13*).

When God's people left Egypt He led them over the longer of two routes. And what was His reason? Their weakness! 'For God said, Lest peradventure the people repent when they see war, and they return to Egypt'

(*Exod. 13:17*). He knew they were not ready for war, and He did not try them with it until they were strong enough to bear it.

On the other hand, if God does call you into fiery trials, His promise will take all responsibility out of your hands: 'When they deliver you up, take no thought' – that is, do not worry – 'how or what ye shall speak: for it shall be given you in that same hour what ye shall speak' (*Matt. 10:19*). It is 'the Spirit of your Father which speaketh in you' (*verse 20*).

There is no mouth which God cannot make eloquent, no back so weak that He cannot strengthen it. And He has promised to go with you wherever your enemies might force you to go; neither fire nor flood can take you away from the Father. These promises make such a soft pillow for the saints' heads that many have experienced marvelous rest when roughly handled by cruel enemies. One persecuted Christian, for example, dated his letter 'from the delectable orchard his prison'; another signed herself 'Your loving friend, as merry as one bound for heaven.' People like these have been far from pitying themselves in their sufferings; in fact, their main sorrow has been that they could not express more thankfulness for them. And where did their supernatural strength and joy come from? The Holy Spirit applied God's promises to them in their time of distress!

II. BELIEVERS' TROUBLES FOR CHRIST'S CAUSE

The ark may shake but it cannot fall; the ship of the church may be tossed but it cannot sink, for Christ is in it and will awaken in plenty of time to keep it safe. Therefore we have no reason to disturb Him with screams of unbelief when storms beat angrily against the church. In times like these our faith is in more danger of sinking than Christ and His church. God's promises hold them securely out of the reach of both men and devils.

Our source of security is an 'everlasting gospel' (*Rev. 14:6*). Heaven and earth will pass away, but not one word of this gospel will perish. 'The word of the Lord endureth for ever' (*1 Pet. 1:25*). It will live to walk over all its enemies' graves, indeed to see the funeral of the whole world when, at the great day of the Lord, it must be everlastingly buried in its own ruins. And as for the church, it is built on a rock: 'The gates of hell shall not prevail against it' (*Matt. 16:18*). It has been thrown into churning seas many times but never drowned; seldom out of the fire but never consumed; sometimes swallowed up by reason but, like Jonah in the fish's belly, thrown right back up again, too heavy for the strongest persecutor to digest.

The faith of this gospel has buoyed up martyrs to their graves with joy even when they swam to it in their own blood, because they knew the church must ultimately win. They left others behind to fight for the victory on earth while they themselves left the battle to triumph in heaven.

Some of these martyrs prophesied that the truths which their enemies tried to bury with them would be gloriously resurrected. John Huss, for instance, both comforted himself and confounded his persecutors by saying that even though they 'burned the goose' – referring to himself – 'a swan' would come to fill the air with sweet songs of deliverance. And Luther subsequently satisfied this prophecy, planting the truth of Christ's grace everywhere he went.

Hiltenius, another German, endured countless miseries in a stinking prison until finally he died for rubbing the monks' sores too hard. But before his earthly life ended he had named the exact year – 1516 – when another ruler would ruin the monks' kingdom. He further prophesied that they would not be able to resist this man's power or fasten a chain on him. And once again, it was a prophecy to be fulfilled in Luther, who continuously evaded the strangling hands of his enemies, despite their thirsting for his blood.

HOW TO USE THE SWORD AGAINST HERETICS

Since it is much more dangerous to part with God's truth than with our lives, heretics or seducers are more to be feared than persecutors. It is far worse to have our souls damned by God than to have our bodies killed by man. If the martyrs had dreaded death more than heresy they could never have walked willingly into persecutors' flames.

The sword of the Spirit in another person's hand will not defend you. If you are to lift it up in victory against this dangerous enemy you must first give yourself completely to the leading of the Spirit in God's Word. The outward expression of Scripture is only the shell, and the meaning is the pearl which you must search for until you find it. 'He that hath an ear, let him hear what the Spirit saith unto the churches' (Rev. 2:7). God spoke an imperative here, not a suggestion – we must listen to what the Spirit says in the Word as we hear or read it, for the one who has an ear for the Spirit will not have an ear for the seducer.

To help you seek and find meaning in the Word, look through these six windows that follow.

1. DO NOT COME TO THE WORD WITH AN UNHOLY
   HEART

The only way you will ever know the mind of God in His Word is for the Spirit to reveal it to you. But the holy God will not take a filthy hand and lead you into understanding: 'None of the wicked shall understand' (Dan. 12:10).

The angel who took Lot's daughters into the house struck the Sodomites with blindness so that they would grope for the door but not find it – and so are those who come to Scripture with unclean hearts. The wicked have the Word of God but only the holy have 'the mind of Christ' (*1 Cor. 2:16*).

Paul persuades Christians with these words: 'Be not conformed to this world: but be ye transformed by the renewing of your mind, that ye may prove what is that good, and acceptable, and perfect, will of God' (*Rom. 12:2*). If we invite truth to be our guest then we must prepare a holy heart for it to live in. When David begged for understanding of the Word he made his desire for holiness the basis of the request: 'Teach me, O Lord, the way of thy statutes; and I shall keep it unto the end. Give me understanding, and I shall keep thy law; yea, I shall observe it with my whole heart' (*Ps. 119:33–34*).

II. DO NOT MAKE YOUR OWN REASON THE RULE BY
WHICH TO MEASURE SCRIPTURAL TRUTHS

The Word reveals things to us that eye has not seen nor ear heard. They are far above reason and have never 'entered into the heart of man' (*1 Cor. 2:9*). In fact the whole array of gospel truths speaks in a foreign tongue to reason; it does not make any sense at all unless faith is there to interpret.

Scripture is like the Red Sea. The Israelites passed through its waters safely but the Egyptians drowned because they lacked faith as their guide. The humble believer passes through the deep mysteries of the Word without plunging into any dangerous mistakes; but the sons of pride, who leave faith and take reason for their navigator, are drowned in damnable errors.

The most treacherous of all errors fathered upon the Scriptures have sprung from this womb. This was the Sadducees' rationale for denying the resurrection of the dead – it seemed impossible to their reason that our bodies, after becoming dust, should stand up in life again. And because their intellect laughed at this truth the Savior indicted them with a serious charge: 'Ye do err, not knowing the scriptures, nor the power of God' (*Matt. 22:29*).

III. DO NOT PREJUDGE THE TEACHINGS OF THE WORD

Too many people read Scripture not to be informed but to be confirmed in ideas of their own. They choose opinions, as Samson selected his wife, because they please them – and then try to make Scripture agree with them. Thus the Jews first adopted idols into their worship and then asked God what to do next. When people like this will not see truth even though it lies squarely in front of their eyes, God gives them up to a foolish heart: 'I the Lord will answer him that cometh according to the multitude of his idols; that I may take the house of Israel in their own heart' (*Ezek. 14:4–5*). And foolish men are desperately trapped in their own hearts by being ensnared in the errors which their own minds weave.

IV. PRAY TO GOD TO UNLOCK THE MYSTERIES OF SCRIPTURE

There is a God in heaven who reveals the secrets of His Word at the throne of grace. 'From the first day,' said the angel, 'that thou didst set thine heart to understand, and to chasten thyself before thy God, thy words were heard, and I am come for thy words' (*Dan. 10:12*). It was the heavenly messenger's only errand to open the Scripture more fully to Daniel. This holy man had gained some knowledge by studying the Word, and this set him to pray, and his prayer was what brought an angel down from heaven to give him more light. Praying rather than plodding brings understanding of the Word.

'When he, the Spirit of truth, is come, he will guide you

into all truth' (*John 16:13*). And the Spirit is the fruit of Christ's intercession: 'I will pray the Father, and he shall give you another Comforter' (*John 14:16*). Now there must be a oneness of our prayers with His intercession – while Jesus our High Priest offers incense within the holy place, we must pray outside for the same thing that He intercedes for within. Let us consider, then, how to pray more fervently for the Holy Spirit to lead us into all truth.

(a) *Experience the dread of Scriptures condemning false doctrine*

It is one facet of Satan's masterplot to reduce drastically the price of error in the thoughts of men. Many think they will not have to pay as much for an error in judgment as for a sin in action. Some even believe that just *any* religion will save a person; and these are the people who become careless and passive in dealing with conviction of sin.

Sins which men think they will never have to pay for rank consistently high in popularity. But woe to those stockbrokers of Satan's market who tempt men to sin by setting cheaper rates than God's Word has done! Once the dread of sin has been worn off the conscience, men leap on it as boldly as the frogs in the fable leaped onto the crocodile which they thought was a log, so still in the river. Fear makes the body more susceptible to infection, it is true, but a clean fear of God protects the soul from the more serious infection of sin.

Now that you realize the danger of drinking in the poison of unsound doctrine, let your mind reflect on a few Scriptures that show its damning nature. In Galatians 5:19-20, heresy is called a work 'of the flesh' and one of those sins which shut the doers of them out of heaven. 'They which do such things shall not inherit the kingdom

[279]

of God' (*verse 21*). Such heresies are called 'doctrines of devils' (*1 Tim. 4:1*). And if they come from him, where can they lead but the way back to hell?

Anything that is against the fundamental principles of the gospel is outside the love and favor of God. In fact, the man who 'abideth not in the doctrine of Christ, hath not God' (*2 John 9*). If this were the only Scripture against heresy, it would be enough to stab the heretic through his loins and make the knees of every seducer knock together.

'There shall be false teachers among you, who privily shall bring in damnable heresies, even denying the Lord that bought them, and bring upon themselves swift destruction' (*2 Pet. 2:1*). So if a person wants to get a head start to hell and arrive there before other sinners, all he has to do is open his sails to the wind of heretical doctrine. His voyage to hell will be short and sure – a 'swift destruction.'

God has left three fearful examples in His Word as patterns and pledges of His divine vengeance on this kind of sinner: in His thrusting out the apostate angels from heaven to hell, in the drowning of the old world, and in the condemnation of Sodom and Gomorrah by raining hell, as it were, out of heaven upon them. But Scripture not only warns and condemns the heretic; it also encourages the saint who wants to walk in the purity of God's truth.

  (b) *Strengthen your faith in the Scriptures, which assure us that no sincere saint will be left to fall finally into soul-damning error*

Christ as Prophet, King, and High Priest preserves us from damnable principles as well as damnable practices. It would not help if He kept us safe from one enemy but left us open to another. But Christ has made sure that His hedge comes all the way around His beloved ones.

Solomon says, 'The mouth of strange women is a deep pit: he that is abhorred of the Lord shall fall therein'

(*Prov. 22:14*). And so is the mouth of a seducer who comes with strange doctrines and whorish opinions. If we look closely we see this pit as Satan's design to trap the saint, for if possible he would 'deceive the very elect' (*Matt. 24:24*). His greatest ambition is to defile the children whom God has washed in the blood of Christ.

But God's intention is to punish the hypocrites and false teachers who would never embrace Christ and His truth. He leaves these people in the pit as prey to corrupt doctrines. 'They received not the love of the truth, that they might be saved. And for this cause God shall send them strong delusion, that they should believe a lie: that they all might be damned who believed not the truth, but had pleasure in unrighteousness' (*2 Thess. 2:10–12*).

These men, like deer running across an open field, are shot down; but the ones inside the pasture fence are safe. It is the outer court that is left to be trampled underfoot. And although God gives up hypocrites to be deceived by false teachers, He speaks comfort to the elect. The same decree which appointed them to salvation provided also for them to embrace truth. And it still serves to show them how to find it. 'But we are bound to give thanks alway to God for you, brethren beloved of the Lord, because God hath from the beginning chosen you to salvation through sanctification of the Spirit and belief of the truth' (*2 Thess. 2:13*). And if God has determined to possess our mind by the power of His truth, and to take our heart by the sufficiency of His sanctifying grace, He will keep both out of Satan's hand.

So go and plead His promises for your preservation. These promises, taken by faith to the throne of grace, will be your best antidote in these times of general infection of Satan's temptations. Do not ever be afraid of going too fast when the promise commands you to go and prosper. The mercy is yours before you ask it; God only wants you to lay claim to it through prayer. And He has written many sweet promises to strengthen your faith and your fervency in prayer: 'And a stranger will they not follow, but will flee from him: for they know not the voice of strangers' (*John 10:5*); 'My Father, which gave them me, is greater than all; and no man is able to pluck them out of my Father's hand' (*John 10:29*); 'For there must be also heresies among you, that they which are approved may be made manifest among you' (*1 Cor. 11:19*); 'That ye may be . . . the sons of God, without rebuke, in the midst of a crooked and perverse nation, among whom ye shine as lights in the world' (*Phil. 2:15*); 'They went out from us, but they were not of us; for if they had been of us, they would no doubt have continued with us: but they went out, that they might be made manifest that they were not all of us' (*1 John 2:19*).

V. COMPARE SCRIPTURE WITH SCRIPTURE

False doctrines, like false witnesses, do not agree among themselves. We might well name them 'Legion,' for they are many. But truth is whole, and one Scripture harmonizes sweetly with another. Thus, although God used many different men to pen His sacred Word, He made sure they all had but one mouth: 'As he spake by the mouth of his holy prophets, which have been since the world began' (*Luke 1:70*). The best way, therefore, to know the mind of God in a particular text is to compare it to another text. The stonecutter uses a diamond to cut another diamond. Like crystal glasses set next to each other, each Scripture casts a peculiar light on the others.

Now in comparing Scripture with Scripture, be careful to interpret the obscure by the more plain, not the clear by the dark. Error creeps into the most shaded places and takes sanctuary there: 'Some things hard to be understood, which they that are . . . unstable wrest' (*2 Pet. 3:16*). But no wonder people stumble in these dark places, when they have turned their backs on the light of plainer passages offering to lead them safely through.

'Whosoever is born of God sinneth not; but he that is begotten of God keepeth himself, and that wicked one toucheth him not' (*1 John 5:18*). Some people run away with this text and rationalize that they can claim perfection and freedom from all sin in this life; but a multitude of plain Scriptures like 1 John 1:8 testify against such a conclusion: 'If we say that we have no sin, we deceive ourselves, and the truth is not in us.' So we must understand, then, that it is in a limited sense that one 'born of God sinneth not.' In other words, he does not sin *finally*, as the carnal man does. And notice a similar example: '. . . that wicked one toucheth him not' (*1 John 5:18*) – this means Satan cannot transfuse his nature into the Christian, as fire touching wood or iron changes and absorbs it into its own nature.

Blessed be God, who has chosen to tame our pride by inserting a few knotty passages in His Word! Yet the necessary saving truths are easy enough even for the person of the poorest ability to understand. There is enough in the plain places of Scripture to keep the weak from starving and in the obscure passages to exalt them above contempt of the strongest.

VI. CONSULT WITH FAITHFUL AUTHORITIES IN THE
     CHURCH

While we must not pin our faith on the preacher's sleeve, we can 'seek the law at his mouth: for he is the messenger of the Lord of hosts' (*Mal. 2:7*). God guides His children for their safety so they will not fall into the hands of false teachers, but will 'go . . . forth by the footsteps of the flock, and feed . . . beside the shepherds' tents' (*Song of Sol. 1:8*).

Satan's strategy works all too well – he sends away the shepherd that he may soon catch the sheep. When has there ever been a time when people have had less respect for ministers of the gospel? Their hearts are so fickle that they follow after strangers, who corrupt their hearers with unsound doctrines, rather than God's chosen shepherds, who must give account to Him.

If you really want to be protected from error, use the sword of the Word which is in your hand. Pray for God to pour divine revelation into your pastor's public ministry – and then wait for Him to do it. If he preaches a message that stirs up doubt, go privately and ask him about it. If he is living up to his name – a faithful minister of the gospel – he will welcome your interest. But make sure you go to learn and build him up, not to ensnare and tear down.

Our Savior was more than willing to satisfy His disciples' questions concerning the doctrine He had preached publicly; when they were alone He opened the Scriptures to them more fully. Yet when they came with questions of little value He replied with reproof: 'If I will that he tarry till I come, what is that to thee? follow thou me' (*John 21:22*). Jesus did not hesitate to change the subject from a trivial question and point Peter toward a necessary ministry.

HOW TO USE THE SWORD AGAINST LUSTS

A third enemy we must fight consists of an army of lusts, captained by Satan and commanded to occupy our heart. If you believe you have a soul that can be lost or saved, how can you refuse to battle this cursed combination of devils and lusts? The Romans fought some nations for honor and glory; but they struggled with Carthage for their very life. In our combat against sin and Satan, both honor and existence are at stake – and this makes it the most noble war of all.

Spiritual warfare is noble because it is just. It is all too true that most people join in political and military battles without ever knowing why. But there is no doubt about the cause of holy war – it is against the only enemy God has who claims the right to rule His world. For this reason God calls all mankind – some by the voice of natural conscience and others by the loud shout of His Word – to join with Him 'against the mighty' (*Judg. 5:23*). He does this not because He needs our help but because He prefers to reward obedience rather than to punish rebellion.

This noble warfare is not only just, but it is also hard. Our stubborn enemy is strong and will do everything he can to try our skill to the limit. Cowards can never hope to overcome him. When sin loses ground it is only an inch at a time, and what it holds it will not easily let go.

Spiritual warfare against lust is enlistment for a lifetime career. If you have a daring, adventurous spirit, here is what you have been looking for. Fighting with men is child's play compared to repelling demons and lusts: 'He that is slow to anger is better than the mighty; and he that ruleth his spirit than he that taketh a city' (*Prov. 16:32*).

It is sad that many of the world's finest swordsmen who courageously risked their lives for freedom have died slaves to sin. Hannibal, for example, enjoyed victory in foreign expeditions but was defeated in his own country. So too many of the bravest heroes, who have had great victories abroad, have been miserably beaten and trampled upon by their own personal corruptions.

But do not be afraid because your enemies are mighty and many; your victory will be so much the greater. And do not worry, either, when you see Caesars stripped of

[285]

their insignias and forced to die in chains of lust. Remember, it is only the unbelieving world – without spiritual arms and abandoned by God – that is left to become the prey of Satan.

You have a God on your side who hands you the consecrated sword of His Word for your defense – a weapon whose cutting edge Satan has already felt. He trembles every time faith draws it. He who created this monster provides a sword adequate to conquer him. And now I want to teach you how to overcome the enemy by effectively using this one weapon in four specific ways.

I. COLLECT SCRIPTURAL PICTURES OF SIN'S DEFORMITY

By placing many views and puzzle pieces of Scripture together you will see the true picture – sketched by a skillful hand – of this enticing lady whose beauty Satan wishes you to embrace. The naive man sins because he believes Satan is offering him a good thing and takes it into his life as Jacob took a wife to his bed before he had studied her face. In the morning he found Leah instead of the beautiful Rachel. Thus when the sinner's conscience wakes up it is too late – in bitter disappointment he sees a hell instead of a paradise. Now Christian, so that you will not be cheated of your heaven, focus on God's Word and recognize the ugly shape of sin without her deceiving masks.

(a) *The birth of sin*.

Who is its father? The holy God disowns it. The sun can produce darkness sooner than the Father of lights can be the author of sin. 'Every good gift and every perfect gift' comes from Him (*James 1:17*). An earthly father loves his own child no matter what the son or daughter looks like; and how much more does our heavenly Father cherish what is His! He looked back on each day's work of creation and was pleased with everything He had fathered – 'it was very good' (*Gen. 1:31*).

But God's Word says exactly what he thinks of sin: 'These six things doth the Lord hate: yea, seven are an abomination unto him: a proud look, a lying tongue, and hands that shed innocent blood, an heart that deviseth wicked imaginations, feet that be swift in running to mischief, a false witness that speaketh lies, and he that soweth discord among brethren' (*Prov. 6:16–18*). God has expressed such hatred of sin that horrible plagues and judgments thunder from the fiery mouth of His most holy law against every form of it.

God throws sin on the devil's doorstep to find its father. 'Ye are of your father the devil, and the lusts of your father ye will do.' And further, 'When he speaketh a lie, he speaketh of his own: for he is a liar, and the father of it' (*John 8:44*). Sin is a bastard which calls Satan both his father and mother. For Satan conceived sin in the womb of his own free will – and as soon as it was born, he threw it down for mankind to feed. How pitiful that whereas God made man to serve and enjoy Him, he chooses to carry around his evil master's child in his arms.

(b) *The names of sin*

God has never made a mistake. If something is sweet he will not say it is bitter; if it is good, He will not call it evil. Do not ever expect to find honey in the pot if God has written 'poison' on its lid. Instead, let us say of sin what Abigail said about her husband – whatever Scripture names it, so it is.

But Satan trains sinners to cover sin with approved nicknames – superstition may become devotion; covetousness, thrift; pride, self-respect; carelessness, freedom; and idle words, cleverness. Sinners have to do this of course; a horsemeat sandwich would make them sick immediately if they knew what it was. Persecutors used to wrap Christians in animal skins so that wild beasts would

[287]

devour them quickly; and Satan sharpens our appetites by sins garnished with appealing temptations which conscience cannot easily recognize and reject.

Are you willing to be cheated like that? Your hand will be just as much charred if you reach out and take a log out of a fire after a hateful fool promises the fire will not burn you. Hear what the God of truth names sin – vomit of dogs; venom of serpents; stench of rotten tombs and sewers; sores, gangrene, and plague. Because even the horrors of hell struggle to find a name repulsive enough for it, the worst expression of its putrid nature is to call it by its own name – 'sinful sin' (*Rom. 7:13*). Now what should we do to the thing that the great God loathes so much, and loads with names of dishonor? We must pursue it with the sword He left us until we have executed the judgment written upon it – utter destruction!

(c) *The nature of sin*

God's Word defines it: 'Sin is the transgression of the law' (*1 John 3:4*). In these few words is enough weight to press the sinning soul into hell for eternity, or to press sin itself to death in the saint's heart, if he seriously considers three truths concerning the nature of sin.

(i) *Whose law is broken?* It is not the law of some petty prince who nervously takes vengeance on every violator who threatens his reputation. Sin is deicide. It is Satan's purpose to destroy the very life of God through sin. God's glory is so interwoven in His being that He cannot outlive the loss of it. Of course God's life and glory are high above the sinner's short arm, but that is no credit to him – his sin deliberately takes accurate aim to dishonor God, though it cannot carry the ammunition all the way to its holy mark.

(ii) *What kind of law is it?* It is not a cruel edict, written in the blood of the people, as laws of some dictators are. But God's law is good, and those who keep it find life.

There is no flaw or unnecessary part in it. 'What iniquity,' asks God, 'have your fathers found in me, that they are gone far from me?' (*Jer. 2:5*). Thus He stoops to reason with sinners, asking why they have forsaken His righteousness. But they have no more reason than has a bull in a fat sweet pasture to break the fence and escape into a barren desert or dirty lane where only starvation waits for him.

(iii) *Who moves sinners to break the law?* When a father's worst enemy hands a weapon to his rebellious son and persuades him to wound his parent, this heaps an added weight of sorrow to the pain. But this is exactly what you do, Christian, every time you break God's law. Does it not make you tremble when He points His finger at your sin and says, 'My precious child, *this* is the enemy that tries to take away My glory and My life, when by grace you owe everything to Me and should be prepared to die for the upholding of My name.' When the love of God fully flames in our hearts we can spit fire in the face of any devil that tempts us to sin against Him.

(d) *The properties of sin*

God's Word exposes the three following characteristics of sin: it defiles, it disturbs, and it damns.

(i) *Sin has a defiling property*. Sin is called 'filthiness of the flesh and spirit' because it damages both (*2 Cor. 7:1*). 'The whole world lieth in wickedness' as an animal revels in its waste, or as a carcass rots in its own slime (*1 John 5:19*). It is leprosy which infects both man and the house he lives in. God sent the flood in Noah's time to wash away that filthy generation from the face of the earth. But because this pest-house of the world is not even yet cleared away, a more thorough purging by fire has been reserved for it on the last day.

Have you ever thought about the beauty of man before

his life was marred by the ravages of sin? Or what glory shone upon the whole creation before sin polluted it by its toxic breath? This poison has so spread its malignancy throughout the soul and body of man and filtered into the whole face of visible creation that it will never be returned to its first loveliness until, like a battered piece of metal, it is melted down and refined by universal fire.

The ermine, it is said, prefers to die rather than defile her beautiful skin in the dirt. And Christian, after it cost Christ His precious blood to purchase His Spirit for your cleansing, will you wallow around in sin's murky cesspools? Ezekiel so dreaded eating defiled bread prepared from dung that he cried out, 'Ah Lord God! behold, my soul hath not been polluted' (*Ezek. 4:14*). Is filthy lust any cleaner for you to eat, Christian, after you have sat at Christ's communion table and tasted of His goodness and purity? We should be ready to cry out with the prophet, 'Oh, Lord God! my soul has not been' – or, do not *let* it be – 'polluted with this abominable thing!'

(ii) *Sin has a disturbing property.* Sin shatters the peace of the soul and of the whole world too; it causes confusion and creates war wherever it comes. Scripture warns that an army of evils encamps at its heels to settle down where it lodges: 'If thou doest not well, sin lieth at the door' (*Gen. 4:7*). And then God puts His hand to the warrant and sentences the sinner to the anguish of a self-torturing conscience.

Who can describe the convulsions that disturb the rest of the sinning soul? 'There is no peace, saith my God, to the wicked' (*Isa. 57:21*). The cries of condemned sinners evidence the disturbing quality inherent in sins of their own choosing: 'There is no soundness in my flesh because of thine anger; neither is there any rest in my bones because of my sin' (*Ps. 38:3*). 'My punishment is greater than I can bear' (*Gen. 4:13*). Perhaps the prime example, though, is Judas. When he was not able to stand up under his guilt he ran from it, and hanged himself, throwing himself into hell to ease the torment of his sin.

Just as sin disturbs the inward peace of a soul, it also interrupts outward peace in the world. What else but sin has caused such confusion? 'From whence come wars and fightings among you? come they not hence, even of your lusts that war in your members?' (*James 4:1*). Delilah betrayed her own husband into the enemies' hands. And Absalom tried to take the life of his dear father. Sin is the subtle whisperer which separates friends and families and even the sweet communion of saints.

Sin has such a kindle-fire nature that its deadly sparks fly not only from one neighbor's house to another but from nation to nation. All the water in the seas cannot quench the wars sin ignites between kingdoms; instead, it makes men who live at one end of the world thirst for the blood and possessions of those who live at the other end. The earth has become an arena where there is little else but fighting and killing. Is this the guest you welcome within your heart?

(iii) *Sin has a damning property.* If sin's damage could be confined to this world, it would be bad enough. Considering our short stay here, we might take a measure of comfort in the fact that it would soon be over. But to be bothered by it here and then damned to eternal torment in the next world – it is unbearable! 'Depart from me, ye cursed, into everlasting fire' (*Matt. 25:41*) – these words should make us seriously question whether or not the desires of sin are worth such a weighty return on our investment.

Sinners already know the best of their pleasures but this does not mean they can know the worst of their

[291]

punishment. It is so severe that it loses most of its emphasis by being translated into our language. What is the fire and brimstone we see and fear now, compared to that burning infernal lake? Little more than painted fire in a mural and blazing logs on the hearth! Earthly fire can be kindled by a tiny puff of wind and quenched by a few drops of water; but 'the breath of the Lord, like a stream of brimstone, doth kindle the fires of hell' (*Isa. 30:33*). And where can man find buckets to put out what God kindles?

Breathing fresh air is a healthy thing to do, and inhaling the smell of this sulfureous pit might prove equally as wholesome in the long run. If more people had descended into hell like this while they were still on earth, their souls might not have dropped into flames when their bodies fell into the grave. Christian, walk often in the Scriptures which describe the damned in hell, and their exquisite torments there. This is the house of mourning, and visiting it through serious meditation is a sovereign means to make us lay the warning to heart. Why would you risk going there, when an indescribable heavenly mansion waits in exchange for your faith and repentance?

II. FIND SCRIPTURAL ANSWERS TO SATAN'S FALSE REASONING

The devil cleverly displays sin under an attractive gloss of reason, urging the soul to accept his best offer. Thus when sin comes to us in a Goliath-like stride it will not be Saul's armour but the 'smooth stones out of the brook' (*1 Sam. 17:40*) – not reasoning but infallible Scripture-arguments –which can protect you and prostrate your enemy.

Where can we possibly find an answer to repel Satan's sophisticated deception? Only by choosing to be 'mighty in the Scriptures,' like Apollos, can we stop the devil's mouth and choke his bullets with a word seasonably interposed between us and temptation. And I see at least three ways to do this.

(a) *Satan minimizes the danger of sin*

Sometimes the father of lies begets sin by using only the slightest insinuation: 'Will this small sin really hurt that much? One mole does not mar the beauty of the face; and one sin cannot spoil the beauty of your soul. If I asked you to welcome several dirty temptations you might well suspect a problem; but why are you so afraid of people seeing this one spot on your robe? Even the finest jewels have flaws – and the holiest saint has faults too.' On and on his loose strings of deception weave a net so tightly about the Christian that only the truth of God's Word can break the snare.

(i) *No sin remains single.* It is not possible to embrace one sin and stay free of others. 'Whosoever shall keep the whole law, and yet offend in one point, he is guilty of all' (*James 2:10*). Even as the entire body suffers from a single wound, all the laws are linked to the tender heart of a holy Father. 'God spake all these words' (*Exod. 20:1*) – they are ten words but just one law.

As a further consequence, the person who violates his conscience in one sin cannot plead conscience against another. 'How then can I do this great wickedness, and sin against God?' asked Joseph in the attractive, available face of temptation (*Gen. 39:9*). Surely his answer would have been the same if his mistress had asked him to lie for her, as when she enticed him to lie with her. The ninth commandment would have bound him as well as the seventh. Thus the apostle urges us not to 'give place to the devil' (*Eph. 4:27*), implying that by yielding in one we lose our ground. And what we lose he gains. When one tiny tack has entered the wood, the skilled workman can drive in a finishing nail the next time.

Thus if you say yes to one sin God will give you over to others. The Gentiles gave themselves to idolatry and God gave them up to beastly lusts. When Judas began to play the thief, I doubt that he ever intended to turn traitor. But treason was his punishment for thievery. He indulged in a secret sin and God gave him up to a more open and hideous one.

(ii) *You cannot serve sin and God at the same time*. 'His servants ye are to whom ye obey' (*Rom. 6:16*). You are Satan's servant if you defend his kingdom in one small castle against God your Ruler. And it will not do any good to say you did not intend to sin. For example, your aim might have been to make profit, not to take Satan's side against God. But even though covetousness has not been your intention, the end of your committed sin will be the charge against you on the last day.

Ahab sold himself 'to work evil in the sight of the Lord' (*1 Kings 21:20*). Now we do not read that he made any direct covenant with the devil, but what he did amounted to the same thing. He knew that if he sinned his soul would eventually have to pay for it. But even knowing the price, he still wanted his lust. So the plain meaning of this invisible but valid covenant is that he sold his soul to enjoy sin.

'No man can serve two masters . . . Ye cannot serve God and mammon [covetousness]' (*Matt. 6:24*). One body could have two souls more easily than a soul two masters. Because a soul has only one love, two cannot have the supremacy of it. A certain man once bragged that he had one soul for God and another for sin. But if he had one soul in hell he would not ever find the other one in heaven.

And do not be deceived – one sin will send you to hell as fast as a thousand. 'Neither fornicators, nor idolaters, nor adulterers, nor effeminate, nor abusers of themselves with mankind, nor thieves, nor covetous, nor drunkards, nor revilers, nor extortioners, shall inherit the kingdom of God' (*I Cor. 6:9–10*). Scripture excludes not only the man who is *all* these, but he who is *any* of them. All men must die, but they do not die of the same disease. And it is just as certain that all unrepentant sinners will be damned – one for a particular sin and another for something else. But they will all meet in the same flaming hell.

(b) *Satan tempts with secret sins*

Saul was ashamed to approach Endor in his princely robe because he had told the world of his hatred of witchcraft, making it punishable by death. But he was not afraid to go to a witch in disguise. What weight it added, then, to the devil's sinister motive when he tempted Christ in the wilderness, soliciting Him to a secret acknowledging of him, just between the two of them. But how much greater was Christ's glory in His victory that day! He won the battle over Satan's assaults with the sword of the Word – and it is time for us to take up His weapon to fight the same enemy. This defense takes on several specific expressions.

(i) *Scripture says God knows every secret sin.* 'Thou hast set our iniquities before thee, our secret sins in the light of thy countenance' (*Ps. 90:8*). God sees secret sins as plainly as we see things at high noon. And He not only knows them but sets them up as targets for His arrows of vengeance.

'The eyes of the Lord are in every place, beholding the evil and the good' (*Prov. 15:3*). He sees when you close your closet door to pray in secret and rewards your sincerity; but He also sees when that door is closed for you to sin in secret – and He will not fail to reward your hypocrisy. It would be better for the whole world to see what you are doing rather than God, for the wrong has been sinned against Him; and a righteous judge cannot let any sin go unpunished.

(ii) *The Word informs your conscience of sin.* You cannot sin fast enough for your conscience not to follow along, witness what you do, and write it down for the court record. The pen of the conscience is sharp and cuts deep into the soul of the sinner, for no torment compares with that of an accusing conscience: 'The spirit of a man will sustain his infirmity; but a wounded spirit who can bear?' (*Prov. 18:14*). Like Regulus in the barrel of nails, whichever way his restlessness turns him he is pricked and wounded. After you have read the Scripture's accounts of what happened to Cain, Saul, and Judas, surely you will be afraid to sin when conscience is standing by the records.

(iii) *The Word usually brings open shame to secret sin.* One of God's names is 'a revealer of secrets' (*Dan. 2:47*). He never forgets to 'bring to light' these 'hidden things of darkness' (*1 Cor. 4:5*) – sins forged in a darker shop than others. God's omniscience is called in question by the man guilty of secret sins, for he behaves as if He were the God of the day but not of the night, as if no one would ever know except his partners in sin. So in order to put fear into the hearts of men God digs these foxes out of their holes and exposes their sin to the world. Ananias and Sapphira committed a secret sin. What happened as a result of it? 'Great fear came upon all the church, and upon as many as heard these things' (*Acts 5:11*).

Men have long considered it an art to hide sin from the world. Gehazi, for instance, played his part cunningly enough and boldly lied to his master's face, never dreaming that Elisha was aware of his sin all the time.

What a strange providence brought his wickedness to light! Gehazi had stolen clothing by lying to Naaman, so God matched his gain with the garment of leprosy – attire not to cover his shame but to show it to everyone. And this garment, unlike the Syrian's suits, refused to wear out but lasted all his life; it was even worn by his children after him.

No matter how hard a person tries to save himself from the shame of sin, his deception paves the most direct path to exposure. Uriah's death, for example, was only an expedient to save David's reputation should his affair with Bathsheba become street talk. But his plot became a catalyst, for ours is a God who is tender in regard to His own reputation: 'Thou didst it secretly: but I will do this thing before all Israel, and before the sun' (*2 Sam.* *12:12*). How sick David became of his sin then. He was more willing to acknowledge it then than he had been to hide it at the time. Wherever Psalm 51 is read to God's people, they are still reminded of David's repentance.

(c) *Satan tempts by others' examples*

An example is an artificial argument, but it carries great force when the person in favor of sin is thought to be high-minded. Sometimes so many people endorse sin that they carry the weak-headed with them as dead fish swim with the stream. These want a crowd to join them in sin and thus take away its shame. Where everyone goes naked, few people blush.

And if the person who occupies a place of respect and wisdom sins, Satan's hand delights to stir and spread the testimony of the wrong. He sees to it that the news spreads far and wide, influencing others to follow this example. When this happens, open the Word and be confident it will draw you away from the temptation with at least two specific warnings.

(i) *Scripture commands us to bring examples to the Word for testing*. Are people constantly quoting opinions? 'To the law and to the testimony: if they speak not according to this word, it is because there is no light in them' (*Isa. 8:20*). We follow a man for the light in his lamp; but if that goes out we leave him. And this Scripture certifies that the person cannot have any light at all unless his opinion has been established in the Word. If he does not know where he is going, how can we know where he might lead us?

Examples are precepts, not warrants. 'Thou shalt not follow a multitude to do evil' (*Exod. 23:2*). An example will not bring acquittal just because you have a precedent to sin. Adam tried that when he said the woman gave him the fruit; yet it did not excuse him from paying the price with her. She was the leader in sin but punishment followed them both. Would you be willing to eat poison if another person offered to taste it first? Does his example make it any less deadly?

(ii) *The Word warns that dedicated saints can sin*. When Paul called others after him, he counseled them to keep their eyes open to see whether he followed Christ: 'Be ye followers of me, even as I also am of Christ' (*1 Cor. 11:1*). The holy life of the best saint on earth is only an imperfect translation of the perfect standard in God's holy Word and therefore must be tried by it. It is the character of sincerity to look to the way rather than to the crowd: 'The highway of the upright is to depart from evil' (*Prov. 16:17*).

I am showing you how this sword of the Word – like the one in the cherubim's hand – may be turned every way to protect the Christian from venturing into sin, no matter how right it seems. But let us continue.

III. HIDE THE WORD IN YOUR HEART

This was David's refuge: 'Thy word have I hid in mine heart, that I might not sin against thee' (*Ps. 119:11*). It was not the Bible in his hand, the Word on his tongue or in his mind, but the hidden Word in his heart, which kept him from sin. It is not the meat on the table, but in the stomach, which nourishes. Scripture uses the word 'heart' for every part of the soul, yet its main twofold meaning is the conscience and the affections.

(a) *Scripture often uses the 'heart' to mean the conscience*
'If our heart condemn us, God is greater than our heart, and knoweth all things' (*1 John 3:20*). When our conscience condemns us justly, it is sad, but God knows more about us than we know about ourselves, and can charge us with many sins which our conscience has overlooked. Hide God's Word in your conscience – let it have a throne room there to keep you in holy fear.

(i) *The Word is stamped with divine authority*. Sin is the traitor's dagger which stabs at God Himself. Sometimes assassins, intending to murder a prince, have been so awed by a few beams of majesty shot from his eyes that they abandon their plot. How much more, then, does the dread of the great God's majesty, darted from His Word into the conscience, keep him from practicing treason against his Maker? 'Princes have persecuted me without a cause: but my heart standeth in awe of thy word' (*Ps. 119:161*), the psalmist's meaning being, 'I had rather face their wrath for my holiness than make Your Word my enemy because of my sin.'

(ii) *The Word will judge you at the last day*. 'God shall judge the secrets of men . . . according to my gospel' (*Rom. 2:16*). The book of your conscience will be opened and compared with the Word, and then Christ the Judge will sentence you to life or death. But you do not have to wait until that last day to find out what your sentence will be. If you cannot stand before the Word now when it is opened by a minister and applied to your conscience, what will you do when it is opened by God's Son? Now your conscience may from the Word condemn you, but not finally; if you repent and have faith, this private court may reverse the sentence of death and justify you before God. But on the day of judgment His decision will be irreversible.

If judgment goes against you then, you are lost for ever. No reversing of the sentence or even a brief stay of execution can be expected. When the Word leaves the Judge's mouth, the sinner will be delivered immediately into the tormentor's hands. Can you still welcome lust, now that you have glimpsed the everlasting chains in which God's Word dooms the sinner to burn?

(b) *Scripture frequently uses the 'heart' to mean the will and affections*

When God said, 'My son, give me thine heart,' He was asking for love (*Prov. 23:26*). Thus if you hide the Word in your heart you have a rare antidote against the poison of sin; for the chains of love are stronger than the chains of fear. Herod's love of Herodias was more powerful than his fear of John. He had some hold of his conscience which bound his hands for a while. But a woman had his affections, and the heart can unbind the hands. His love for her made him shake off his respect for John – and at last drench his hands in his blood.

The man who is a prisoner of the command – and bound to good behavior only by chains of fear in the conscience – may somehow have these removed, and then he will shake off his obedience too. But one who loves the Word, and the purity of its precepts, cannot turn traitor. When this person sins, he makes a wound as deep in his own heart as in the law, and trembles at displeasing God: 'I love thy testimonies. My flesh trembleth for fear of thee' (*Ps. 119:119–20*). Blessed fear is the daughter of love! But now to kindle your heart with love for God's Word, think on these two truths – the Word is your most faithful monitor and the sweetest comforter you have in all the world.

(i) *The Word is your most faithful monitor*. Scripture tells you plainly what your faults are and will not let sin lie upon you; instead it points to the enemy who stalks the very life of the soul. It discovers every design which Satan and your own lusts plot against you. This protection is one thing which made David love the Scriptures so dearly: 'Moreover by them is thy servant warned' (*Ps. 19:11*).

Besides warning of danger, God's Word shows you how to escape it. King Ahasuerus heaped favor upon Mordecai because he had once saved his life from attempted treason. How much more, then, should you reverence Scripture, which has saved you from the enemy many times? David was so thankful for Abigail's wisdom that he rewarded her kindness by taking her to be his wife. God's Word offers such necessary intimate counsel every day that you should not be ashamed to fall in love with it without reserve.

(ii) *The Word is your sweetest comforter*. When you are bogged down in the quicksand of guilt, how puny this world's pleasures and treasures become! A person can no more comfort you than a man on the seashore who sees his friend drowning but cannot get out to him. The Word alone can walk on these waters and come to the soul's relief.

You may be as desperate as those sailors who were about to die, when the Word stands up – like Paul – and brings relief: 'You should have listened to me in the first place and not have untied your obedience from God's fair haven of safety. But repent of your sin and turn to God in Christ Jesus; then you will not lose your life.'

There is forgiveness with the Lord Jesus. No matter what the trouble, this truth brings comfort to saints. You know how a cool spring is welcomed in a parched desert.

And when you recall what sweet refreshment you have had from God's wells of salvation you will cry out with David: 'I will never forget thy precepts: for with them thou hast quickened me' (*Ps. 119:93*). It is no surprise that Satan tries to stop your well of comfort; but it is more than tragic if he can persuade you to do it yourself.

IV. PLEAD THE PROMISE AGAINST SIN AT THE THRONE OF GRACE

As the veins in the body have arteries to bring them life, so precepts in the Word have promises to encourage and empower Christians to perform their vows to God. Is there a command to play? There is also a promise: 'Likewise the Spirit also helpeth our infirmities: for we know not what we should pray for as we ought: but the Spirit itself maketh intercession for us with groanings which cannot be uttered' (*Rom. 8:26*). Does God ask for your heart? The promise says, 'A new heart also will I give you' (*Ezek. 36:26*). Does He require us to crucify the flesh? Not without His promise: 'Sin shall not have dominion over you' (*Rom. 6:14*). But to make this promise serve your need, you must humbly and boldly press it believingly at the throne of grace. What the precept commands, the prayer of faith begs and receives. In other words, first conquer heaven and then you do not need to fear overcoming hell.

Do not forget – you are warring at God's expense, not your own. David was a military man who could handle one enemy as well as another, but he dared not promise himself success until he had heard from God: 'Order my steps in thy word: and let not any iniquity have dominion over me' (*Ps. 119:133*). But if you have decided to steal victory in your own strength, expect an overthrow. It will be a mercy, for defeat will bring humility with it but victory will only increase your pride in your own strength.

Jehoshaphat chose the right battle plan by admitting to God that he did not know what to do. Almost a million men were available at his call, yet he cried out for God's help as if he were alone: 'We have no might against this great company that cometh against us; neither know we what to do: but our eyes are upon thee' (*2 Chron. 20:12*). If Caesar had headed such an army, he probably would have known what to do. But the humble man knew better; a host of mighty warriors count for nothing unless God is with them.

HOW TO USE THE SWORD OF THE WORD AGAINST AFFLICTIONS

The Christian stands open to storms and tempests from every direction. He is not like a fenced house that is so sheltered by hills or woods that the wind comes against only one side. Like the strange wind which 'smote the four corners' of Job's house, the Christian's afflictions leave no corner unassaulted. Often he is attacked by financial stresses, physical problems, and a wounded spirit all at once. And when so many seas of sorrows meet, it is not easy for the Christian's heart to stand unbroken by their violent waves.

My task here is to counsel the weak Christian how to use this sword of the Word for defense and comfort in any affliction which may attack him. I cannot confine this teaching to detailed examples but instead must give the following general rules which will apply in all instances.

I. KNOW YOUR RIGHT TO GOD'S PROMISES

This is the hinge on which the dispute between you and Satan will move in the day of trouble. How pathetic for a Christian to stand at the door of promise in the darkest night of affliction and be afraid to turn the knob! That is the very time when we should go right in and find shelter as a child runs into his father's arms. 'Come, my people, enter thou into thy chambers, and shut thy doors about thee: hide thyself as it were for a little moment, until the indignation be overpast' (*Isa. 26:20*).

When a believer holds the title to a promise proved true to his conscience from Scripture, he will not easily be wrangled out of his comfort. Job produced his evidence for heaven: 'Till I die I will not remove mine integrity from me' (*Job 27:5*). Satan did his best to make Job tear it up, but his title was clear and Job knew it. Even when God seemed to disown him he testified before heaven and hell that he refused to let Satan dispute him out of his right: 'Thou knowest that I am not wicked' (*Job 10:7*). This assurance was what kept the chariot of his hope on its wheels along the rough road of suffering; it shook and rattled but nothing could overturn it.

But how can we be sure that we really do have this right to God's promises? The answer will come after we have asked three more questions.

(a) *Are you united to Christ by faith?*
The promises are not a pig-pen for swine to root in; they are Christ's sheep-walk for His flock to feed in. 'If ye be Christ's, then are ye Abraham's seed, and heirs according to the promise' (*Gal. 3:29*). The promise is the joining which takes place only when the Person of Christ is taken in marriage. And faith is the grace by which the soul gives consent to accept Christ as the gospel offers Him, a union called the receiving of Christ.

Surely you have heard the same question concerning Jesus which was asked Rebekah about her taking Isaac as her husband: 'Wilt thou go with this man?' (*Gen. 24:58*). From God's Word you have seen Christ in His glory and the vows that are requisite before you can go with Him as His beloved into the bedchamber of His heart.

(i) *Send away all other lovers.* Christ will not endure a competitor or partner with Him in your affections. First the names of Baalim were taken out of Israel's mouth and then God married Himself to her.

(ii) *Embrace His law as well as His love.* Christ will not be your Husband without being your Lord.

(iii) *Take Him for better and for worse – with His cross as well as with with His crown.* He wants you to be ready to suffer with Him as well as to reign with Him. Is Christ so precious that He inflames you with an insatiable desire for Him? Can you freely put away all your lusts and carnal pleasures to be taken into His embrace? In a word, are you so in love with Him that you can neither live without Him, nor enjoy yourself except when you enjoy Him? Your heart is wounded with the arrows which His love and loveliness have sent into it, and He alone has the ointment which can heal it.

Let Him ask anything and you will do it. If He tells you to leave your father's house you will go after Him, even if it is to the other end of the world. If He tells you to be poor in the world for His sake, you are glad to beg with Him rather than reign without Him, or die for Him rather than live without Him.

Come forth now, you blessed of the Lord, and put on the bracelets of the promises; they are love tokens which I am delivering from Christ's hand and in His Name to promise marriage to you. He has betrothed you to Himself. So put away your unbelieving fears; it is not in the Savior's heart to reject your love after you have given it to Him.

(b) *What effect does the promise have on your soul?*
The person who has a right to the promise is transformed by that promise. Satan shed his venomous seed into Eve's heart by a promise: 'Ye shall not surely die' (*Gen. 3:4*);

and she conceived with sin and was changed into the wicked nature of the devil himself. So how much more, then, does God use gospel promises – called 'incorruptible seed' – to beget His own likeness in the hearts of His elect? They are 'exceeding great and precious promises: that by these ye might be partakers of the divine nature' (*2 Pet. 1:4*).

When the Holy Spirit applies the promises to a Christian, their virtue purifies the heart as well as calms the conscience. 'Now you are clean,' said Christ to His disciples, 'through the word which I have spoken unto you' (*John 15:3*). Have God's promises sanctified you?

Some try to use promises as a protection for sin rather than an argument against it. Because sin works all kinds of evil in the carnal mind, many people sin even more freely because they do have the promise – like sideshow quacks who swallow poison because they are confident of their antidote. Which way does the promise work in your heart? Unless the seal of the promise impresses God's image, it does you no good. And if it does not produce holiness it will not bring joy either. But if you can find the likeness of God within, this assures His love and favor to you.

(c) *How does your heart respond to God's command?*
It is not hard to smile at the promise, but does your countenance change to a frown when you remember that you need to obey God's command? As if He were some stern master who breaks the backs of His servants with heavy burdens! If only you could ignore a command now and then without giving up your claim to His promise! If the shoe fits, you have wandered away from the comforting lap of God's promises.

On the other hand, you may not be offended by the command at all, but by your own failure to obey perfectly. Although your foot may slip often, yet your heart cleaves to God's commands and will not let you lie where you fell, but you get up again, resolved to watch your step better. Know this, then, that your sincere respect for the commandment is ample evidence of your title to the promise.

When David confessed his love for God's law he did not question his title to the promise: 'I hate vain thoughts: but thy law do I love' (*Ps. 119:113*). He did not say that he was free *from* vain thoughts but that he hated them. And he did not say that he *fully* kept the law but that he loved it, even though he sometimes failed in total obedience. Because of the testimony which conscience gave concerning David's love for the law, his faith settled the question once for all: 'Thou art my hiding place and my shield: I hope in thy word' (*Ps. 119:114*).

II. GATHER AND SORT THE PROMISES INTO THEIR
 DIFFERENT APPLICATIONS

God does allow his children to walk through many different trials and temptations: 'Many are the afflictions of the righteous' (*Ps. 34:19*). But Scripture is a garden which grows a comforting promise for every sorrow. And a wise Christian gathers one of every kind and writes them down as a doctor keeps records of tried and proven prescriptions for diseases.

The best time, of course, to get ready is before the need comes. The fisherman mends his nets in the harbor before he puts out to sea. And the shrewd saint, in health, stores up promises for sickness and, in peace, for future crises. It is too late for a man to run home for his overcoat when he is already caught in the downpour: 'A prudent man foreseeth the evil, and hideth himself: but the simple pass on, and are punished' (*Prov. 22:3*).

III. TAKE IN THE FULL BREADTH OF GOD'S PROMISES

Christ has children of all sizes in His family – some little

Christians and some tall ones. And His covenant of grace takes in the weak as well as the strong: 'if children, then heirs' (*Rom. 8:17*). Scripture does not specify 'mature' or 'bright' members, but 'children.' Even if you are still in the cradle spiritually, the promise is your portion as well as Peter and Paul's: 'All the promises of God in him are yea, and in him Amen' (*2 Cor. 1:20*).

We distort God's promises every time we try to make them fit one saint but not another. They belong to the whole body of Christ. 'He that believeth on the Son hath everlasting life' (*John 3:36*). Does Scripture say Christ provides eternal life only for believers who never doubt? No, He tells us to receive the weak in faith because He Himself will never turn them away.

IV. MEDITATE ON GOD'S PROMISES

It is human nature to think more about our problem than about God's promise. But the promise holds in itself the very power to restore the spirit. When a crying baby takes the nourishment he needs, he falls asleep at the breast. And the Christian stops complaining about his affliction as soon as he takes hold of the promise and enjoys its sweetness in his heart: 'In the multitude of my thoughts within me thy comforts delight my soul' (*Ps. 94:19*).

When a swarm of bees dislodge themselves they are in confusion, flying everywhere without any order, until they enter their hive again. Then the uproar ends and they get back to work as peaceably as before. And it is just as true in the Christian's heart. God, in the promise, is the soul's hive. Let the saint turn his thoughts loose and they riot in fear of the affliction or temptation facing him. But as soon as he collects his straying thoughts and settles his heart on the promise, he recovers his comfort. The Spirit of God sounds a call to retreat from troubled thoughts and come into Him, where there is a quietness and confidence: 'Rest in the Lord, and wait patiently for him' (*Ps. 37:7*).

The Christian's heart is the color which his most abiding thoughts have stained it. Transient ideas, even if they are comfortably neutral, do not have much effect on the soul either for joy or for sorrow. Poison cannot kill and food will not nourish unless they stay in the body. But when a person's thoughts lie steeped in sorrow every day and bitter fears soak into his heart he will probably become bowed down with 'a spirit of infirmity' (*Luke 13:11*). Then he is unable to raise his heart from the thought of his cross to meditate on the refreshing promise of resurrection.

On the other hand, God's promise works effectually when the believer wakes with it and walks with it bound to his heart. No pain he feels nor danger he fears can ever take the promise away from him; but as Samson went on his way eating the honeycomb, the Christian feeds on the sweetness of the promise. Here is the saint who can spend the hours of his affliction singing while others are sighing, and praising while they are murmuring.

Be careful, Christian, to *practice* this duty of meditation. Do not just chat with the promise in passing; but like Abraham with the angels, invite it to stay in your tent door so you can enjoy it fully. This is how saints through the centuries have caused their faith to triumph over the most tragic troubles. 'My beloved,' said the woman, 'shall lie all night betwixt my breasts' (*Song of Sol. 1:13*). In other words, when sorrows press in to cause fear she will spend the night meditating on the love and loveliness of Jesus, on His beauty and tenderness toward her. When you have learned to do this you will not feel the severity of affliction any more than you feel the bitter cold of a north wind as you wait by a glowing fireplace.

[309]

Julius Palmer, an English martyr, shared how he lifted his thoughts above suffering by heavenly meditation on God's 'great and precious promises': 'To them that have their mind fettered to the body as a thief's foot is to a pair of stocks, it is hard to die. But if any be able to separate his soul from his body, then by the help of God's Spirit, it is no more mastery for such a one than to drink this cup.' A soul in heaven feels none of the struggles we have here on earth. Here, Christian, is the most glorious picture to be seen this side of heaven!

When a Christian can stand upon this Pisgah of meditation and look with the eye of faith across the panorama of the great and precious things which the faithful God has prepared for him, it is easy to turn from the world's love and rejection alike. But it is hard for some of us to get up there because we get tired after only a few steps of climbing toward God's mount. That is when we must call out, 'Lead me to the rock that is higher than I.' Who will lift us up to this holy hill of meditation, higher than the surging waves that dash upon us from beneath? God's Spirit will pick us up in His everlasting arms and take us there.

If only we could put to better purpose the hours we lavish on inferior pleasures and worldly entertainment, the Spirit would surely meet us on the way. But if we take in just one lust to play with – even for a moment of leisure – Satan will be right there to help. Instead, we must spread our sails and let the Holy Spirit fill them with His own breath.

If we are willing priests and lay the wood and sacrifice in order, fire from heaven will come down upon it. But be careful to provide fuel – gather your truth for meditation from the promises and put your thoughts to work on it. Then the Spirit of God will kindle your affections: 'While

I was musing,' David said, 'the fire burned: then spake I with my tongue' (*Ps. 39:3*).

V. PLEAD THE PROMISES AT THE THRONE OF GRACE

We load the gun in vain if we never pull the trigger. Meditation fills the heart with heavenly matter but prayer gives the discharge which pours it forth on God and moves Him to give desired relief to the Christian.

Although it is some comfort to a penniless person to read through his statements and find that someone owes him money, this alone will not supply bread for his next meal. Payment of the debt does this. By meditating on God's promise we can see there is deliverance from affliction; but it will not happen until the prayer of faith calls in the debt: 'Your heart shall live that seek God' (*Ps. 69:32*). 'They looked unto him, and were lightened' (*Ps. 34:5*). If you hold back prayer God holds back His mercy.

Meditation is like the lawyer's preparation of the case in order to plead it at the bar. After you have viewed the promise, and disposed your heart to the riches of it, then get you to the throne of grace and spread it before the Lord, as David did: 'Remember the word unto thy servant, upon which thou hast caused me to hope' (*Ps. 119:49*).

VI. ACT IN FAITH THAT GOD WILL PERFORM HIS
    PROMISES

The Christian's safety lies in the faithfulness and strength of God who is the Promiser; but that security will not be a reality unless faith believes He will perform His Word. Reason may try to discourage you, and if your faith is weak or based only on sense and reason, you will draw little satisfaction from the promise. Thus all Christians are out of danger concerning the worst that could happen – eternal separation from God in hell – but too many of them are bound by fears because their faith acts weakly on a mighty God.

[311]

'Why are ye fearful, O ye of little faith?' (*Matt. 8:26*). Here you can see the leak where the water came in to sink their spirits – they had 'little faith.' It is not what God is but what we understand Him to be which makes the difference between victory and defeat. If a man thinks his house will collapse in a tornado – though it is as unmovable as a rock – that person will probably stay outside in the storm rather than trust the shelter to cover him.

To keep up the energy of faith on the power of God's promises, we must somehow dismiss sense and reason from being our counselors. Why did Abraham not stagger in his faith, although the promise was such a strange one? 'He considered not his own body now dead' (*Rom. 4:19*). And, on the other hand, what made Zacharias falter? He listened to the counsel of reason and assumed he was too old to have a child. Like Thomas, we are prone to carry our faith on the tips of our fingers – to trust God no further than our hand of sense can reach. God is very often on His way to perform a promise and deliver joyful news to His afflicted servants, when sense and reason close the case as being hopeless.

Sense, *reason*, and *faith* are separate entities and must not be confused with one another. We know some things by sense but cannot understand them by reason. Other realities we accept by reason that cannot be discerned by sense, like the size of the sun exceeding the circumference of the earth – when judging by the eye it can be covered with one's hat. And other things too, which eclipse both sense and reason, are clear to faith. By faith Paul knew, even when all hope was gone, that not a man would die in the sea storm: 'Be of good cheer: for I believe God, that it shall be even as it was told me' (*Acts 27:25*).

When the angel struck Peter and told him, 'Arise up quickly . . . and follow me,' Peter did not let reason respond to the impossibility of the whole thing (*Acts 12:7–*

8). How could he walk quickly in chains? Or what about the iron gate which fastened him in? He did not give common sense a turn to ask questions but stood up and saw his chains fall off – just before the gate opened itself to them! So do not say it is impossible to bear your affliction or escape a certain temptation. Give faith free reign to follow the promise and God will loose the knots which reason and sense have tied.

Luther admonished Christians everywhere to crucify the word 'how' – how can you possibly go through this trouble or withstand such a hard attack? Has not God been faithful to give plenty of promises to stand between you and all harm? 'I will never leave thee, nor forsake thee' (*Heb. 13:5*); and 'My grace is sufficient for thee' (*2 Cor. 12:9*). Nothing 'shall be able to separate us from the love of God, which is in Christ Jesus our Lord' (*Rom. 8:39*).

A Jewish proverb says, 'Shut the windows and the house will be light.' In other words, do not judge by sense but by faith in an omnipotent God. It is the highest act of faith to believe those things which seem most improbable; and it is the highest act of love, for Christ's sake, to endure patiently the things which bring pain. In these we are denying carnal reasoning which disputes against God's power and strength.

EXHORTATION TO MINISTERS CONCERNING THE SWORD OF THE WORD

God has placed the sword of the Word in the hands of His ministers in an especial manner. He 'hath committed unto us the word of reconciliation' (*2 Cor. 5:19*). You are *ambassadors* from the great God to take eternal peace from the gospel to sinners, His *under-workmen* to build up His temple in men's hearts by laying every stone by the line and rule of the Word. And you are *stewards* to give His family their portions from His storehouse in due season. In a word, you are God's *shepherds* to lead and feed His flock in the pastures which are His.

If the terms of peace are not concluded, the ambassador is sure to be called in to account for the fault; if the house is poorly built, the negligent workman must take the blame. And what will the steward do if the family starves? Should the sheep wander or die because of neglect, the shepherd must pay for the loss. Now to help you fulfill this public trust let me point to two specific duties – one to be performed in your study and the other in your pulpit.

I. KNOW THE WORD OF GOD

The same diligent way a layman searches Scripture may constitute negligence in a minister's study. No farmer uses his various tools more constantly than the minister who digs in this mine of Scripture. It is not enough for him to read a chapter now and then as his secular schedule permits – or steal an hour from his academic studies to look into the Bible in passing. Instead, it must be his regular exercise, his plodding work. Everything else must stoop to this requirement.

Even if you know all that Plato, Aristotle, and other princes of worldly learning have written but remain unlearned in the Word of righteousness, you will remain as unfit to minister as an attorney would be to perform surgery. Now I do not recommend, as some fanatics do, that you burn all books except the Bible; but I do exhort you to prefer it above them. As the bee flies over the whole garden and brings the honey she collects from each flower into the hive, so should the minister direct his supply from other sources to the building up of Scripture knowledge.

We ministers are only 'younger brothers' to the apostles. Christ left them gifts as a father leaves the inheritance to his oldest son and heir. But we must work for our living. Like Jacob's venison, their knowledge of the Word was brought to them without hunting; but if we desire to know the mind of God, we must trace it out with diligence, always taking prayer with us as we do so. This was Paul's charge to Timothy: 'Give attendance to reading' (*1 Tim. 4:13*). And 'meditate upon these things; give thyself wholly to them' (*verse 15*).

How can the people grow spiritually if their minister is not growing? And how will he grow, unless he daily drinks in more than he pours out? Study and pray; pray and study again. But do not ever think your week's work has been done when Sunday is past. Take a deep breath and get back to work, like a farmer who sits down to rest after he has planted a long row of seed, and then gets up and puts his hand to the plow again.

Is the parent supposed to care for his estate and time and provide for his children? And should not the spiritual father have a similar affection for his people? How strenuous a physical and mental calling the pastor has, and if his congregation understood that, they would surely encourage and furnish practical help to him. Otherwise their complacency forces him into the world to earn bread for his family when he should be providing bread for their souls.

II. USE NO SWORD BUT SCRIPTURE IN THE PULPIT
     AND HANDLE IT FAITHFULLY

Remember whose work you are doing; and then perform it purely and freely.

(a) *Use the sword of the Word purely*
In a threefold respect, work hard to keep this ministry pure – from error, from passion, and from vanity.

[315]

(i) *Pure from error*. Every word of your sermon must claim Scripture as its source. That is, do not preach your own dreams and visions in God's name. 'He that hath my word, let him speak my word faithfully' (*Jer. 23:28*) – and purely, without the alloy of your own opinions. 'What is the chaff to the wheat? saith the Lord' (*verse 28*).

Let me say it again – do not stamp God's image on your own coin. Many people are not satisfied with the plain truths of God's Word and exalt their own ideas so high that they have flown out of sight of Scripture and drift into dangerous errors. Be sure it is pure truth before you give it to the people.

Do not choose the pulpit for your stage by performing phenomenal experiments upon the people. Never deliver something doubtful which has not been refined in the furnace. It is always better to feed your people with a simple meal of sound doctrine than to create an exotic dish garnished with an original topping. It takes but one wild gourd to bring death to their spiritual diet.

(ii) *Pure from passion*. Beware of the strange fire of venting personal discontent in the pulpit. The man of God must be gentle and meek, speaking words of wisdom. A little oil makes the nail drive in without splitting the board. And the Word never enters the heart more kindly than when it falls gently. 'Ride prosperously because of truth and meekness' (*Ps. 45:4*).

Do you need to take the rod of reproof in your hand now and then? Let the people see it is love, and not anger, which gives the blow. Nurses are careful not to heat their milk, knowing it would make the baby sick. And even so, the preached Word flows best from a warm heart. A feverish heat would breed prejudice in the hearers and make them throw up the milk with it.

I am not warning about zeal if it is pure and peaceable.

[316]

Just save it for God and do not spend it on your own cause. Moses' meekness is a good example. Although he received a stinging insult at the hands of Aaron and Miriam, he did not rail against them. That would have been for personal justification; and it was enough that God knew about it. Yet whenever a sin was committed against God, this meek man's righteous anger flared: 'Who is on God's side? who?' Remember, the minister who can take the greatest freedom in roughly reproving his people's sins against God is the one who confidently and quietly digs a grave and buries personal injuries against himself.

(iii) *Pure from levity and vanity*. God's Word is too sacred to be played with like a toy. Some ministers use a sermon to show off their own sense of humor or colorful personality. It is like a baby's stuffed doll – unpin the story, unfasten the ruffles, take off that shocking introduction and gaudy conclusion, and you have nothing left inside but sawdust. If we mean to do God's work we must come not in words only but in demonstration of power in the Holy Spirit.

A thousand quips and quotable clichés will not end Satan's control over lives. But draw the sword of the Word and strike with its naked edge – this is the only way to pierce your people's consciences and spill the blood of their sins. I am in no way discouraging your efforts to be a good speaker; for this is one of our duties: 'Because the preacher was wise . . . he sought to find out acceptable words' (*Eccles. 12:9–10*). The doctor prescribes medicine which can be swallowed easily and maybe even pleasantly sometimes. But he is careful not to weaken its effectiveness by mixing in a thick sugar coating. While these are 'acceptable words,' they must also be upright, 'words of truth' (*verse 10*).

(b) *Use the sword of the Word freely*

Do not make God's Word a slave to the preference of the most affluent members of your congregation. It is required that a steward be 'faithful' (*1 Cor. 4:2*). Now the preacher's faithfulness is toward the One who anointed him. And it is highly unlikely, in handing out provisions, that a steward can please every servant in the house. If your goal is to please all men you have an endless and needless work. A good and wise doctor seeks to cure, not to please, his patients. In fact the patient may actually complain for a while because his medication tastes bitter – until it makes him well; then he is sincerely thankful for it.

The apostle Paul walked right past critical thoughts of men on his way to the prize of the high calling of God. 'With me it is a very small thing I should be judged of you' (*1 Cor. 4:3*). He was saying, 'My Master will decide whether or not I have been faithful; there will be plenty of time then to have my name righted, when He comes to vindicate His own.' Micaiah stood up for the kind of freedom God desires for His ministers: 'As the Lord liveth, what the Lord saith unto me, that will I speak' (*1 Kings 22:14*).

Ironically, Paul might have remained a free man rather than a prisoner if he had settled for the Word's being bound occasionally in his ministry. But he was too faithful to buy freedom with imprisonment of the truth through sinful silence. 'Wherein,' he declared, 'I suffer trouble, as an evil doer, even unto bonds; but the word of God is not bound' (*2 Tim. 2:9*).

If ever there was a time of temptation to ministers – and a need to stir them up in it to hold to the Word of God's patience – it is now in these last tumultous days of the world, when most men do 'not endure sound doctrine'

[318]

(*2 Tim. 4:3*). To hold forth the truth in such a perverse generation, ministers must have more power and boldness than flesh and blood can furnish.

It is no trial for a minister to speak truth freely among its friends, but among those who despise it and are enraged with the messenger for delivering his Master's mind without compromise. This makes the confession of our Lord even more glorious when He witnessed the whole counsel of God before Pontius Pilate, a bloody enemy against Him. Even though our messages must sometimes go against the grain of people's consciences, we have our commission directly from the Most High God: 'I have set thee for a tower and a fortress among my people, that thou mayest know and try their way' (*Jer. 6:27*).